In Poe's Wake

TRAVELS IN THE GRAPHIC
AND THE ATMOSPHERIC

Jonathan Elmer

The University of Chicago Press   CHICAGO AND LONDON

The University of Chicago Press, Chicago 60637
The University of Chicago Press, Ltd., London
© 2024 by The University of Chicago
All rights reserved. No part of this book may be used or reproduced in any
manner whatsoever without written permission, except in the case of brief
quotations in critical articles and reviews. For more information, contact
the University of Chicago Press, 1427 East 60th Street, Chicago, IL 60637.
Published 2024
Printed in the United States of America

33 32 31 30 29 28 27 26 25 24   1 2 3 4 5

ISBN-13: 978-0-226-83347-7 (cloth)
ISBN-13: 978-0-226-83349-1 (paper)
ISBN-13: 978-0-226-83348-4 (e-book)
DOI: https://doi.org/10.7208/chicago/9780226833484.001.0001

Library of Congress Cataloging-in-Publication Data

Names: Elmer, Jonathan, 1961– author.
Title: In Poe's wake : travels in the graphic and the atmospheric /
    Jonathan Elmer.
Description: Chicago : The University of Chicago Press, 2024. | Includes
    bibliographical references and index.
Identifiers: LCCN 2023039682 | ISBN 9780226833477 (cloth) |
    ISBN 9780226833491 (paperback) | ISBN 9780226833484 (ebook)
Subjects: LCSH: Poe, Edgar Allan, 1809–1849—Appreciation. | Poe, Edgar
    Allan, 1809–1849—Illustrations. | Poe, Edgar Allan, 1809–1849—Film
    adaptations—History and criticism. | Poe, Edgar Allan, 1809–1849—
    Songs and music—History and criticism.
Classification: LCC PS2638 .E56 2024 | DDC 818/.309—dc23/
    eng/20230921
LC record available at https://lccn.loc.gov/2023039682

♾ This paper meets the requirements of ANSI/NISO Z39.48-1992
(Permanence of Paper).

Contents

Plates follow page 90.

Introduction

The Face, the Brand

There is no escaping the face. It's everywhere: on the "Poe me some more coffee" mug, on the "writer's block" paperweight, on the bobbleheads, and on the T-shirts with a raven perched on the shoulder. It's on the cover of the Beatles' "Sgt. Pepper's Lonely Hearts Club Band," right at the top, separated off from the pile of other faces, as if for easier recognition.

Given that most of the faces on that famous album cover are celebrities who are easily identified, we might think Poe's presence is part of a message about celebrity. But we get a better clue about Poe's inclusion here from "I Am the Walrus": "Man, you should have seen them kicking Edgar Allan Poe." The kicking of Edgar Allan Poe began early, arguably at birth; in terms of posthumous fame, it began with Rufus Wilmot Griswold's biographical "Memoir of the Author," included in his edition of *The Works of the Late Edgar Allan Poe*, published a year after Poe's death.

In Griswold's "Memoir," we are told of Poe's erratic behavior, his dissolute habits, his disagreeable egotism. We are told he had virtually no friends, that he was an outcast in his own society. Charles Baudelaire used Griswold's edition for his many translations of Poe, but where the editor was opprobrious, Baudelaire was admiring. "[Poe] was at all times a dreamer," griped Griswold, "dwelling in ideal realms—in heaven or hell—peopled with the creatures and the accidents of his brain. He walked the streets, in madness or melancholy, with lips moving in indistinct curses, or with eyes upturned in passionate prayer." This melancholy flaneur hurling "indistinct curses" into the void is quickly assimilated into the Baudelairean playbook for the poète maudit. Poe is a model to be emulated for Baudelaire.

It's not news that Baudelaire savored "madness or melancholy" and wore his damnation in the eyes of the world as a badge of honor. And like

FIGURE 0.1. The face. The "Ultima Thule" daguerreotype of Edgar Allan Poe, 1848. Courtesy of the American Antiquarian Society.

Baudelaire, we like our Poe well-kicked. The face we see reproduced everywhere testifies to this. Taken just days after an attempted suicide, the daguerreotype of 1848 is called the "Ultima Thule" daguerreotype (see figure 0.1).

If Poe is so consistently associated with doom and gloom, it is probably due to this image as much as anything he wrote. The face stands for life-catastrophe—Poe's own, certainly, but by extension all creative souls destroyed by the indifference of society. This is why Laura Howell, in her witty graphic summary of Poe's life, can assimilate the "Ultima Thule" portrait to Munch's *The Scream*: existential angst of a distinctly modern kind lies coiled in Poe's dark eyes (see figure 0.2).

Poe's face, sometimes accompanied by a raven, is what advertisers and graphic designers call a "mark." It is meant to identify a Poe "brand" instantaneously. No treatment of the extraordinary range of Poe-inspired artworks that follow in his wake can evade this brand: this is what it means to say there is no escaping the face. Poe's works and his person fuse in the brand. In a way unlike any other author, Poe appears *as a character* in adaptations of his own works, such as when Poe is conflated with the speaker in "The Raven." He also appears as a character in works that are *not* written by him but that are self-consciously part of the Poe "brand." In Netflix's recent film, *The Pale Blue Eye* (2023), for example, Poe (Harry Melling) appears as a West Point cadet who helps the detective (Christian Bale) solve a grisly series of murders. Three elements of the brand are here combined: a tidbit from Poe's life (he was in fact a cadet at West Point for a year), the activation of a genre associated with Poe (the detective tale; that is, ratiocination trained on acts of extreme violence—think "The Murders in the Rue Morgue"), and some fragment of his literary corpus, here reduced to the title, *The Pale Blue Eye*—words borrowed from "The Tell-Tale Heart" that have no relevance to the action of the film.

The Poe brand allows for this kind of freewheeling mix-and-match attitude to Poe's words, works, and biography. Edgar G. Ulmer can produce a film for Universal Studios, *The Black Cat* (1934), that has nothing more than a title in common with Poe's story and yet it remains true to the brand, as I argue in chapter 2. In this book I consider films and illustrations and prints and paintings and artist's books and songs and operas and free improvisations and comic books and conceptual art installations and music videos and animations and cartoons and video games. Some of these works have only glancing connections to the particulars of Poe's life and texts, but many others reveal complex transformations of Poe's themes and formal devices. As inescapable as the brand is, it can also be a problem, a scrim that both makes it clear there is something behind it and makes it hard to access that something. But we cannot understand Poe's extraordinary influence on creators in nonliterary media if we stop at the face. We need to dig deeper.

If there's no way of getting around the face, then perhaps we can go through it. In 2011, Universal Studios in Florida erected a haunted house

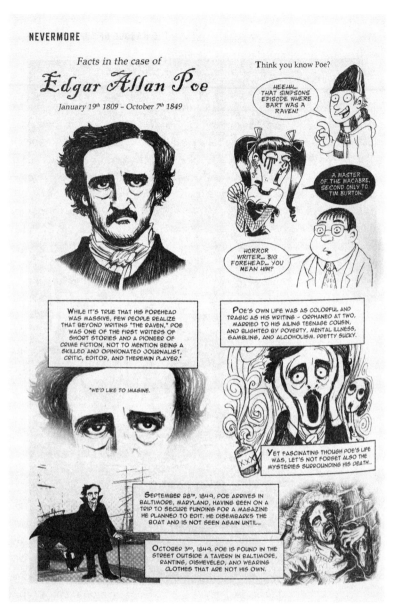

FIGURE O.2. The face and *The Scream.* "The Facts in the Case of Edgar Allan Poe." Illustration by Laura Howell for *Nevermore: A Graphic Adaptation of Edgar Allan Poe's Short Stories* (London: SelfMadeHero, 2007). Courtesy of Laura Howell and SelfMadeHero.

entertainment. Thrill seekers had to wend their way past a line of recycling bins to reach the entrance to "Nevermore: The Madness of Edgar Allan Poe." There they would find a facade resembling giant sheets of scrawled-over manuscript paper, out of which Poe's face emerged: you entered via the face. Once in the haunted house, viewers were led through a series of rooms, all associated with either Poe's tales or his biography. In the room dedicated to "The Pit and the Pendulum," for example, "the main character is seen on a table getting sliced in half by the pendulum as the Spanish Inquisitors attack the guests, holding severed body parts of victims." Moving on, "guests enter Poe's portrait gallery, and see Poe calling out to his late wife Virginia Eliza Clemm Poe, as she and multiple other women from Poe's life attack guests throughout the room." Poe's life, his mind, turn out to be the real horror show: "The madness of Edgar Allan Poe's greatest works has come to life. Step into the mind of the iconic writer, where every turn of the page takes you closer to the brink of insanity."

Haunted house entertainments go back a long way. If confronting "guests" in a confined space with realistic depictions of severed body parts is the criterion, then we could go back to Madame Tussaud's wax-figure "Chamber of Horrors" in the early nineteenth century. In the United States, the haunted house assumed its modern form during the 1930s to keep teenagers from vandalizing things on Halloween. Disney installed its first "Haunted Mansion" at Disneyland in 1969, effectively inaugurating the "haunted attraction industry."

Prior to all these developments, though, the haunted house was a literary device. One could thus argue that the modern "haunted attraction" is *always* a kind of homage to literature. The metaphor of the mind as a haunted house is one Poe embraced, most insistently in "The Fall of the House of Usher," in which the ancestral home (with its "vacant eye-like windows") forms an organic unity with its two lonely inhabitants. In other words, Poe has *already* imagined something quite like this attraction, right down to its embrace of overkill. The relation between this attraction and Poe's imagination begins to seem quite close. Even the forced march through themed rooms, each more grisly than the last, could make one think of "The Masque of the Red Death" and its color-coded itinerary of horror.

But the relation between this theme-park experience and Poe's legacy lies still deeper. Film historian Tom Gunning has dubbed the earliest years of film (up to around 1906) the "cinema of attractions." These early films are a "harnessing of visibility," Gunning argues, an "act of showing and exhibition." In this sense, early cinema participated in what has been memorably called the "frenzy of the visible" that seized publics in the latter half of the nineteenth century. These (necessarily) short early films aimed less to tell a story than to produce an effect. They were much closer to amusement park rides (or "attractions," according to the term still in active use today) than to theatrical experiences.

Gunning borrowed this idea from Sergei Eisenstein, whose essay "Montage of Attractions" (1923) offers the following programmatic statement: "An attraction (in relation to the theatre) is any aggressive aspect of the theatre; that is, any element of the theatre that subjects the spectator to a sensual or psychological impact, experimentally regulated and mathematically calculated to produce in him certain emotional shocks which, when placed in their proper sequence within the totality of the production, become the only means that enable the spectator to perceive the ideological side of what is being demonstrated—the ultimate ideological *conclusion*."

Attractions are "aggressive," they aim to induce sensual, psychological, and emotional "impact" or "shocks." At the same time, they are aggressively controlled: "experimentally regulated and mathematically calculated," always with a view toward the "totality" of the production and its "*conclusion*."

If you take the word "ideological" out of Eisenstein's statement, you have a near-perfect reprise of Poe's aesthetics of "effect." Poe articulated an aesthetic principle about his short works that was also immediately legible to many who came after him. That principle was the "unity of effect": the composition of any work should start from the effect it wishes to produce and strive to make the development of plot, setting, character, and symbol subservient to a felt sense of the "unity" of the effect. As with Eisenstein, one finds in Poe's aesthetic an emphasis on violent, sensual, emotional, and psychological effects aimed at a reader but handled with great control, with a coolness of method. One of Poe's most outrageous (and hence memorable; certainly influential) statements is that the composition of "The Raven" "proceeded, step by step, to its completion with the precision and rigid consequence of a mathematical problem." As in Eisenstein, "totality" is the fundamental value—everything leads to a "conclusion" that is experienced as a fusion of sensational effect and the apprehension of form.

It's not impossible Eisenstein derived his theory of attractions and effects from Poe directly. But it doesn't much matter: by Eisenstein's time, these ideas had seeped into the groundwater. Both Poe (in "The Philosophy of Composition," from which I have just quoted) and Eisenstein invoke mathematics, but the more important idea is that their "productions" can be "experimentally regulated." A story or a poem or a play is not an outpouring from the soul—it is an *experiment*. John Tresch made this point best, and most consistently, as it relates to Poe: "Poe treated literary 'genres' as a form of mass production. Applying the habits of his engineering training to the writing of fiction, Poe surveyed the field, analyzed the construction of earlier products, and applied these formulas in a series of works of his own. . . . Poe optimized his formulas, magnifying them into 'grotesques,' or rarefying them into more concentrated forms."

This experimental ethos helps make sense of the repetitions and variations in Poe's work. Put the corpse beneath the floorboards, behind a wall, in a crypt, in a ship's bunk; have the tale explode with a cat's cry, a beating heart, a tinkling bell, a glutinous voice. Play around with codes and ciphers—as a clue to buried treasure, as mysterious glyphs on cavern walls, as a blizzard of printing errors. Set the drama of detection in a blood-smeared apartment or an elegant royal chamber.

Poe's poems and tales are simultaneously indelible and provisional: you never forget them, but you can always change them. Being *experimental*, Poe's works always have endings, but they are not finished. They are *extensible*: later artists feel that work on them can be continued. This might take the form of actually continuing a story, as Jules Verne extends *The Narrative of Arthur Gordon Pym of Nantucket* in his novel *Le sphinx des glaces*, or of recasting it, as Mat Johnson does with his novel *Pym*. But it more often takes the form of tinkering with Poe's tales, adding and subtracting plot elements or characters. This tinkering, finally, points to a third trait: Poe's tales are *modular*. Because there are so many continuities across different works, later artists feel free to grab and go, to reassemble elements in new configurations: hence, the prevalence of the mash-up in the archive of Poe remediations. Finally, because Poe's works exemplify a method as much as they send a message, they are often taken as a whole, as a corpus. Hence the attraction of the *anthology* (many artists redoing Poe, gathered in one work) and the *series* (one artist redoing Poe across several works).

Poe's signature themes—intense grief, intense fear, revenge, perversity, the analysis of signs, and the workings of ratiocination—are very often staged as dramas of extreme sensation. The intensity of affective experience is increased by the separation of sense modalities: his characters might have preternaturally acute hearing, for example, or be completely blinded in a dark space, or whirled about in waters of "hideous velocity." For those coming after Poe, who are trying to understand and create with recorded sound, moving image, the nine-panel-grid, or the point-and-click video game, to take just a few examples, Poe's analytic of the senses offered puzzles and provocations that could be addressed in new ways, according to the affordances of these new media.

Much will be said about Poe's formal flexibility in what follows, but the gist is this: Poe wrote tales and poems that have a strong emphasis on closure—and its breakdown. The narrator of "The Tell-Tale Heart" kills a man and secretes his dismembered corpse beneath the floorboards: closure. Then he pulls up the floorboards: disclosure. This emphasis on vivid formal reversals is so insistent that form often becomes a theme in Poe. The maelstrom or vortex, for example, is not just a plot device; it is a figure of form. The same is true of Poe's dark rooms, what I will call the "black box." This combination of form as device and form as theme also appeals in special ways to later artists, as they seek ways to harness the powers of new media and platforms. The recursiveness of form encouraged a self-consciousness about medium as well.

In short, Poe exemplifies a modern method of aesthetic production for those in his wake: this is why he is so attractive to them. It's as if he left his experimental works and his box of tools lying around for others to pick up and play with. The bundle of Poe traits—his thematic emphasis on extreme sensation, his flexible sense of form, his experimental and modular method, and, yes, his iconic personal profile—all feed into what I have been calling the Poe brand. But it is the argument of this book that those many artists and creators traveling in Poe's wake make visible, beneath the face and the brand, fundamental categories of aesthetic experience applicable across the range of media that has developed since Poe's death. I call these categories of aesthetic experience the graphic and the atmospheric.

Graphic and Atmospheric

If you say to someone familiar with Poe that his works are often quite graphic and also powerfully atmospheric, that person might respond: "That sounds plausible. Some are certainly quite violent. I remember the scene with a guy gouging out a cat's eye. And the woman shoved headfirst up the chimney. Oh! and the dismembered corpse—'The Tell-Tale Heart,' right? As for atmospheric—do you mean moody? Some stories—'The Fall of the House of Usher' comes to mind—are kind of creepy or uncanny. Lots of shadows and vagueness—and a pervasive feeling that sadness or madness, or both, are at work. OK, I see your point."

I indulge in this imaginary conversation to suggest that both the graphic and the atmospheric are vernacular aesthetic categories—they are broadly available as terms we can apply to artworks and aesthetic commodities we encounter today. We might criticize the *graphic* violence that is the stock in trade of, say, the *Saw* franchise. We might revel in the inky shadows and anxious air of menace of our favorite noir films by calling them *atmospheric*. The terms are not meant to be all that precise: they are not technical analytic terms, like *sfumato* or *free indirect discourse*. But they are not meaningless just because they are imprecise or ambiguous. People find the terms useful. Because so many of the works I look at in this book are frankly mass cultural or popular, the vernacular dimension of aesthetic understanding is never far from the conversation.

As I made my way through (a portion of) the vast archive of remediations of Poe's work in writing this book, I found myself gravitating toward these two vernacular aesthetic categories as both descriptive and sufficiently capacious to accommodate the many kinds of aesthetic objects I wished to discuss. It came to seem fundamental to me that Poe's uptake had been massively visual—the face is part of this, but so is the enormous body of work by graphic artists of all kinds, from Manet to comic books. Equally important was the fact that Poe's works are highly influential on the depiction of extreme—of graphic—violence. He is both kitschy and edgy, finding a niche in the world of tchotchkes as well as torture porn. His legacy is both mass cultural and avant-garde. I will argue that what is graphic in Poe applies across this range.

I organize this complex visual legacy by dividing it into two approaches. Both represent developments in visual media that Poe saw emerging in his time, and that deeply fascinated him. The practice of publishing illustrations to accompany literary works was rapidly accelerating during his career, though he was low enough on the publishing pecking order that it largely bypassed him. He did produce four "Plate Articles," however—prose pieces written to accompany an already-made image. This saturation of mass-produced images in print environments engaged many graphic artists, especially in the latter half of the nineteenth century, and forced them to ask new questions about the relation between image and word. Poe's aesthetics of darkness, something I explore in detail in chapter 1, proved especially provocative to many graphic artists, leading to innovation with the format of the book and explorations of the limits to vision and the visual.

The other approach to Poe's "graphicality" (a word he coined) is via photography, a technology introduced only a decade before Poe's death, about which he published some remarkably visionary words. For Poe, there seemed literally no limit to this new graphic art (for photography, as its name indicates, is graphic—the marks left not by the hand but by light): what it could show was literally beyond human comprehension, "infinitely" verisimilar. Poe's aesthetic of darkness—all those closed rooms, pitch-black torture chambers, graves; what I call his "black boxes"—would need to be entirely revised under the conditions of photography's "infinite" capacity to make the world visible. And it was revised—but in translating Poe's darkness into light, cinema confronted a different limit: not what cannot be seen but what *should* not or *must* not be seen, not the indiscernible but the unwatchable. This is the problem explored in chapter 2.

Poe's "atmospheric" qualities presented a different problem. Many of his tales and poems are brooding, weird, and shadowy. They are "moody," and thinking about mood, feeling, or affect seems the quickest way in analytically. When we invoke "atmosphere," after all, we are often talking about an inchoate mood, about diffuse affective states. But Poe's engagement with "atmosphere" seems to me not adequately described by such an analytic approach: Poe's works, for the analysis of the human senses, seem less psychological and more formal, less everyday and more cosmic. Three extraordinary essays by Leo Spitzer helped me sort my treatment of the atmospheric into two lines of approach. In "Milieu and Ambiance: An Essay in Historical Semantics" (1942), Spitzer shows how concepts of the cosmic surround have evolved from the ancients to today: what was a kind of vast holding environment for the Greeks discloses in modernity a fundamental homelessness, disorientation, or determinism. A decade after this essay, Spitzer published on Poe's "The Fall of the House of Usher," which he interpreted as an exemplary illustration of this disorientation and determinism. Following Spitzer's lead, in chapter 3, I base my investigation of atmosphere and form around that complex story.

After Spitzer published "Milieu and Ambiance" in 1942, a colleague suggested that he expand one of its footnotes into a separate essay about the origins of the term *Stimmung*—mood, or attunement. Spitzer's fundamental labor here was to recall Stimmung to its sonic origins: the "attunement" in play concerns the music of the spheres, or more broadly, what he calls in his title "Classical and Christian Ideas of World Harmony" (1945). But here again modernity records a collapse: we are not gathered into harmony, attuned to it, so much as impinged upon, awash in, or buffeted about by sound. This insight allowed me to address, in chapter 4, the sonic dimension in Poe's works, which has been often overlooked but which has inspired many ingenious treatments in recorded sound, radio, vocal performance, and music, from the era of spiritualist dictation to that of children's cartoons.

Method and Mosaic

Two aesthetic categories, then, and two chapters devoted to each. My tactic has been to unfold the implications of these ideas bit by bit, as I explore the wide variety of works traveling in Poe's wake. This book is, in other words, structured the way it was written: inductively and itinerantly. I published a book in 1995 that advanced a series of arguments about Poe's discerning relationship to the incipient mass culture of his day. The book was generous with its theoretical argumentation but less so with its range of example. This book is a kind of sequel, one that reverses the balance between argument and example. I do turn, in the afterword, to some theoretical takeaways from these travels, however, exploring how they compare to contemporary thinking about topics such as adaptation studies, graphic violence and form, and the interest in the "atmospheric" as a category conjoining environment, affect, and art.

In Poe's Wake has been constructed by placing smallish pieces next to one another. Sometimes the tiles feel very closely linked—like tiles of the same color or shape in a mosaic—and sometimes there is a contrasting note, a sudden jump. It is my aim to produce enough sense of connection between tiles, even the ones that contrast, that my reader will be able to make out a larger-scale design emerging from the positioning of the tiles. Any study like this will lead readers to propose other examples than the ones I bring forward. Different examples will alter the mosaic design, of course, but if such a revisionist believes a different design is possible with counterexamples, I will have achieved a central goal. Although I am pursuing a wide-ranging exploration of the graphic and the atmospheric in these pages, I also understand myself to be providing materials for other approaches and conclusions.

Because of my commitment to as full an array of remediations as can be managed, I am continually poaching on fields of expertise that are not

my own. In this book, I talk about illustration practices, the comics controversy of the 1950s, René Magritte, French expressionist cinema, Lou
Reed's interest in Poe, and point-and-click video games—the list goes on
and on. There are so many fields and historical moments that I needed to
pack light in each foray if I was ever going to emerge again. What is more,
I am very often brushing up against complex historical and theoretical
debates that could easily become the focus of the discussion.

These circumstances required adopting what is (for me) an unusual attitude toward citation. Because I wanted to read these objects closely, I have
given them pride of place; and to avoid cluttering the text with names, I
largely (though not entirely) avoid including the names of anyone not
involved in the production of the object under discussion. To keep the
reader focused on the objects and not on scholarly discussions, I have
avoided footnotes, offering instead references keyed to page number at the
back of the book. My familiarity with historical and theoretical debates
should also be clear from the references at the end of the book.

Mosaics are meant to be taken in as comprehensively as a painted canvas—as a totality, in one go. That's true, but also in another sense less
than the whole story—because what is often the most beguiling aspect
of mosaic art is that it remains visible as an assemblage. It is visibly ad hoc
and at the same time intricately planned and composed. The pieces—
the tiles—are basically what is available, and they retain that aura of the
"found object," even when (as we know) they are sought and gathered
with intent.

The sequential aspect of writing—the expectation that you proceed in
order, just as we must do to make sense of any single sentence—weights
a reader's expectation toward continuous development, toward argument
and visible logical connection. But there are critical minds—William
Empson and Walter Benjamin come to mind—who make something of a
specialty of assemblage, who favor the power of examples and lean away
from the power of an argument to make those examples "fit right in." (In
the Platonic ideal of argument, to "fit right in" is to *disappear* as a refractory
particular). I, too, want the individual tiles to retain their integrity, even
as they gain in interest by their juxtaposition to others.

Practiced as a style of critical writing, this mosaic method has a natural
affinity with the essay. The essay, as distinguished from the argument, embraces its provisional, even unfinished, nature. It is, in its basic meaning, a

trial, an experiment, an attempt. Following along with great essayists can be a disorienting experience—Why have we turned down *this* path?— but also one with unexpected pleasures. I hope to produce some similar pleasures in what follows. The essays that follow are truly "travels in the graphic and the atmospheric."

This book presents Poe less as a prognosticator of our world than as a resource for it; he does not so much anticipate us as we confirm him, and in doing so we make visible a shared aesthetic history. The book is an attempt to understand some aspects of aesthetic experience in a fully multimedia world, one in which distinctions between art and commerce are not of great moment. *In Poe's Wake* explores values of aesthetic production and experience that are not restricted to certain media or economic circumstances but that travel from "high" to "low," and from word to image to moving image to sound, taking in all intermediate stops. This train is a local. I hope you have an enjoyable trip.

PART I

Graphic

The Black Box and the Eye

Graphicality

A man grabs his cat by the scruff of the neck, takes out a penknife, and carves out one of its eyes. Another man lies tied to a table, rats running over him, waiting for a blade attached to a pendulum to cut him in two. Yet another man visits his cousin's grave, and in some kind of trance state, he removes all her teeth.

People carry around durable impressions of Poe and his work: that he was a drunk, an outsider, an unappreciated genius; that his women all die, and he was very sad and a little mad; that the worlds he imagines are either weird or grisly, or both at once. Above all, they carry around certain startling, violent, vivid images.

An insulted man binds his tormentors, improbably hoists them aloft in a great mass, and sets them on fire. Another insulted man lures his frenemy to a subterranean vault, where he walls him up alive. Yet another man, not insulted by his victim, as far as we know—"I loved the old man"—kills him nevertheless and dismembers the corpse and deposits it beneath the floorboards.

Although Poe was a self-consciously literary writer, his uptake has been massively visual. Many of Poe's tales, like the ones I synopsized above, are "graphic," in the sense of excessive or extreme, which is how the word is used by the ratings board of the Motion Picture Association (MPA), formerly the Motion Picture Association of America (MPAA), when they advise that "graphic depictions or graphic descriptions . . . may lead a film to receive an R or NC-17 rating."

What's the difference between a *depiction* and a *description*? Depictions are pictures, as the word suggests. Descriptions, by contrast, are scripts; they have a necessary relation to language, to writing or inscribing. "Graphic depictions," we presume, are thus visual presentations: we actually *see* the man carve out the cat's eye. "Graphic descriptions," by contrast, would be more a matter of language: in a film, perhaps it is a character or voice-over *describing* what it looked like, felt like, to carve out a cat's eye. By using both *depiction* and *description*, the MPA simultaneously brings together and keeps separate pictures and words.

This is true to the root meaning of "graphic." In Greek, the word *graphein* means to make a mark, and thus includes both drawing and writing. This inclusive sense of "graphic" is what allows us to use it as a suffix for all kinds of modern markmakings that are neither writing nor drawing in the strict sense: photo*graphy*, cinemato*graphy*. A great deal of the modern media environment, in other words, would seem to be implicated in the concept of the graphic. We might even say that "graphic," as used in our contemporary world, refers broadly to our pervasively visual culture. Such usage remains true to the root sense of *graphein,* in that it includes not just words and images but diagrams, the windows and icons on our screens, logos, infographics, emojis, advertisements, animations—any and all aspects of "graphic design" or "visual communication" as the designers call it.

The graphic—a mark of any kind—needs a support, something that receives the mark. And these supports must last, extending past the moment of marking. Descriptions or depictions are graphic because they *endure* as marks; they leave a trace. But if the ratings board at the MPA needs to add "graphic" in front of the words "description" and "depiction"—words that that are *already* graphic—perhaps it is because the board reasons that, although we are completely awash in depictions and descriptions all the time, not all of them are graphic in the sense they intend. In fact, it seems that as our culture has become more and more pervasively graphic, we have felt the need to reassert an older idea of the graphic as a scoring or a scarring.

If you run a search for "graphic sex" and "graphic violence" on Google's Ngram Viewer, the online search engine that charts word and phrase frequencies in printed sources between 1500 and 2019, you will find a very sharp increase in use of these phrases since around 1980. Like the MPA, we evidently need to retain "graphic" as an intensifier. Perhaps *truly* graphic descriptions and depictions are ones that use *us* as their support, scar *us* rather than paper or metal plate. They are depictions that linger—perhaps unwanted—in the mind's eye. Once we have seen or read Poe's narrator mutilate his cat, we can never erase that mark.

I remember when Bret Easton Ellis's *American Psycho* was causing a scandal, I picked up a copy off a bookstore table. It fell open at the scene in which Patrick Bateman is describing in great detail his attack on two women with a power drill. I was genuinely horrified—more than I would have thought possible. I remember hastily closing the book and putting it back on the table—and deciding that perhaps I did not need to read this book. But I remember the scene anyway.

What is it that I remember? To some extent, the over-the-top gore of the scene; but more upsetting was the way this carnage and the feelings and motivations accompanying it—the feelings of the victims, the motivations of the perpetrator—could not be brought into the same representational space as the gore. A gulf separated them: one was visible, all-too-visible; the other was, as we say, "unimaginable"—I could not find an image for it. What caused my heart to race in that bookstore, what marked and scarred me, was both what I saw and what I couldn't picture, both the all-too-vivid and the obscure.

Patrick Bateman is a "psycho" because he can be bloviating about Phil Collins one moment and in the next giving detailed descriptions of his mutilation of other human beings. Ellis puts the reader in Bateman's head, where in one sense everything is very brightly lit and in another as black as pitch. Poe was one of the first writers to present "psychos" like this.

> It is impossible to say how first the idea entered my brain; but once conceived, it haunted me day and night. Object there was none. Passion there was none. I loved the old man. He had never wronged me. He had never given me insult. For his gold I had no desire. I think it was his eye! yes, it was this! He had the eye of a vulture—a pale blue eye, with a film over it. Whenever it fell upon me, my blood ran cold; and so by degrees—very gradually—I made up my mind to take the life of the old man, and thus rid myself of the eye forever.

The nameless narrator of "The Tell-Tale Heart," like Patrick Bateman, is an open book—he hides nothing from us. He reasons with us; he explains clearly that he "loved the old man." He insists he is not mad, that he can tell you the whole story, in order and in detail. But there is a black hole at the center of the story, sucking up all the light: the intolerable provocation of the old man's eye.

Poe had a special feel for the graphic, and people recognized it. As an aspiring young writer, he submitted a sheaf of stories for a contest. He had hand-lettered the manuscript to look like print, perhaps hoping that if the judges saw his text as it might look when published, it would *be* published. And, in fact, the *Baltimore Saturday Visiter* did publish one of the stories, "MS. Found in a Bottle," in October 1832.

"MS. Found in a Bottle" is an uncanny tale about a ghost ship on a one-way trip to the bottom of the vortex that lies at the South Pole. Announcing the prize, the editors wrote that Poe's story "will be found highly graphic in its style of Composition." There are indeed many vivid touches in this story: sublime oceanic imagery, weird archaic people and clothing, and so on. But the editors say it is "graphic in *its style of Composition*," which presumably means something a bit more complex than mere imagery.

In puzzling this out, we might note that Poe's narrative is both oppressively close to the action (the narrator is still scribbling even as the ship goes down) and fundamentally inaccessible: the "never-to-be-imparted secret" that the narrator anticipates remains just that for his reader—unimparted. The "style of composition," to put it simply, conjoins the very concrete and the very abstract. There is an uncanny moment in the story when the narrator realizes that he is *invisible* to the sailors on the ghost ship (an effect Poe recycles in "The Man of the Crowd"). He sees them in great detail, but they do not see him. In this story, the rules of visibility do not conform to our everyday understanding: the narrator describes all he sees in detail but remains invisible himself. Oddly, this combination of visibility and its default makes the story more vivid, more graphic.

In Poe's time, if the word graphic was applied to literature, it meant above all vivid, or striking, a calling up in the mind's eye of a scene or image. Poe invokes this sense of graphic in a review of Margaret Fuller's *Summer on the Lakes* in 1846, but he also complicates it: "Many of the *descriptions* in this volume are unrivaled for *graphicality*, (why is there not such a word?) for the force with which they convey the true by the novel or unexpected, by the introduction of touches which other artists would be sure to omit as irrelevant to the subject. This faculty, too, springs from her subjectiveness, which leads her to paint a scene less by its features than by its effects."

Poe first aligns "graphicality" with a practice that seeks "the true" in the "novel or unexpected," as opposed to a pedestrian or naturalistic understanding that confuses the true with the probable or normal. Let's call this practice the search for the *striking*. What is striking is not merely a feature of the external world; its novelty is only confirmed by its *effect* on someone in the scene (or on someone reading or viewing the scene). This is what Poe calls Fuller's "subjectiveness." This combination of *strikingness* and *subjectiveness* also changes the details or "touches." In much naturalistic depiction, details are inert because they signify the normal—they are *supposed* to be there. But in scenes dedicated to the striking, they become "touches" that take on a lively, often uncanny, aspect; they become conductors of energy between the striking and the subjective.

The narrator of "MS. Found in a Bottle" tells us he is invisible to the other sailors on the ship. This detail is striking—to him, to us—not simply because it is a vivid visual particular but because something in the scene— the narrator himself—is also *not* in the scene, is not registered. A dynamic of (in)visibility is at work, a painting of the scene "less by its features than by its effects"—here an uncanny one. Poe's tale suggests that what is "graphic" in a "style of composition" cannot finally be reduced to the visual register alone.

Early readers of Poe recognized that he had a skill for presenting scenes in which clarity and obscurity intertwined to strange effect. Fyodor Dostoevsky, whose landlady-killing Raskolnikov bears more than a passing resemblance to the narrator of "The Tell-Tale Heart," observed in 1861 that Poe "chooses as a rule the most extravagant reality, places his hero in a most extraordinary . . . psychological situation, and, then, describes the inner state of that person with marvelous acumen." What Dostoevsky refers to as Poe's "stupendous plasticity" only gains in impact by visualizing situations that "never actually occurred and even never could happen." Poe's "fantasticalness," Dostoevsky concludes, is "strangely 'material.'"

In America, too, and during his lifetime, many readers remarked on Poe's knack for being both concrete and abstract, simultaneously vivid and vague: "Mr. Poe possesses an extraordinary faculty. He paints the palpable obscure with strange power," wrote one contemporary. "The images are dim, but distinct; shadowy but well-defined. The outline is all we see; but here they stand, shrouded in darkness, and fright us with the mystery which defies further scrutiny." The poet James Russell Lowell wrote that Poe "combines in a very remarkable manner two faculties which are seldom united; a power of influencing the mind of the reader by the impalpable shadows of mystery, and a minuteness of detail which does not leave a pin or button unnoticed." Outline and shadow; detail and indefiniteness. The "graphic" in Poe's hands combines visibility and its limits.

Graphic/Literature

In Poe's day, the word "graphic" was most often used not in a literary context but rather to refer generally to the "graphic arts"—etching, wood-cuts, lithography, and so on. In this sense, the graphic encroached on the precincts of the literary not through aesthetic considerations but through the publishing revolution of the nineteenth century. Improvements in the ability to incorporate images into print publications meant that texts were increasingly saturated by mass-produced images, frequently taking the form of "illustration." Poe's "The Gold-Bug" was published with a few illustrations, but that was a rare exception in his career.

Elsewhere, however, and with bigger literary stars, illustration became in-tegral to literary publishing. Balzac's vexed collaboration with Grandville began in 1840, and Dickens worked closely with "Phiz" (Hablot Knight Browne) as early as *The Pickwick Papers* (1836). The first illustrated weekly news magazine was the *Illustrated London News* (1842). *The Graphic* came along in 1869, and the New York–based *Daily Graphic* in 1873. The trend was the same in Europe and North America: graphic imagery became more and more central to the world of publishing.

"The history of culture is in part the story of a protracted struggle for dominance between pictorial and linguistic signs," writes W. J. T. Mitchell. "The dialectic of word and image seems to be a constant in the fabric of signs that a culture weaves around itself. What varies is the precise nature of the weave, the relation of warp and woof." In the latter half of the nine-teenth century, one theater of this "protracted struggle" was the relation between literary publishing and the arts of illustration. The jostling for status between literary artists and graphic artists took place not just in journals and newspapers—it extended to the form of the book itself. The artists I now turn to engage with Poe's stories and poems not just at a thematic level but also at the level of form; and the "dialectic of word and image" often takes place against the backdrop of the format of the book, which itself becomes a site of innovation.

Two Spanish scholars have recently argued that 1884 represents a water-shed year in the reception of Poe. That year, two ambitious illustrated editions were released—*The Works of Edgar Allan Poe*, edited by Richard

Henry Stoddard in the United States, and Albert Quantin's republished Baudelaire translations of *Histoires extraordinaires* and *Nouvelles histoires extraordinaires* in France. Both editions were extensively illustrated by teams of artists—Quantin used no fewer than seven across the two volumes. These were major investments and indicated, if nothing else, that Poe had arrived as a literary icon worthy of such treatment.

It has been said that volumes like Quantin's that use "a consortium of illustrators" are a "Victorian oddity." But the format is alive and well. A publication from 2007, *Nevermore: A Graphic Adaptation of Edgar Allan Poe's Short Stories*, is a gathering of nine texts by Poe (eight stories and "The Raven," plus the graphic "Facts in the Case of Edgar Allan Poe" by Laura Howell mentioned in the introduction), each entry the work of a different artist. The effect of this book—and in this it is not that different from the 1884 editions—is the realization that Poe lends himself to graphic experimentation or, to take it further, that Poe's "literariness" is fundamentally tied up with his "graphicality." He can seemingly be thrown into any style, the details of his stories can be radically altered—"The Tell-Tale Heart" is illustrated in *Nevermore* by Alice Duke to feature a woman as the murderer—and he still comes out Poe.

By 1884 Poe had become a literary icon: both a celebrity (making publishers think they will make money on new editions) but also especially amenable to graphic illustration (which makes the model of "consortium of illustrators" an appealing way of making that money). Another publishing event at this time takes a different approach but testifies even more directly to Poe's star status. Toward the end of his life, Gustave Doré was commissioned by Harper & Brothers in the United States to produce a set of illustrations for "The Raven." The first print run was set at ten thousand, indicating that the publishers had dollar signs in their eyes, and necessitating that Doré's images be engraved on steel plates, which bear up better under repeated printings than copper plates. The volume is sumptuous and imposing—a folio weighing in at seven pounds. Doré was probably the most famous literary illustrator of the nineteenth century and had produced astonishing and intricate illustrations of the Bible, Dante, Cervantes, Milton, and many more. If Doré illustrated you, that meant you were "literature."

The Doré "Raven" can stand as a second model of how to package graphic literature. Here it is not a team of illustrators but a single artist's vision: if you bought the Doré "Raven," it was probably because of Doré more than

Poe. This single-artist model has produced some of the most powerful and influential illustrations of Poe's work, by Harry Clarke, Edmund Dulac, Arthur Rackham, and many others. For sheer opulence, the four volumes released in 1927 and 1928 by KRA publishers in Paris, with Baudelaire's translations and etchings by Neapolitan artist Carlo Farneti, may take the prize.

"The Raven" was one of the most beloved poems in English of the nineteenth century. Everyone knew the story: a man grieving by the fire for his lost love, Lenore, is interrupted by a tapping at the door. He opens the door—"Darkness there and nothing more." After whispering the name of his love into the void of the night, he returns to his chair by the fire, only to be arrested a second time by a tapping, this time at the window. He opens it and in flies a raven, which alights on the bust of Pallas Athena above his door. The bird has one word it croaks—"Nevermore." There follows a series of exchanges between the narrator and the bird, in which what Poe called the "human thirst for self-torture" is slaked, as the narrator feeds questions to the bird for which the inevitable reply "Nevermore" incrementally increases his despair. A final stanza tells us that the bird "still is sitting, still is sitting" on the bust and that the narrator's "soul from out that shadow that lies floating on the floor / Shall be lifted—Nevermore!"

It is a dark poem. In fact, it is a poem *about* darkness, darkness invading a space that is illuminated, if only feebly ("each dying ember wrought its ghost upon the floor"). The bird, like a terrible shard shot from "Night's Plutonian shore," explodes into the fragile haven of light, bringing darkness with it. By the end, there is no escape from the "shadow that lies floating on the floor."

Doré was a master of the deep blacks that could be rendered through engraving. He used such darkness to powerful effect in many of his illustrations from Dante, for example. In "The Raven," however, he adopted a different approach (see plate 1).

The raven here is backlit by a radiant fan of light that illuminates the room rather than darkens it. The room itself, so essential to the poem's drama of closure, opens out, perhaps to give egress to the troupe of angels flowing past the astonished man. The effect is of a space somehow both unconfined and cluttered. In other plates in the series, Doré plays more with shadow properly speaking, but the overall shimmery tonality of his treatment is in line with the image shown here. The raven is impressively commanding in its spotlight but reads more like a heavenly apparition than a light-canceling denizen of night's Plutonian shore.

Doré's extensive sequence of images, many giving form to the narrator's hallucinatory visions, has been compared to the proto-cinematic medium of the "magic lantern," the popular nineteenth-century entertainment in which viewers sat in darkened rooms watching projected images. It is surprising that there is only one known treatment of Poe's work in magic-lantern format. It is not surprising, however, that it takes "The Raven" as its subject.

Magic-lantern displays borrowed a "presentational approach" from theatrical melodrama: heightened emotions are read off from coded gestures, and we sit before the image somewhat as we sit before a stage set with an empty foreground. The histrionic gesture of the grieving man is a cue. The acting style of stage melodrama was transferred to early cinema. But there is another feature of the medium that makes it proto-cinematic. The slides featuring angels, like one painted by Joseph Boggs Beale and dated by experts to 1894 (see plate 2), were made to transition at a faster rate (linked to the live recitation of the poem accompanying the images), an effect anticipating the moving images of cinema. And slides, like the camera eye, could offer multiple perspectives of a kind not possible in a stage drama.

In Beale's image the angels are really getting out of hand. We see the "rare and radiant maiden whom the angels name Lenore" being bundled off under the expressionless supervision of the bird, while the man gestures in melodramatic dismay. For a magic-lantern show, it makes sense to depict a scene with the word "radiant" in it, even if in the poem the raven cancels this vision like all the others. The overwhelming impression of this slide is—pink. The only black elements are the bird and the man's suit. The magic lantern—proto-cinematic form that it was—concerned itself more with making visible things that were not normally visible—here the hovering angels—than with portraying a darkness visible.

Of course, cinema would develop its own love affair with shadow and obscurity—with noir—but the ontology of the medium remains illumination. As with photography, the graphic in cinematography is a marking by light, not a scoring by black. I will take up these issues in the next chapter. What I would emphasize is that if, as I have suggested in my brief recounting of Poe's poem, "The Raven" is about an invasion of darkness, Beale's painted lantern slide offers a different interpretation. And to the extent that Doré's engravings project a kind of luminescence that looks ahead to the blinding coloration of Beale, they do too.

The Black Box

Poe was a name to conjure with around 1884, and publishers who saw in his work and reputation a chance to bring literature and graphic illustration together had no difficulty finding big names—Doré being the biggest—to contribute their talents to such a project. Nowhere was Poe more iconic, more a byword for literature itself as a modern force in the world, than in France, due to Baudelaire's translations of the American writer. "The young writers who adopted [Odilon] Redon in the early 1880s 'talked incessantly' of Poe and Baudelaire." One of these young writers was Stéphane Mallarmé. Redon would eventually produce four beautiful and enigmatic images intended for publication with Mallarmé's landmark experiment in bookmaking, *Un coup de dés*. But Mallarmé's rethinking of literature and the book in the graphic age started much earlier, and with a different artist—Édouard Manet, the giant of modern painting.

Published in 1875, *Le corbeau* paired Mallarmé's translation of Poe's "The Raven" with accompanying transfer lithographs by Manet. It is a folio-sized production, unbound, in which Poe's words alternate with Mallarmé's translation, and with Manet's full-page images interspersed throughout "between the printed pages," effectively "declaring the autonomy of the series of plates." It is an extraordinarily avant-garde work, widely viewed as the first "artist's book," or *livre de peintre*. Avant-garde or not, Manet and Mallarmé seemed to have hoped to make money on it. For a brief period, a rich American was considering bringing the volume out in the United States, and Manet, hoping to keep the ball rolling, wrote to Mallarmé to see "if he could find some other unknown thing by Poe to do" ("*si vous pouvez trouver quelque machin inconnue de Poe à faire*"). *Le corbeau* was in the end a financial failure, but what is important is that for both Mallarmé and Manet, the venture was part of a more concerted effort to engage the changing conditions of publishing and the relation between word and image, to make the painter, in fact, a kind of author.

The collaboration has been seen in the context of the "etching revival" of the 1860s: "Writers were drawn to printmakers by virtue of resemblance. The graphic artist and the writer are laborers in black and white, sharing the basic tools of the trade: paper and ink." Etching was the technique thought to be closest to writing: "As an art of paper and ink, etching provided a powerful model of graphic writing that encompassed both physical immediacy and mobility, qualities central to the construction of modernity." This "physical immediacy and mobility" was not restricted to etching, however. Constantin Guys, praised by Baudelaire in "The Painter of Modern Life" (1863) for his exquisite sensitivity to the passing moment as embodied in his gestural line, was not an etcher, and the "intense and idiosyncratic markmaking" so prized in the "etching revival" could assert itself—as we will now see—in lithographs as much as in etchings. Although most reviews of *Le corbeau* mistakenly took Manet's image to be *eaux-fortes*, or etchings, they are in fact transfer lithographs.

Le corbeau is further evidence that "graphic Poe" provoked experimentations in format—we have here a word-image collaboration that doubles down on the book format and undoes it at the same time. It is, at all events, an aesthetic engagement of singular force and strangeness. (I leave to one side Mallarmé's translation; one publisher who declined the work wrote to Manet: "The translation offers such insanities that it is not possible for a serious publishing house to publish it"). Manet provides two images of the raven itself—a frontispiece and an ex libris—and four transfer lithographs that track the story. These latter plates exhibit "intense and idiosyncratic markmaking," if any ever did.

Looking at all four, one comes away with the feeling that the hero of the tale is blackness itself. The first depiction of the narrator at his desk in a pool of light surrounded by pitch black is followed by one showing the admission of the raven through the window. In the third plate, we are shown what can only be called the submission of the narrator before the darkness of the raven, "pressed into the chair, almost erotically." And, in the fourth and final plate, one that "has arguably no equivalent in the history of illustration," the room is emptied of everything but viscous shadow. These images startled contemporary viewers, who were "struck by the stark and 'brutal' simplicity of Manet's broad unmodulated strokes," and they startle still.

The angle of the man's head in this third image (see figure 1.1) and his placement in the bottom right corner emphasize his abasement before the raven. The heavy black lines that radiate from the raven's perch and pool to the right of the man's head connote a field of force—the moving and encroaching force of shadow, of blackness. That this is a darkness filling an enclosed space is emphasized by the carefully rectilinear closed door. One feels the thrust of the hand that laid these lines: one modern commenta-

FIGURE 1.1. The raven's domination. Transfer lithograph by Édouard Manet in *Le corbeau* (Paris: Richard Lesclide, 1875). Courtesy of Lilly Library, Indiana University.

tor suggests that the "brushmark neither depicts an object nor expressive feeling—it is neither figurative, nor abstract, nor expressive." This may seem to overstate the case—the four images form a series, after all, and recognizably follow the poem's narrative shape. But art historians largely agree with Michèle Hannoosh, who discerns in Manet's images "forms which hover between abstraction and figure, which emerge from a background of white page or of blank darkness of which they are simultaneously part."

"The Raven," as I have been suggesting, tells the story of darkness breaking into a perilously protected space and filling that space by degrees, until darkness is all there is. And this is what Manet delivers in his final image (see figure 1.2).

FIGURE 1.2. "That shadow that lies floating on the floor." Transfer lithograph by Édouard Manet in *Le corbeau* (Paris: Richard Lesclide, 1875). Courtesy of Lilly Library, Indiana University.

This astonishingly modern image piles black lines on top of one another, voiding the human figure, leaving only some tarry marks hovering over his seat. This is Manet's treatment of the end of the poem, when the "raven still is sitting, *still* is sitting" and has become one with the "shadow that lies floating on the floor." The raven inhabits this darkness, evident from its recognizable shape in the shadow, while the shadow cast behind the man's chair is misshapen—humanoid rather than human. We might take this shadow as that cast by the chair itself, but given the carefully managed voiding of the speaker from the scene—pushed first to the bottom right corner and then removed altogether—the idea that this shadow is the trace of the speaker's disappearance is compelling. In place of the human figure for which it substitutes, we have a pure "graphisme": observing that Manet's signature in this last plate, floating in empty space at the bottom left, is essentially illegible, Ségolène Le Men suggests that the "loss of legibility of the signature seems to accompany the disappearance of the subject. . . . Shadow and signature represent nothing other than a graphisme."

Note, finally, that Manet again underscores the closure of the scene, sketching the flats and uprights of the room, the shelter that human ingenuity has erected, unsuccessfully, against the invading darkness. A strong sense of closure is the prevailing effect on the reader/viewer, as one contemporary recognized: "By what kind of light, and where the light comes from, is a question for artists to settle," but the impact of the whole is "grandly grim and self-contained."

What Manet's "markmaking" shows, in effect, is light giving out, visibility collapsing into darkness, marks collapsing into the "indecipherable" and "illegibility." The strangeness of these marks, then, comes partly from the paradox they embody: they represent unrepresentability. *Le corbeau* may have been a minor effort for Manet; when he asked whether there was another "Poe thing" he and Mallarmé might collaborate on, he may have been thinking first about money and getting his work before the public, but his contribution to this volume remains a searching engagement with Poe's poem nevertheless. It was possible, as we have seen in the Doré and Beale treatments, to seize on Poe's mention of celestial worlds and to emphasize seraphim, angels, and radiant maidens. Manet takes another tack, one closer to the true force of Poe's poem: his focus is this world below, and its darkening close.

We have now reached something fundamental in Poe's work, an aesthetic of darkness to which graphic artists are drawn as if to a limit to their own medium's capacities. I will call it the black box. Phenomenologically, it is a zone of existential terror, the navel of the nightmare: a confined and confining space from which one cannot escape and in which one cannot see. Formally, what is at stake in the black box is *closure*—a narrative or spatial delimitation that conveys force. Inside the box, all is existential powerlessness, but from the outside, and if you can handle it, the box brings aesthetic power. Manet increases the impact of his radiant darkness, for example, by sketching the door and the walls of the room. The black box, as I conceive it here, is both terrifyingly concrete and wholly abstract. For this reason, it can be translated into many formats: it can be a story, or a frame, or a room, or a page. It can be the grave. If Poe has ever seemed graphic to you, if you have been marked or scarred by reading him, it is probably from some encounter with the black box.

Harry Clarke's illustration for Poe's "The Premature Burial" provides a graphic example of the black box (see figure 1.3).

The claustrophobic terror of the man in his coffin is distilled and exacerbated by the expanse of black soil that dominates the composition; it's as if Clarke wanted to portray the blackness of death itself, not just the unfortunate man who has been buried alive. The coffin is an index of the black box, but Clarke's black-bordered page itself is the more visually striking version of it. The rhythm of the image is one of breaking out followed by a larger and blacker recontainment.

Here is how the narrator of "The Pit and the Pendulum" negotiates the terror of the black box:

> So far, I had not opened my eyes. I felt that I lay upon my back, unbound. I reached out my hand, and it fell heavily upon something damp and hard. There I suffered it to remain for many minutes, while I strove to imagine where and *what* I could be. I longed, yet dared not employ my vision. I dreaded the first glance at objects around me. It was not that I feared to look upon things horrible, but that I grew aghast lest there should be *nothing* to see.

The man knows himself to be imprisoned in a torture chamber. He is not yet bound—that will come later, when he lies beneath the pendulum's swinging blade—but he has already been robbed of his very self: "I strove to imagine . . . *what* I could be." Cast into absolute darkness, the man's other senses kick into gear, but the compensation does not restore psychic

DEEP, DEEP, AND FOR EVER, INTO SOME ORDINARY
AND NAMELESS *GRAVE*

342

FIGURE 1.3. The black box. Illustration by Harry Clarke for "The Premature Burial" in Edgar Allan Poe, *Tales of Mystery and Imagination* (New York: George Harrap & Co., 1919). Courtesy of Lilly Library, Indiana University.

integrity. Despite the man's exercise of ratiocination, he remains unable to conjure any sense of wholeness, to "imagine . . . *what* I could be."

Rimbaud suggested in 1871 that it was possible to "reach the unknown through the unsettling of *all the senses*" ("*dérèglement des tous les sens*"). *Dérèglement* can be translated as unsettling, as it is here—or as disturbance, or perhaps as disordering. You can create disturbances of sensation by amplification, or by suppressing one sense modality so that others become more acute, or by transposing sense experiences, so that the ear feels, for example. The synesthetic poetics so important to symbolists such as Rimbaud depends on an analytics of the sensorium, on the conviction that different sense modalities can be understood, and manipulated, in isolation. You can't put the senses back together in unusual ways if you can't separate them first.

In recent years, historians of science, of art, and of media have shown how experimental work on the senses was central to all three domains over the course of the nineteenth century. Physiologists and psychophysicists produced experimental results that defined sense experience in newly precise ways, results that directly informed the development of technical media, such as phonography. And both the science and the emerging media opened new aesthetic possibilities for artists in the latter half of the century. But Poe was already at work on Rimbaud's project in the 1830s and 1840s. His texts constitute an extensive interrogation of aberrant sensation. This is one major reason for his continued relevance to the age of technical media.

There was a very important precursor to the black box, one that in fact models the intertwining of science, art, and technology mentioned in the last paragraph—the *camera obscura*. Although versions of the camera obscura go back to the ancient world, it was in the seventeenth century that it began its career as an experimental setup for asking questions about vision and sight. Pretty quickly, it became a metaphor for the understanding itself, for how sensation and cognition fit together. This is how John Locke, in *An Essay concerning Human Understanding* (1690), uses it:

> External and internal sensation are . . . the windows by which light is let into this DARK ROOM. For, methinks, the understanding is not much unlike a closet wholly shut from light, with only some little openings left, to let in external visible resemblances, or ideas of things without: which, would they but stay there, and lie so orderly as to be found upon occasion,

it would very much resemble the understanding of a man, in reference to all objects of sight, and the ideas of them.

It has been suggested that the camera obscura becomes "inseparable from a certain metaphysics of interiority: it is a figure for both the observer who is nominally a free sovereign individual and a privatized subject confined in a quasi-domestic space, cut off from a public exterior world." Locke seems to imagine that his sensations might "lie so orderly as to be found upon occasion," like papers that can be retrieved even on a messy desk. The fundamental passivity of Locke's perceiver does not, in any case, seem threatening in this description.

Poe's black box works entirely differently. Poe's characters often try to review their sensation, but never at leisure; sensations seize the pitiful human figures. The black box is a place of extreme vulnerability and, frequently, outright terror. Kircher and Locke were primarily interested in the scientific uses of the camera obscura. But the ability to project images in this way was from very early on also exploited for purposes of entertainment. Because of this, Athanasius Kircher thought it was important for viewers to understand the workings of the mechanism that brought them these images, so that they were not confused, mystified, or manipulated by them. There is a whole prehistory of film tied up in the evolutions of the camera obscura—into phantasmagoria, the magic lantern, and so on.

All the elements of the story of the camera obscura—its role in science and technology, its isolation of an idea of the spectator—are in play in Poe's uptake of this tradition. But these elements have become disturbed and displaced in his hands—they have undergone a *dérèglement*. Consider "The Tell-Tale Heart." The story evokes the model of the camera obscura only to provide a dark parody of it. And it does so in a way that emphasizes the role of technological apparatus. Night after night, the narrator tells us, for seven nights, he very slowly puts his head, along with his dark lantern—"a portable device with a sliding shutter, which makes it possible to either direct a narrow beam of light or conceal the illumination altogether"—into the old man's room while he sleeps. On the seventh night, the man awakes, and the narrator opens his dark lantern: "you cannot imagine how stealthily, stealthily—until, at length, a single dim ray, like the thread of a spider, shot from out the crevice and fell upon the vulture eye."

It has been suggested that Poe's tale also evokes the technology of daguerreotype, invented only five years before the story's publication. Poe's narrator "carefully wields an instrument that enhances his vision, adjusts its aperture, calculates the length of exposure, and focuses a single ray of light—all to obtain an image of someone else." But there is something essentially different going on here: both the camera obscura and the daguerreotype were technologies for the capture of natural light and produced what were experienced as marvelously enhanced effects of natural vision. But Poe's tale has no relation to either natural light or natural vision. When the narrator's "dark lantern" sends out a dim ray "like the thread of a spider," it is not seeing—it is seizing.

If there is a metaphor of vision here, it is the premodern one of "extramission," the idea that vision is the result of the eye sending out light rays to its object. And at the other end of this "single ray" is the object that precipitates murderous rage, the "vulture eye." This eye is no more "natural" than the dark lantern. It is an eye at once in default—it has a pale blue film over it; it cannot see, or only imperfectly—and in excess: it seems to threaten a kind of inhuman surveillance. It feels to the narrator, we surmise, like a kind of "dead eye" watching *him* all the time.

The old man's "vulture eye" looks forward to our world, in other words, symbolizing at once the outsourced, unsleeping, inhuman vision of our apparatuses and the vulnerable, enfeebled eyes lodged in our own bodies. The field of vision is not a safely secured chamber, any more than the bedroom is for the old man or the space beneath the floorboards is for the narrator. The forthright treatment of this blind all-seeingness in "The Tell-Tale Heart" opens a fundamental dimension of visuality and the graphic as we live it today.

Poe's manipulations of the black box can be seen in hindsight as an early, influential instance of art's participation in, and reflection on, the massive transformation of the human sensorium that began during his lifetime and has accelerated right into the present, a cultural sea-change interweaving scientific and artistic experimentation, evermore astonishing media prosthetics, and the economic directives that reward the ability to seize the attention of individuals, what is sometimes called the competition for "eyeballs."

The Eye

In the last two decades of the nineteenth century, the French artist Odilon Redon produced a multitude of graphic works that are called his "noirs." These often took the form of albums—a series of images linked by theme, often literary in inspiration. His second such album was titled *À Edgar Poe* (1882) and featured six enigmatic images with oblique captions of Redon's own devising. (One of these images—the eye-balloon—is among his best-known; it is on the cover of Penguin's edition of *The Science Fiction of Edgar Allan Poe*.) As with the Mallarmé-Manet collaboration, which Redon certainly knew, we find here an engagement with Poe leading to experimentation in format. Redon's albums could also be called *livres d'artistes*.

Redon's approach was aimed at a particular public: the "very format of the albums that established Redon's reputation in the narrower art circles during the early 1880s corresponds to the mode of perception and appropriation cultivated by the *littérateurs* who made up his first admirers." That is, they read more like books than pictures. Like pages, Redon's images could be given a sequential reading on a table, rather than hung on a wall, where the force of sequencing might be dissipated. At the same time, the sequence could also be left to the discretion of the reader/viewer. Like Manet's plates slipped unbound between the leaves of Mallarmé's translation, what looks like supplemental illustration is in fact an assertion of autonomy: "Redon's formula of a series of lithographs conceived as a tribute to a writer . . . allowed him to combine the benefit of a literary association with a maximum of freedom and autonomy."

No matter how "literary" Redon's lithographs were, he resisted understanding them as conventional illustrations: "I have never used the defective word 'illustration,'" Redon wrote to a friend in 1898. "You will not find it in my catalogues. The right term has not yet been coined. I can only think of transmission, of interpretation." The idea that Redon's images work as "interpretations" of his literary sources makes sense. Consider one of the images in *À Edgar Poe*, titled (or captioned) "*À l'horizon, l'ange des certitudes, et, dans le ciel sombre, un regard interrogateur*" (see figure 1.4).

This peculiar image cannot be linked to any Poe text in particular and is thus not an illustration. The title phrase or caption was apparently misunderstood by many contemporaries to be Poe's words, but Poe never wrote those words. What Redon has done here, I think, is *allude* to Poe's most visionary style, exemplified perhaps by one of the "angelic dialogues" such as "The Colloquy of Monos and Una" (1841). This evocation of Poe clears a space, as it were, in which Redon can pursue his own vision of the relation between the angel's certitude and the eye's questioning glance. Redon shares this visionary and morose space with Poe, a space in which the vivid and the obscure are combined, and the eye only uncloses within

A l'horizon, l'Ange des CERTITUDES, et dans le ciel sombre un regard interrogateur.

FIGURE 1.4. A questioning glance. *À l'horizon, l'ange des certitudes, et dans le ciel sombre, un regard interrogateur*. Lithograph by Odilon Redon, 1882. Courtesy of the Art Institute of Chicago.

a surrounding darkness. Such convergences led Redon to appear to his contemporaries as "a kind of Edgar Poe of the graphic arts."

L'ange des certitudes also reminds us that disarticulated, solitary eyeballs are more the rule than the exception in Redon's work, and not just in his literary albums. *Les origines* (1883), the series Redon produced under the influence of his extensive reading in the evolutionary literature of the day, includes *Il y eut peut-être une première vision essayée dans le fleur* ("There was perhaps a first vision attempted in the flower") (see figure 1.5).

Looking at this new interrogating eye—the form itself is a backward question mark—we get the sense that for Redon vision was less the privileged sense-mode of the sovereign human subject, what Descartes called "the noblest of the senses," than a capacity of the cosmos. This has implications for his audience: Redon's work looks back at his viewers, and in a sense, he wants their seeing to be seen.

Shortly after he completed his album *À Edgar Poe*, Redon's writer friend Émile Hennequin convinced him to produce four images for a proposed volume of Poe's works with new translations by Hennequin. I wish to look closely at one in particular. Redon reportedly called it *After Reading Edgar Poe; or, The Eye*, but the image has come to be called *Le coeur révélateur*— "The Tell-Tale Heart" (see plate 3).

A single eye hangs in black space. It is a left eye. There might be an eyebrow, but those black marks could also be the beginning of the shadow. The eye and its surroundings seem oddly continuous with one another. The smudgy patch below the eye looks like the shaded bits of the wood, while the knot in the board toward the top suggests another eye. The hanging eye is wide open but strangely expressionless. Perhaps it is spying on someone (perhaps on us) through the slats that frame it. Or are we doing the spying, and the eye monitors us warily? Is this gaze threatening or frightened? It is hard to say. In a strange way, we find ourselves on both sides of the separating boards.

This image was meant to accompany Hennequin's translation of "The Tell-Tale Heart," so we are entitled to think of it as an illustration. But what exactly is it illustrating? A first thought is that this is the eye of the narrator as, night after night, he peers through the crack of the barely opened door, looking for the moment to kill the old man. Redon's hanging eye recalls this sinister, watchful eye. But the boards through which it peers do not look like a doorway; they look like floorboards. So we begin to think this

FIGURE 1.5. The eye-flower. *Il y eut peut-être une vision première essayée dans la fleur.* Lithograph by Odilon Redon, 1883. Courtesy of the Art Institute of Chicago.

might be the old man's eye, unblinkingly gazing up from beneath the floor under which the narrator has deposited the old man's remains.

The most detailed interpretation of this image is by Dario Gamboni, for whom Redon's image "evokes the moment in which the light introduced through a door by the narrator . . . falls upon the eye of an old man." This implies that the pictured eye may be the old man's *before* the murder. But Gamboni concedes that the boards look like flooring and thus the image may allude to the story's conclusion (although there is no return of the dead man's eye mentioned in the tale—there is only the beating of a heart). What's more, if this is the old man's eye, dead or alive, it does not seem to have any special grotesque film over it. It seems like an entirely normal eye. Indeed, that is part of why it is unsettling.

There are two other eyes we might consider—those belonging to the reader of Poe and to the viewer of Redon. As I mentioned, Redon called this *After Reading Edgar Poe; or, The Eye*, a title suggesting, perhaps, that Poe's tales are the kind that keep you up at night in anxious watchfulness. The reader, in this view, is a target of the text and thus brought into proximity to both the narrator and the old man in "The Tell-Tale Heart," neither of whom gets much sleep either. Seeing and being seen are reversible in Poe's tale, which dramatizes a web in which predator becomes prey.

The idea that the reader, too, is caught in this web would be consistent with Poe's practice. Celebrating the power of shorter forms, Poe emphasizes with some relish that "during the hour of perusal the soul of the reader is at the writer's control." Turning back to Redon's hanging eyeball, and emphasizing its ambiguous power as both fixed and fixating, we might see here an analogy to Poe's "control" of his audience. If it illustrates "The Tell-Tale Heart," I would suggest finally, Redon's image does so by distilling in one striking image an entire narrative logic, becoming a visual version of what Poe prized as "unity of effect." Redon's image is a coup d'oeil, something that is taken in as a whole and quickly, in a glance, and also forcefully, a kind of blow (*coup*). On this interpretation, the image becomes what Redon called a "transmission"—a kind of energy transfer—of Poe's entire problematization of sight and blindness, rather than a mere illustration of a narrative moment, which in the nature of things must be partial, not a "unity."

The many fugitive eyeballs in Redon's work testify to his sustained focus on sight and visibility as capacities that outstrip the scale of the human. But like Manet, Redon found something profound in Poe's work, something that advanced his own project of investigating the graphic. That investigation, I think, is less about sight or visibility taken on their own than about the capture and fixation of attention more generally. The coup d'oeil works because of all that lies coiled *behind* the visible surface, what I called Redon's transmission of the narrative economy of Poe's tale.

We cannot help feeling as if we occupy both sides of Redon's image, I have suggested, and thus occupy the positions of both seer and seen. Our appropriation of the image, we might say, is in suspense—as indeed is the eyeball. And Poe's tale, of course, is fundamentally driven by a narrative logic of suspense. The narrator taking an hour to open the door wide enough to see into the old man's bedroom; the narrator returning night after night to perform this agonizing exercise; the narrator trying to keep from confessing to the policemen; the narrator appealing to us not to condemn him as a madman—the mode of suspense permeates every aspect of the tale, and of its telling.

But suspense is not eternal. It is a matter of coil and recoil; what has been stretched tight has to snap. And Poe's tales have snap. This aspect of his narrative art explains a great deal of his later impact. The genre of the detective story, which he invented, is based on snap: the locked room always gets unlocked in the end. And this is true of what I have called his black boxes too. "The Tell-Tale Heart" is indeed claustrophobic, a series of enclosures, from the walls of the old man's bedroom to the floorboards covering his body. But what makes for the story's snap is that the labor of enclosure recoils on itself in a climax of disclosure. The old man's room is eventually entered, the grave beneath the floorboards gives up its secret after all, and of course the narrator's confession *to us* opens everything up again: right from the start, enclosure and disclosure are woven together.

This is true of many of Poe's tales of enclosure: "The Black Cat" and "The Fall of the House of Usher," to take two examples, are also tales of the failure to wall up or to hide. Other tales represent variants: Egaeus, in "Berenice," digs up in a trance state the body of his cousin; and if we take the tiny tinkling of the bell in "The Cask of Amontillado" as the sign of something escaping the crypt, something that eventually leads to the confession that is the tale itself, we can include that story in the series. Indeed, many of the most memorable moments in Poe's work are these moments of disclosure—the cat's cry from within the wall, Madeline's bloody return from the tomb, the thumping of the heart that pushes the narrator of "The Tell-Tale Heart" over the brink.

If you ask strangers what they remember about Poe, it will often be these scenes of disclosure. The concept of closure as used in literary studies describes an experience of narrative shape as satisfyingly gathered and rounded off—"the sense of an ending." Closure is memorable. If what I have called the black box is a formal feature capable of transfer across media, it is in part because Poe's tales are memorable and portable. But it is also because they model closure in terms of this dynamic, a seemingly paradoxical weave of enclosure and disclosure. The coup d'oeil of Redon's hanging eyeball captures this dynamic in visual terms—and captures us in the process. Redon, too, has a version of the black box in play. We can see it in the inky strip of darkness out of which the eye gazes.

Disclosure

"Mr. Clarke can make a daisy look corrupt." So wrote a reviewer in 1920, reviewing Harry Clarke's illustrated *Tales of Mystery and Imagination*, brought out by George Harrap & Co. in 1919. And it's true. Clarke, who divided his time between work in stained glass and book illustration, was a leading figure in the Irish Arts and Crafts Movement who inherited from symbolism and art nouveau a tendency to portray the fecund as monstrous. Consider his illustration from "Morella," one of Poe's tales in which a beloved woman comes back from the dead (see figure 1.6).

What first strikes the viewer is the intricacy and textural detail—the sheer busyness of it all. And yet it imposes itself as a unity, even as we may struggle to understand the details. The frame can barely contain all this activity. The image "evinces a *horror vacui*" made all the more convincing by the glimpse of the void at the top left and top right. This is a black box that, like Poe's stories, displays an effort at enclosure against the ever-present threat of its failure. Like Redon, Clarke had a feel for the natural world in its evolutionary monstrosity; while Redon imagined primitive flowers that were eyes, Clarke gives us a series of exfoliating faces rising from a slurry of shell and hair. The living and the dead are in uncertain commerce here, as the artifice of jewels and patterned clothing becomes one with the organic flow of flower. Even as the narrator's obsession conjures forth multiples of Morella back from the dead, he himself seems to subside beneath the encrustations of a grasping life that cling to him like barnacles on a shipwrecked hull.

Clarke's images are among the most celebrated and influential in the vast canon of images of Poe's work. As tempting as it is to linger on them, I want to stay focused on the hints about Poe's appeal to graphic artists that Redon's treatment provided. Those hints were about how the dynamic of enclosure and disclosure might be dramatized by the graphic artist, how Poe's black box might be translated in terms of the single image whose frame or surface becomes an agitated element in the whole. The nearly bursting frame of Clarke's illustration for "Morella" offers one example.

A more explicit example, though no less complicated for all that, can be seen in Clarke's illustration of "The Tell-Tale Heart" (see figure 1.7).

FIGURE 1.6. *Horror vacui.* Illustration by Harry Clarke for "Morella" in Edgar Allan Poe, *Tales of Mystery and Imagination* (New York: George Harrap & Co., 1919). Courtesy of Lilly Library, Indiana University.

At first sight, this image behaves more like a conventional illustration than Redon's: it pictures a delimited narrative moment, something we saw that Redon's hanging eyeball resisted doing. Clarke's image even has a caption: "But, for many minutes, the heart beat on with a muffled sound." Like Redon, Clarke has intuited that this sonic denouement does

FIGURE 1.7. Sound as vision. Illustration by Harry Clarke of "The Tell-Tale Heart" in Edgar Allan Poe, *Tales of Mystery and Imagination* (New York: George Harrap & Co., 1919). Courtesy of Lilly Library, Indiana University.

not mean we have left the play of eyes behind: the murderous narrator stares out at us—or maybe through us, given his obviously preoccupied state—but so too does the dead man, muffled under the covers. Clarke has conflated the murder scene—a bed—with the burial scene under the floorboards.

Most striking of all, a very Redonesque isolated eyeball perches atop the plant-like growth that emerges from where the dead man lies and that climbs up the side of the image. This climbing growth seems to allude to the organic ornamentation of borders so characteristic of art nouveau illustration. If so, the exfoliation on the right border captures visually what the story tells us narratively, namely that what you thought was outside the frame, or safely contained beneath the boards, is curling into the space itself, compromising its enclosure.

Clarke takes on a problem that Redon avoids: how does one depict the beating of the heart itself in this moment of climax? Clarke here reaches for the resources of icon and emblem that would become only more prevalent in the graphic arts over the next century—and by graphic arts, I mean all the inheritors of the tradition of nineteenth-century illustration—advertising, cartoons, comics, graphic novels, animation, and so on. Look closely again at how Clarke represents the sound of the beating heart (see figure 1.8).

Under the watchful gaze of the eyestalk, two tendrils curl toward the murderer. The most elaborate growth captures the repetitiveness of the heartbeats by fanning out a series of heart icons that culminate in a perfectly centered heart-form that reads like some kind of sick-joke Valentine: "I ❤ the old man." This is Clarke at his most cartoony. But notice also the strange pendant hanging beneath. As if to balance the nonnaturalistic iconicity of his heart shapes, Clarke hangs something shaped suspiciously like a *real* heart. And the other, higher, tendril seems to split the difference: heart icons but veinous and drippy like the pendant organ below.

I want to pull two threads from this discussion of Clarke's images. The first is that, like Redon, Clarke seeks to project visually the dynamic of containment and its failure that he finds in Poe's work, and he does so with the means most immediately at his disposal: the edge, border, or frame marking off the image and the black void that seems to lie behind it. The second thread concerns use of visual icons, such as the heart shape in the image above: such icons represent a turn toward the more pervasively iconic visual vocabulary of the rest of the twentieth century, the vocabulary of advertising and design, comics and cartoons—all forms that place a premium on rapid intelligibility, the coup d'oeil.

In 1940, a limited edition was released in Urbino titled *Quattro racconti di Edgardo Allan Poë*. The engravings are by Pietrino Vicenzi, and they are weird. Throughout the series, Vicenzi summons deep blacks, perhaps

FIGURE 1.8. Hearts and the eye-flower. Illustration (detail) by Harry Clarke of "The Tell-Tale Heart" in Edgar Allan Poe, *Tales of Mystery and Imagination* (New York: George Harrap & Co., 1919). Courtesy of Lilly Library, Indiana University.

through resin-treated aquatint technique, but also stipples and scratches his images until they seem to crackle and flow with mysterious energies. The style is largely expressionist. Vicenzi gives yet another treatment of "The Tell-Tale Heart" (see figure 1.9).

The wide margins and tall, narrow format isolate the image, adding to a sense of stark, almost coffin-like, enclosure that contracts even more extremely through perspective effects. Rather than threatening to burst the frame, Vicenzi's image seems to implode. The violence of the scene literally bends space, as the entire bed becomes a flexible weapon in the hands of the murderer.

Like Clarke, Vicenzi brings eye and heart into emblematic proximity (see figure 1.10). The old man's eye looks out at us, but it is the heart that takes on the role of the inhuman eye, sending out rays of brilliant light. Vicenzi captures in his own way the play of visibility and blindness that structurers Poe's tale: the murderer here, in stamping out life, is stamping out light. Rather than play with the frame, though, Vicenzi suggests that the dynamic of enclosure and disclosure plays itself out in the center of the image, as emanating light and vorticial darkness fight for dominance.

FIGURE 1.9. Murder of the old man. Engraving by Pietrino Vicenzi of "The Tell-Tale Heart" in Edgar Allan Poe, *Quattro racconti di Edgardo Allan Poë* (Urbino: R. Istituto d'arte di Urbino, 1940). Courtesy of the Newberry Library, Chicago. Call number ZP 935.I87.

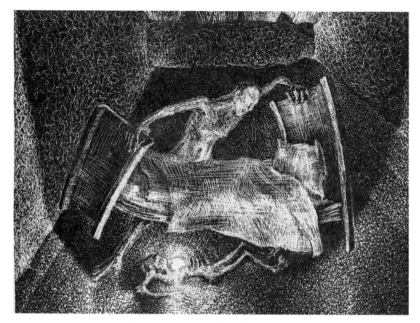

FIGURE 1.10. Eye and heart. Engraving (detail) by Pietrino Vicenzi of "The Tell-Tale Heart" in Edgar Allan Poe, *Quattro racconti di Edgardo Allan Poë* (Urbino: R. Istituto d'arte di Urbino, 1940). Courtesy of the Newberry Library, Chicago. Call number ZP 935.I87.

Another example of locating representational limits at the heart rather than at edge of the image is provided by Abner Epstein's treatment of "The Fall of the House of Usher" in 1931. Epstein was the nephew of the renowned modernist sculptor Jacob Epstein, and under the name "Abner Dean," he became a significant and offbeat cartoonist for the *New Yorker* and other publications. Exploiting the muscular effects possible with woodcuts, Epstein sucks us in to the image, even more than Vicenzi (see figure 1.11).

The sightlines here hurtle across an electrified field toward a small, darkened rectangle edging off the right border. This could be Roderick eyeing intently the door through which he knows Madeline will return, or perhaps Madeline herself looking toward the door she will open to disastrous effect. In either case, something may enter or exit from this black box. The uncanny emergence of Madeline may be the *theme* of the image, but its *flow* is in the opposite direction, as if the world might be sucked into the distant doorway.

In Poe's story, there is a remarkable passage in which the narrator struggles to describe the effect of one of Usher's paintings:

> One of the phantasmagoric conceptions of my friend, partaking not so rigidly of the spirit of abstraction, may be shadowed forth, although feebly, in words. A small picture presented the interior of an immensely long and rectangular vault or tunnel, with low walls, smooth, white, and without interruption or device. Certain accessory points of the design served well to convey the idea that this excavation lay at an exceeding depth below the surface of the earth. No outlet was observed in any portion of its vast extent, and no torch, or other artificial source of light was discernible; yet a flood of intense rays rolled throughout, and bathed the whole in a ghastly and inappropriate splendor.

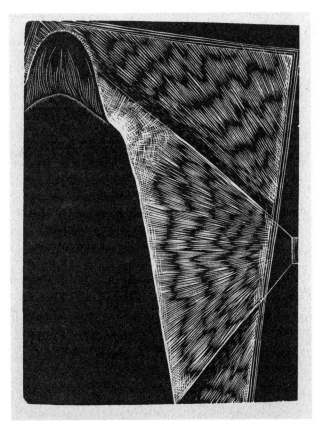

FIGURE 1.11. The black box disappearing into itself. Woodcut by Abner Epstein for Edgar Allan Poe, *The Fall of the House of Usher* (New York: Cheshire House, 1931). Courtesy of the Newberry Library, Chicago. Call number ZP 983.E464.

We cannot help thinking that Roderick has imaged the grave itself, a crypt or mausoleum: a "long and rectangular vault or tunnel . . . at an exceeding depth below the surface of the earth." Poe has included within his tale a description of the internal limit of his own fiction, the black box that lies at the heart of his paradoxical aesthetic project of casting nothingness itself—the absolutely dark—"in a ghastly and inappropriate splendor." Epstein's woodcut captures perfectly the way Poe's description functions as a miniaturization of the whole: the distant rectangle that draws the figure to it as if through some kind of magnetic attraction draws us as well, sucking *our* rectangle—the image as a whole—into the black hole of its own model.

My discussion of the images of Clarke, Vicenzi, and Epstein demonstrates that what I have called Poe's black box—with its dramatization of enclosure and disclosure and its investigation of blindness and visibility, blackness and "ghastly and inappropriate splendor"—has been taken up by some talented graphic artists as a challenge and a chance. I am not claiming that "the best" artists follow this path. Doré is a master illustrator, and there are many other sophisticated engagements with Poe—by Arthur Rackham, Alexandre Alexeieff, Aubrey Beardsley, Richard Corben, and others—that seize on different aspects of Poe's work.

But the problems being worked out by the artists I have surveyed tell us something essential about how Poe's work helps to realize an aesthetics of the *graphic*, as we experience that mode today. The graphic lays stress on certain formal features—closure, impact, the coup d'oeil—that have become increasingly fundamental to our way of looking at images over the 170 years since Poe's death.

This is the second thread I promised to follow out of the discussion of Clarke's images. I noted that in his illustration of the climax of "The Tell-Tale Heart" Clarke avails himself of the conventional icon of a heart to depict what he cannot picture—the sonic phenomenon of the repeated heartbeats. It is as if the very artificiality of this icon was the appropriate way to index the impossibility of the representational task at hand. Perhaps the weird distortions present in the images we have been looking at—distortions of bodily shape, of perspective, of space, of what can be seen and what not, of what gives off light and what swallows it up—are also in service to such an acknowledgment of representational limits.

Artifice and exaggeration here would not be marks of aesthetic failure, then, but rather signs to the viewer that certain aesthetic failures are built in, inescapable. The artifice of the icon, on this reading, would not be merely a labor-saving device in search of dramatic impact; it would also be a kind of metamessage about the representational task at hand, and its limits. This may help explain why some artists reach beyond the icon to something more closely resembling the emblem. A single-image illustration of "The Tell-Tale Heart" by John Coulthart is all about immediate visual impact, and it uses naturalistic imagery—the heart and the eye are immediately legible as such—in service of a grotesque, exaggerated, and decidedly nonnaturalistic composition—an eyeball lodged in a heart. One's attention can be grabbed by Coulthart's image, whether one has read the story or not. But it assumes, I think, a viewer who also knows Poe's tale—its play with eyes and heart, confessional agony, and so on. Not unlike a Renaissance emblem, we are meant to decode this highly artificial image in line with a preexisting field of meaning, in this case Poe's text.

Others have turned to this emblematic approach. One of the four illustrations Redon offered Hennequin was for "Berenice," and it consisted of a set of teeth with wings flying out of a library: you need to know Poe's tale to see this image as anything other than merely bizarre. René Magritte, lifelong devotee of Poe, also produced an emblem for "Berenice" (1948) that consisted of a pair of closed red lips surrounded by extracted teeth. I suppose one can find Magritte's image both beautiful and grisly and be seized by it even if you do not know the story. But having once read Poe's beautiful and grisly tale about a man who becomes obsessed with his cousin's teeth and then, in a trance, removes all thirty-two of them, one does not forget it. And it is that reader, I presume, whom Magritte addresses with this visual emblem of the tale, teeth liberated from the mouth. In its way, this too is an image of disclosure.

To conclude this exploration of gestures of graphic disclosure, I turn to a remarkable treatment of "The Tell-Tale Heart" by Argentinian comics artist Alberto Breccia. Widely celebrated for his artwork in the science-fiction/horror comics series *Mort Cinder* (1962–64), Breccia also had an abiding fascination with Poe, illustrating "The Facts in the Case of M. Valdemar," "The Black Cat," "William Wilson," and "The Masque of the Red Death." These are all powerful treatments—the "Valdemar" especially—whose expressionist drawing and patchy coloring bring out the kind of queasy feeling we often get reading Poe. But Breccia's first attempt was "The Tell-Tale Heart" (1974), and it is in an entirely different style (see figure 1.12).

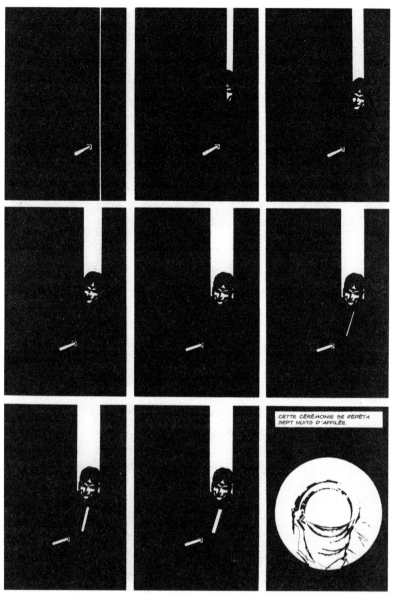

FIGURE 1.12. The black box and the gutter. Comic by Alberto Breccia of Edgar Allan Poe's "The Tell-Tale Heart." © Estate of Alberto Breccia. Reproduced by permission of Rackham Editions.

Breccia understands two crucial things about Poe's tale—it is about the black box, and it produces suspense by repetition. Here the default form of the comic-book format—the nine-panel grid—is used to great effect, as over eight of the panels, Poe's murderous narrator slowly inserts himself into the darkness. In Redon's hanging eyeball, the darkness lay without, but Breccia places the reader squarely within the blackness of the old man's room. The absolute uniformity of the panel size produces an effect of clocklike repetition against which the glacial change introduced by the intruder stands out vividly.

Breccia uses the same effect during the waiting game with the policemen at the end (see figure 1.13). Very little changes here. The policemen are identical in all six panels in which they appear. There is a slow zoom in on the narrator in the left-hand panels, and of course the beating heart—depicted, as the graphic idiom of comics allows, as a lettered sound effect—grows in volume. But Breccia uses the grid primarily to indicate how little is happening.

Look back to the previous image now. Notice what comics artists call the "gutter"—the spacing between panels. Scott McCloud, in *Understanding Comics*, has pointed out that the "gutter" is essential to the narrative goals of comics art, since in navigating the void between images the reader is forced to supply all the missing action between panels. McCloud calls this collaboration between artist and reader "closure." It's a complex idea. In "closure" we fill in what's missing, but we can only be asked to do that if we have to confront the absence that *is* the gutter. "Closure" lies behind one of the special traits of the comics medium, namely that we both "see" (all in one go) and "read" (in a certain order) the page before us. We "see" the suspense of the story in Breccia's repetitive nine-panel grid even before we "read" the incremental changes ratcheting up the suspense.

In the page depicting the opening of the old man's door, Breccia offers a kind of second-order refinement of this process. What we see, in effect, as the strip of light widens with the slow opening of the door, is the incursion of the gutter into the panel, or perhaps the creation of a new gutter. I have been insisting that the "closure" of Poe's tales, the snap that we remember and that thus becomes portable to other media, is a dynamic tension between enclosure and disclosure. This apparent contradiction is structural to the comics medium as well—no unity without the gutter, no closure unless we incorporate the empty spaces between the closed-off panels.

FIGURE 1.13. The black box, repetition, and suspense. Comic by Alberto Breccia of Edgar Allan Poe's "The Tell-Tale Heart." © Estate of Alberto Breccia. Reproduced by permission of Rackham Editions.

What's graphic in Poe is what's graphic in Breccia; in remediating the former, the latter both uses and comments on the formal traits they share.

The artists I have been looking at do not turn to Poe only because he was famous, or because his work offered gripping narratives to illustrate—though such considerations are surely in play. In their explorations of the nature of graphic representation, they unearth *formal* arguments from Poe's work about the essence of the graphic: namely, that it combines the vivid and the obscure in uneasy balance, that unity of effect depends on a paradoxical commingling of enclosure and disclosure. Issues of format—the artist's book, the album, the anthology—are often important, and Poe's status as an icon of "literariness" is everywhere present. But my overarching aim has been to use Poe's striking works, and their uptake by visual artists, to fill out a concept of the graphic that is faithful to its semantic root in the Greek *graphein*—both mark and letter—and that thus "belongs" neither to literature nor to visual art exclusively, but rather brings the two together.

Facing the Unreadable

I have been tracking the several ways in which visual artists develop an idea of the graphic in dialogue with Poe's works: they have taken from Poe powerful models of closure and disclosure, and they have mined his tales as well for a dynamic in which the visible and the invisible, the eye and its dispossession, come to play a role in graphic art. As I bring this first chapter to a close, I want to look at two more radical engagements with the format of the book, as that is put under pressure by the contradiction at the heart of the graphic.

An obscure artist's book by Heinz Veuhoff from the 1960s, *The Haunted Palace*, knots several of our threads together in a strikingly idiosyncratic way. Poe's poem "The Haunted Palace," originally published in 1839, was later incorporated into "The Fall of the House of Usher." The poem unfolds an allegory in which a "fair and stately palace— / Radiant palace—reared its head" only, in time, to become haunted by madness. One of Veuhoff's facing-page images is captioned "Radiant Palace" (see figure 1.14).

Veuhoff is fully alive to the allegory of Poe's poem: this "palace" looks humanoid, if not human. Vaguely architectural elements are surmounted by what can be read as a face with a wild spray of wiry hair; a kind of squid eye slides off the right side of the face. Rather than radiant, though, this palace seems already to have succumbed to disordered madness. Its radiance, we

might say, is like that of Roderick's abstract painting, emanating the kind of "ghastly and inappropriate splendor" found in a crypt.

The image feels a bit like a frontispiece. "'Frontispiece' has come to mean any illustration facing the title page, but initially it meant to look at head-on," Andrew Piper tells us in his wonderful *Book Was There*. "*Frontispicium*, from *fons* (forehead) and *specio* (look). In its earliest form it applied to architecture, meaning a 'façade.' . . . [It] was Pindar who first equated writing with building (as in his sixth Olympic Ode: 'As when we contrive a stately mansion, supporting on golden pillars the well-built portal of the edifice, we will construct the hymn')." The frontispiece is a face or head, in other words, and it is a building, and it is a page. Veuhoff's image does not face the title page, it is not an image of the author, it is not a facade in any obvious way. And yet it evokes all of those. In its allusion to the form of the frontispiece, the image cuts into deeply sedimented layers of book arts.

Helga Schiskowsky, Veuhoff's dealer and publisher, tells us about the process of the book's composition. Veuhoff began by thinking he'd provide "realistic and illustrating" images, but he vetoed that idea, then toyed with taking existing images and "intuitively placing them into the book," discarded that idea as well, and then made a series of twenty-five drawings, cut them apart, pasted them into different arrangements, and added "linework woven into them." These too were destroyed. Nothing served: "Nothing seemed to come close to that vague, the abstract idea [Veuhoff] had of the book as a whole body. Nothing was intensive, nothing seemed to have the continuous flow which he wanted in combination of text and drawing."

"That vague, abstract idea of the book as a whole body." The concreteness of a book, of a body, is accompanied, as it were, by its own vague and abstract dimension. Schiskowsky tells us that Veuhoff settled at last on a collage technique, using different typefaces for letters and word fragments, and "finally a network of lines was spun in between, above and behind them, connecting letters and wordfragments." This "gave him the stability and continuous flow of the book as a whole." On the one hand, Veuhoff is availing himself of the techniques of the "electric information age book": such play with fonts, collage, and phototypography was common in the 1960s, as for example in Marshall McLuhan's *The Medium Is the Massage*. On the other hand, such wildness gives way to something more primitive, something we encountered earlier with reference to Manet: "intense and idiosyncratic markmaking."

Veuhoff thought of his work in organic terms, likening his process to a slow and imponderable process of ripening. But if so, this is a reconstructed organism—it is an artificial organism, a cut-up—one in which letter, line, and composite image seek both "stability and flow." This body—the abstract body of the book, the graphic body—is not a human body; it is a body that has both stability and flow, the letters often serving as seeming attractors for energies and currents visible in the abstract lines. The lines seem at times to hint at striations and sedimentations that are well-nigh

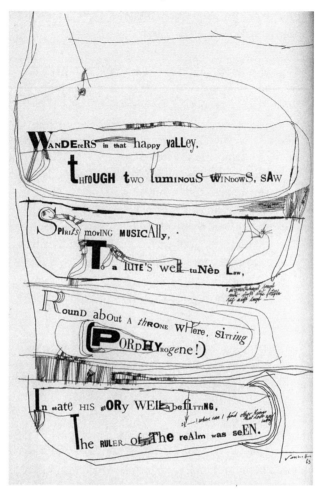

FIGURE 1.15. "Porphyrogene!" Illustration by Heinz Veuhoff in Edgar Allan Poe, *The Haunted Palace* (New York: H. Schiskowsky, 1963). Courtesy of the Newberry Library, Chicago. Call number ZP 983.V594.

geological, and at other times they suggest spider's silk, that substance simultaneously flimsy and extraordinarily strong (see figure 1.15).

Why does Poe present himself to Veuhoff as a resource for this experimentation with graphic abstraction? I have hinted at one reason already. The very literariness of Poe's poem—a classic conceit poem in which the human mind is likened to a palace—unearths conventions of book arts that speak to Veuhoff, such as his play with the frontispiece in the image captioned "Radiant Palace." The geological, sedimented aspect of the linework is at the same time a "network"—that is, an image of filiation.

And make no mistake, Poe's poem is literary—even excessively so. "Porphyrogene!" Who uses such a word? Well, poets do. Specifically, the kinds of poets that Daniel Tiffany has in mind when he argues that it is in the ornate, artificial language of pre-Romantic poetry that we find the origin of *kitsch*: "The schism underlying the emergence of kitsch occurred not between literature and popular culture as we know it today but between the residual genre of poetry and the emergent supergenre of literature. A recalcitrant but also renegade school of poetry—the precursor of kitsch—assembled a fossilized language from archaic diction and a radicalized vernacular to avoid the middle ground of 'polite conversation'—the purity of diction—cultivated polemically by the new school of *literary* poets (Wordsworth and his followers)."

(Wordsworth would never use the word "Porphyrogene." Then again, Poe didn't have much time for Wordsworth, about whose work he commented drily: "I love a sheep from the bottom of my heart").

Veuhoff's "Haunted Palace" is, I think, a work of power, intricacy, and imaginative freedom. But it is not a work of subtlety. As we have seen, Poe does not feed into projects of politeness and subtlety. His work—radically abstract and mythic, as Northrop Frye correctly observes—challenges later artists on a different level. One of those levels, as Tiffany allows us to see, is kitsch. Poe's poem uses "fossilized language" and "archaic diction" in what Tiffany calls a "refractory and militant form of poeticism." And that is just what Veuhoff, interested in the abstract body of the book, likes about it. Looked at the right way, Veuhoff's practice begins to look kitschy—in other words, as if he is less interested in the words themselves and what they mean (do we need to know what "porphyrogene" means to revel in its artifice?) than in how they might serve as a vehicle for encrustations.

In the final analysis, Veuhoff's text sends the graphic past intelligibility. Who needs it to be readable? What is essential is that one experience the cosmic energy of artifice itself, submit to it, be carried away. Stability and flow, as in the furious and yet somehow settled blur of lines captioned "To a Lute's Well-Tuned Law." Poe provokes in Veuhoff, too, "intense and idiosyncratic markmaking" (see figure 1.16).

FIGURE 1.16. The black box filling up. "To a Lute's Well-Tuned Law." Illustration by Heinz Veuhoff in Edgar Allan Poe, *The Haunted Palace* (New York: H. Schiskowsky, 1963). Courtesy of the Newberry Library, Chicago. Call number ZP 983.V594.

We might call the abstraction of this page a field of graphic energy: word and line, page and print, everything gets raveled up in the insistence of markmaking evident here, as it is throughout Veuhoff's strange art book. It is the black box filling up—vivid and vague, darkness visible.

In 1937, Edward James, René Magritte's English patron, commissioned three canvases from the Belgian surrealist. One of them is a portrait of James (see plate 4).

Magritte titled this canvas *La reproduction interdite*, usually translated as "Not to be Reproduced." It is a phrase common in the legal language prohibiting unauthorized use of images or texts, as in *"toute reproduction interdite sans l'autorisation écrite expresse des éditeurs."* The title is a kind of puzzle, as it often is with Magritte. What, exactly, is not to be reproduced? The painting itself—"no photographs, please"? Edward James's face? If the latter, Magritte could be commenting on the genre of portrait painting, as if to say, "You and I both know, Mr. James, that portrait painting is thoroughly archaic in this modern age, and in any case pretends to capture and reproduce a uniqueness that cannot be so captured. So why pretend?"

But as always with Magritte, the play of frames is decisive. The frame around the canvas contains a second frame: a mirror, angling to the back left, giving a sense of window being half opened. Mirrors in portraits are common, of course; and in self-portraits, *very* common, serving as a way both to show off the painter's skill at likeness and to fold into the painting the drama of the scene of its making. This mirror is a bit strange, however, and not only because it reflects the back of James's body rather than the front. The man's body is reflected straight on, rather than slightly from the side, as the angle of the mirror should dictate. The body seems copied, in other words, rather than reflected. Magritte's legalistic title points beyond the values of likeness, reflection, or the artisanal production of unique artifacts that are asserted in the mirror/portrait convention. It points to the world of mechanical reproducibility and the circulation of identical copies—and the prohibition on such circulation. It points, in fact, to the only mechanically reproduced item in the picture—the book on the mantel (see plate 5).

It is a copy of Poe's *The Narrative of Arthur Gordon Pym of Nantucket* in French translation. And unlike the face and front of the man standing before the mirror, the book is accurately reflected there—that is to say, it is reversed. The unique person standing before the mirror confronts merely a cutout copy of himself that does not obey the laws of optics; the book, native inhabitant of the world of copies, is accurately reflected, but that means that it can't be properly read. (That is, as it exists in the mirror, the book could be read only by translating back the inverted letters). Both book and face are deprived of their essential offering to the world in this mirror reflection: the face cannot be seen, and the book cannot be read.

Magritte was an eminently graphic painter, in the sense that interests us: he concerned himself with the relation between word and image, letter and line. In his short book on the painter, Michel Foucault suggests we approach Magritte's work through the calligram, the shape-poem made famous in French literature by Apollinaire. The calligram enforces the distinction between looking and reading by confusing them. It is a bit like the duck/rabbit: you see they are a whole, but you can't see both aspects of the figure simultaneously: "Thus the calligram aspires playfully to efface the oldest oppositions of our alphabetical civilization: to show and to name; to shape and to say; to reproduce and to articulate; to imitate and to signify; to look and to read."

We could say that Magritte literalizes such an "effacement" in *La reproduction interdite*—except that to "literalize" anything sends us back to letters and words, which it is not clear Magritte wants to do. The graphic, as "dialectic of word and image," is always a scene of contest, a jockeying for primacy. Certain conventions—illustration in a book, captioning beneath an image—can stabilize things for a while, but the contest is irresolvable. Foucault suggests that Magritte is intent on presenting that irresolvability itself: instead of taking a position in the ongoing dialectic of word and image, Magritte gives us a face-off.

Ultimately, it is the system of representation itself, that unstable conjunction of "plastic representation (which implies resemblance) and linguistic reference (which excludes it)" that Magritte questions: instead of resemblance, Magritte gives us "similitude": "Resemblance serves representation, which rules over it; similitude serves repetition, which ranges across it. Resemblance predicates itself upon a model it must return to and reveal; similitude circulates the simulacrum as an indefinite and reversible relation of the similar to the similar." In refusing to depict Edward James's face, Magritte foils resemblance; in having the book's letters reflect accurately, he installs similitude.

Face, book. Interface. Facebook. Facing pages: a frontispiece is an image facing the title page of a book, originally the face of the author. In *Book Was There*, Andrew Piper explores the intricate linkages between the face and the book. "The face is where reading and seeing merge. We see letters and we read faces." Well, yes, though we also read letters and see faces. And that's Piper's point: the face is the privileged location for the always unstable but inescapable conjunction of reading and seeing, word and image. There resides an experience or perhaps fantasy of transparency: we train ourselves to see through the letters on the page—in a sense, to not see them—to attain an "image" in our head conjured by the words. We feel sometimes that we can read someone—read them like a book—by scrutinizing their face. But the face is also of course often inscrutable, opaque: the place where the structural *non*coincidence of reading and seeing becomes visible.

At the end of Poe's story "The Man of the Crowd" (1840), the narrator, who had been trailing a peripatetic old man all day and night, finally stops "fully in front of the wanderer" and gazes at him "steadfastly in the face": "He noticed me not, but resumed his solemn walk." Shaken, the narrator philosophizes: "This old man . . . is the type and genius of deep crime. He refuses to be alone. He is *the man of the crowd*. It will be in vain to follow; for I shall learn no more of him, nor of his deeds. The worst heart of the world is a grosser book than the *Hortulus Animae*, and perhaps it is one of the great mercies of God that '*er lasst sich nicht lesen*.'"

The German phrase, translated at the beginning of the tale as "it does not permit itself to be read," has never been traced by scholars; Poe may have made it up. But its meaning in context is fairly clear: the old man is unreadable, and what's more, that's a good thing. The narrator suggests that it's the "heart" that can't be read, but the action of the story makes it a matter of faces. Gazing "steadfastly in the face" of the old man, he gains no knowledge, and it is implied that the old man's failure to *acknowledge* the narrator at all is somehow tied up with this unsettling failure. "Who can read the heart of man?" is a cliché, but it's much more uncanny to arrive at this idea through the experience of being invisible to the very person into whose face you are gazing. The failure of Edward James's face to appear in the mirror is uncanny in this way.

We arrive, then, at the delayed question: Why a book by Poe? Why *this* book? *The Narrative of Arthur Gordon Pym of Nantucket*, in Baudelaire's 1858 translation, has a unique place in French letters. Jules Verne wrote a sequel to it, and in *À rebours*, Joris-Karl Huysmans has his narrator dedicate an entire room to maritime fantasy, tricked out with porthole window and artificial seaweed; the only book is a volume of *Pym*, bound in seacalf leather. Magritte's well-thumbed paperback is hardly so grand, but its singular placement suggests that *Pym* retains for him a fetishistic power.

Of course, Poe's novel also features some memorable thematizations of the problems of reading/seeing: disappearing ink, huge characters carved into rockface in an unknown language. Poe scholars have also demonstrated how Poe's text is structured by symmetry and inversion, right down to the typography of the title page, which offers a shape suggestive of a ship above the midline and its inversion below, as if mirrored in the water. The novel features much puzzling play with frame narrations: perhaps Magritte, ever a fan of play with frames, is thinking of that. And as one strong recent interpretation points out, Poe's novel itself plays games with facial (un)recognizability. But for my purposes here, it doesn't much matter if we find a specific reason. It could be none or (less plausibly) all of these features of Poe's tale that make it ready to hand for Magritte's purposes here.

Magritte's engagement with Poe was deep and wide, and it spanned his entire career—*La démon de la perversité* dates from 1928 and *Le domaine d'Arnheim* from 1962. Poe reached Magritte on several frequencies. I have already mentioned the unnerving image Magritte created from Poe's "Berenice," extracted teeth circling a closed mouth. This grisly tale, it turns out, played a special role in the development of surrealism: both Max Ernst (who also produced a canvas titled *Berenice*) and Magritte reported that reading about Egaeus's trancelike attentiveness echoed powerfully their own experiences of vision.

Egaeus tells us he was wont to "muse for long unwearied hours with my attention rivetted to some frivolous device upon the margin, or in the typography of a book." In his autobiographical essay, "La ligne de vie" (1938), Magritte tells of an Egaeus-like "prolonged contemplative experience" in a Brussels brasserie, in which he gets caught up in the "mysterious quality" of the "moldings on a door." We might call Egaeus's fixation on a feature of typography a kind of misreading, but more consequential for his narrative is his misreading of Berenice's face: in her illness, Berenice appears before him with melancholy countenance and lusterless eyes, but what Poe delivers at this moment is a kind of lap dissolve from her visage as a composed whole to an isolated set of teeth within the mouth. The face is erased as the teeth come forward.

Magritte is a puzzling artist. His visual idiom is simplified, even child-like: everyday iconic objects—a pipe, a bowler hat, a wooden wall—are placed in strange juxtapositions. His titles and the use of words within his compositions can sometimes feel like little more than brain teasers. It is certainly true that neither Poe nor Magritte was interested in putting their work in the service of any aesthetic ideology of growth or maturity. Rather, they are artists of the impasse, of transparencies and opacities so extreme that they come to resemble one another in causing misfires or blockages in received systems of meaning-making.

I have argued throughout this chapter that the concept of the graphic, released from the conventions developed to stabilize the contest between word and image, tends toward its own undoing—toward blackness or il-legibility inscribed as a kind of sinkhole within representations seeming to promise precisely the opposite. Nothing could seem on its surface more given to understanding than Magritte's simple graphic elements. But they are never fully legible. In *La reproduction interdite*, with Poe carefully placed as tutelary presence, Magritte places his own art, as a technique of resemblance, under the sign of the unreadable, that which is striking and visible yet finally opaque. And thus does the graphic achieve repose at its own dark heart.

Unwatchable

The Frenzy of the Visible and the Grave of the Eye

In the latter half of the nineteenth century, the proliferation of things to see—photographs of exotic locales, a horse caught midcanter, one's own face on a carte de visite—incited "a frenzy of the visible," an importunate desire to inspect, to "*'get closer' to things*." Early cinema provides many instances of this phenomenon. Edison's film *The Kiss* (1896), for example, is simple enough: two stage actors reproduce for the camera the kiss they share in a popular play. If you were to see it in the theater, you would watch from a distance as two people kissed, but the film shows the kiss itself, as it were, up close. The kiss is shown in *graphic detail* in Edison's film, by which I mean that something actually existing in the world has been rendered unusually explicit.

Less than six months after the first public announcement of the invention of the daguerreotype, Poe went on record about the new technology. He does not hold back: "The Daguerreotyped plate is infinitely (we use the term advisedly) is *infinitely* more accurate in its representation than any painting by human hands." The daguerreotype can satisfy any craving to get closer to things, and then some; it turns out the craving is finite while the technology is not. "If we examine a work of ordinary art, by means of a powerful microscope, all traces of resemblance to nature will disappear—but the closest scrutiny of the photogenic drawing discloses only a more absolute truth, a more perfect identity of aspect with the thing represented." The daguerreotype, or "photogenic drawing," places in our hands a power of visualization greater than we can in fact verify: a "more absolute truth, a more perfect identity of aspect with the thing represented" will always lie, infinitely receding, beyond our powers of observation. What we see by subjecting the painting to microscopic scrutiny is how the painter disguises the fact that he cannot represent the world perfectly; what we see looking at the daguerreotype with equivalent intensity is a visible world in the "supremeness of its perfection," and thus beyond not just our powers to reproduce by the arts of resemblance but beyond our very capacities to apprehend. The daguerreotype both extends the power of our eye and exposes its limits.

The Kiss was a runaway hit, but it also provoked considerable backlash from religious and cultural authorities. We are so familiar with the dynamic in which graphic representation provokes a backlash of criticism, condemnation, even censorship, that it is hard to think about it clearly. The message of the critics is this: *just because something can be shown doesn't mean it should be seen*. Of course, such proscriptions are common in everyday life: just because a naked body *can* be shown does not mean it *should* be seen. But the advent of photography and then cinema exacerbated this conflict between showing and seeing. Somehow the camera eye's superhuman power to see things exposed the vulnerability of the merely human eye. No longer sovereign, the human eye could now be assaulted—or protected.

This vulnerability is not ultimately about the perceptual limitations of the human eye, *pace* Poe, or its organic identity. It was not about what the human eye could not see, finally, but what it *could* see—if the camera showed it. In the previous treatment of the "graphic," I argued that Poe's work appealed to graphic artists because "the black box"—an image of closure that at its limit holds absolute darkness, an eye opening on nothingness— provoked in these artists experimentation with their medium, which was after all markmaking, and thus dark-making. But photography and cinema are graphic *with light*. If Poe's "black box" was to be usable in this new graphic medium, it would need to be illuminated. (And, as we will see, it was). After photography and cinema, the problem of the graphic is the fact that everything can be seen.

"Graphic" representations have only accelerated in our time, whether we consider online pornography or the carnage depicted in film, videogames, and television or recorded on cell phones. But the term "graphic" meaning extreme representation rides piggyback on the "graphic" aspects of our everyday world, one saturated by images accessible to all, every one of them reminding us that there's more that can be shown than any one of us can, or should, see. As I noted earlier, when the Motion Picture Association feels the need to add "graphic" (for extreme) before "depiction" (which is graphic in its normal condition), it is this doubleness of the graphic that is at work. Perhaps we could say that the drive toward the extreme and excessive is now normal.

Think again about Edison's *The Kiss*. What could be more normal than a kiss? Ah yes, but is that same kiss seen in extreme close-up still normal? Is it not, perhaps, obscene?

In what follows, I extend my exploration of the aesthetics of the graphic by tracking how a visual culture of the normally extreme plays out in different historical moments. This culture is one in which the power to show is everywhere affirmed, but the ability—even the right—to see is cast into doubt. The triumph of total visibility as a principle is always shadowed by a reckoning with the vulnerability of the eye. This reckoning takes a variety of forms: attempts at censorship, the production of ceaseless discourse about what should be seen or shown, and thematizations of vision and of violence to the eye within individual works.

Nothing is unwatchable, not in and of itself. Rather, the "unwatchable" always refers to discourses about seeing and showing, not seeing and not showing. The "unwatchable" names the idea that at the heart of total visibility there is a limit, a blind spot, a blockage. In a recent collection of essays titled, precisely, *Unwatchable*, we find a variety of expressions of this idea. For example, "It is striking that the discourse around these images is often shaped not by the simple binary of showing and not showing, but rather by hybrid formations of both modes at once: One doesn't exhibit the images but talks about them at length; one withholds them but reports what *could have been seen* in them. In this way a curious dialectic is activated involving showing and hiding, seeing and imagining, not viewing and wanting to watch."

Jean-Louis Comolli, to whom we owe the memorable phrase "frenzy of the visible," offers another pithy comment: "The photograph stands at once as the triumph and the grave of the eye." To speak of the "grave" of the eye may sound hyperbolic. But the "frenzy of the visible" that unfolded from the mid-nineteenth century well into the twentieth was indeed shadowed by a "denigration of vision" that took many different forms. We can think of philosophical treatments of the limits of vision, or we can reach for literary mistreatments of the human eye, as in Georges Bataille's surrealist *L'histoire de l'oeil* (1928). Or we can turn to film, where denigration sometimes became overt aggression: the slitting of the eyeball in *Un chien Andalou* (1929) was shocking precisely because the power to see and the vulnerability of the eye were made to collide, a collision that seemed to destabilize the very institution of cinema, our seeing not just seen but destroyed.

Now consider the nearly contemporary film *Maniac* (1934), directed by Dwain Esper. *Maniac* is an example of what has come to be known as "exploitation" film—very low-budget affairs that evaded the censor's grasp by being shown in "grindhouse" venues rather than in the network of theaters tied to Hollywood. Not yet porn, but certainly not respectable cinema, "exploitation" films carried over from the early "cinema of attractions" a commitment to striking spectacle at the expense of narrative coherence and convention. For this reason, there is no point in rehearsing the "plot" of *Maniac*. But like *Un chien Andalou*, *Maniac* has a knowing relation to its medium, and it announces that fact by doing violence to an eyeball.

Dwain Esper's *Maniac* turns to Edgar Allan Poe for some of its most extreme ideas. Poe's "The Black Cat" features some egregious eye gouging: in the grip of the "imp of the perverse," which incites a desire to do wrong for its own sake, Poe's narrator grabs his cat and carves out one of its eyes. So, too, in *Maniac*: having discovered that a cat has eaten some of the heart that had been revived in a twisted experiment, the "maniac" of the film squeezes the creature so hard that one of its eyes pops out. And at this point a kind of one-upmanship takes over: the "maniac" pops the eyeball into his mouth and remarks, "Why, not unlike an oyster, or a grape!"

This eyeball-eating is a more complicated gesture than it may seem. First, it is gross, and thus participates in a fundamental drive of horror cinema, in particular—the celebration of the difficult-to-watch special effect. In its echo of the eyeball-slitting of *Un chien Andalou*, moreover, Esper's *Maniac* reminds us that one can often find avant-garde effects in lowbrow entertainments, now repeated as farce. The staged exaggeration, the embrace of artificiality, the winking tone—all these elements are present in Poe's aesthetic program as far back as the 1830s. In justifying the extremely macabre early tale "Berenice" to his publisher, Poe wrote: "But whether the articles of which I speak"—articles like "Berenice"—"are, or are not in bad taste is little to the purpose. To be appreciated you must be *read*, and these things are invariably sought after with avidity." Poe then offers a formula for his production of excess: "the ludicrous heightened into the grotesque: the fearful coloured into the horrible: the witty exaggerated into the burlesque: the singular wrought out into the strange and mystical."

If the "graphic" in the age of cinema expresses a frenzy of the visible, it does so accompanied by a range of aversive strategies—simple looking away; the imposition of censorship; a sheathing of the visible by tonal irony, "exaggerated into the burlesque"; or—perhaps the most widespread strategy of all—endless chatter about what constitutes the "unwatchable" for an eye on the edge of its grave.

The Black Box, Illuminated

In 1909, D. W. Griffith made two short films inspired by Poe and his works. The first, *Edgar Allen Poe* [*sic*], is a biopic. Poe's wife, Virginia, is ill; a raven appears; Poe writes his great poem and rushes out to sell the work so he can buy food and medicine; after several tries, he does sell it, buys the supplies, and returns triumphantly to Virginia, only to discover that she has died while he was gone. The film is an early example of the durable tradition of merging Poe's life and his works. Later that year, Griffith produced *The Sealed Room*, drawing on both Poe's "Cask of Amontillado" (1846) and Balzac's "La grande bretèche" (1831). Having constructed a kind of love niche for his wife, a nobleman discovers her in it, canoodling with the court musician. Even as they play their love games, the nobleman walls them up.

What makes Poe attractive to a filmmaker like Griffith? We know that much early cinema turned to literary sources not just for stories but also to raise its own cultural status. Observing that 1909 was the centenary of Poe's birth, Griffith saw an opportunity to bask in the glory of his subject, described by the publicists as "the most original poetic genius ever produced by America." It has been suggested that the same motives lie behind the production of *The Sealed Room* later in the year, and perhaps that is true. But this second film avails itself of the themes of Poe's work and not just the tragedy of his life. And it explores technical challenges in a way that *Edgar Allen Poe* did not.

The Sealed Room provides early instances of crosscutting, for example, as the narrative moves rapidly between the lovers and the avenger supervising their live burial. But there is a deeper message about the medium at work here, namely that *for the camera eye there is no such thing as "a sealed room."* In Poe's "Cask," the subterranean setting and especially the rising wall created by Montresor leads to a climactic moment in which the avenger can no longer see into the niche. He thrusts in a torch to no avail. He knows Fortunato is in there, alive, because he can hear him. But he cannot see him. In Griffith's version, however, there is nothing that cannot be seen: the camera moves frictionlessly between inside and outside the room.

The niche in which Fortunato is walled up is a classic example of what I called in the previous chapter a "black box." Much of the terror of the narrative lies in our imagining being inside it, able to see, perhaps, but able to see nothing. And Griffith's film is reasonably successful in harnessing the terror and the sadism we find in Poe and Balzac. "The sealed room" itself, however, must remain visible to us—as indeed it does to the film's victims, who gesticulate wildly in an illuminated space, despite there being now no natural source of light.

The prolific Alice Guy-Blaché produced a film just a few years after Griffith's that confirms the same logic. Only the first reel of *The Pit and the Pendulum* has survived, but we know from reviews as well as lobby cards and stills that Guy-Blaché rendered the torture scene in considerable detail. Live rats were brought in to scamper over the strapped down victim. (After the shooting, the rats proved difficult to dispose of: a cat and a bulldog having declined to attack them, the rats had to be bludgeoned). As with Griffith's "sealed room," the torture chamber, which in Poe's tale is pitch black, is here well lighted, so much so that we can watch the victim watching the swinging blade.

That Guy-Blaché was testing boundaries is clear enough in the reviews. Stephen Bush reviewed the film in *Moving Picture World*, saying he was "astonished at the effectiveness with which the fearful tortures of the story's hero have been illustrated by the Solax producer." Bush is rapt before "all the mechanisms of torture, including the cell with the pit in its floor down which we see skulls and crawling serpents." On the other hand, "R. R.," writing for the *Exhibitors' Times*, recoils from just this frank depiction: "The one great drawback of this film portrayal was the entirely unnecessary torture scene. There was absolutely no legitimate reason for showing us the agony of a woman on the rack, to say nothing of a man, to all outward intent, actually being racked. . . . The great dramatists and stage directors carefully avoid the presentation of such scenes not only because they are too revolting, but because a more powerful effect may be gained by suggestion." Being a writer, not a filmmaker, Poe sided with "R. R." and declined to specify what was in the pit.

The "pre-code" era of moviemaking was notoriously eager to sell sex and violence—or both at once, as in the scenes of a bare-chested Valentino being tortured in *Son of the Sheik* (1926). In 1934, the Production Code Administration was instituted, and Joseph Breen, publicist and prominent catholic layman, was put in charge. One of the first movies Breen had to consider was *The Black Cat* (1934), directed by Edgar G. Ulmer, another in the famous series of horror movies released by Universal Studios that began with *Dracula* and *Frankenstein*—both from 1931. Initially Breen was put off by a number of things in the shooting script—the Aleister Crowley–inspired black mass, for example, or the climactic scene in which Dr. Vitus Werdegast (Bela Lugosi) takes his revenge on Hjalmar Poelzig (Boris Karloff) by flaying him alive. Breen wanted to make sure this scene was depicted only in silhouette, if at all, and in fact we see Lugosi begin the grisly process in silhouette. Although many other things Breen had flagged remained unchanged, his office breezily approved *The Black Cat* on April 2, 1934, concluding that the film "contains little, if anything, that is reasonably censorable." As one modern film historian exclaims incredulously: "How did Ulmer get this far with so perverse a script?"

Let us now ask our persistent question: Why does Ulmer turn to Poe? What does it allow him to do as a filmmaker? The answer to the first question is, Ulmer doesn't turn to Poe, Universal Studios does. Junior Laemmle was trying to continue the successes of *Dracula* and *Frankenstein*, and he did it in the way studios always do: by devising a formula and iterating a series. The association of Poe's name with multiple horror titles is ideal for this strategy, and indeed Universal had already produced *The Murders in the Rue Morgue* (1932) and followed *The Black Cat* with *The Raven* (1935). None of these films pays close attention to the details of its putative source text—*The Black Cat* least of all. As Ulmer later said, his film has "nothing" to do with Poe's story.

To be fair, the film is advertised as "based on" Poe's story, but aside from there being a black cat, there is no other connection. All this makes Ulmer's film a good test of our theory that Poe is a brand more than an author. If, as one film historian suggests, Poe's name signified at this moment themes of "depravity, melancholy, psychological trauma, and sadism," then Ulmer's movie was entirely true to the brand. Depravity? Poelzig holds satanic rituals and embalms his sacrificial victims, one of whom is Werdegast's former wife. Melancholy and psychological trauma? Werdegast has spent fifteen years in prison and is consumed by the loss of his wife and daughter. Sadism? Werdegast straps Poelzig to his own embalming apparatus and begins to skin him alive.

Ulmer's triumph in this movie is to have taken some core features of the Poe brand—necrophilia, transmigration of souls, subterranean torture—and made them graphic according to the means of the cinematic medium. Poelzig is a sophisticate, an engineer in a designer house that is all open-plan rooms, sweeping stairs, and tasteful sculptures. The house is *rational*,

FIGURE 2.1. Madness and the grid. Bela Lugosi, Boris Karloff, and Lucille Lund in *The Black Cat*, directed by Edgar G. Ulmer (Universal Studios, 1934).

a fact advertised visually by the prevalence of the grid. Poelzig's grand stairway is backlit by a wall of faintly glowing glass brick. Even his subterranean chambers retain this feature. The chilling scene in which Poelzig reveals Werdegast's former wife in her embalmed state takes place against a wall resembling graph paper but which, as if commenting on the fragility of the works of reason, is revealed to be glass when Werdegast falls against it (see figure 2.1).

The single most effective horror Ulmer draws from the Poe brand is the complete transformation of the black box. Poelzig preserves his white-robed women—the implication is that they have been human sacrifices at the black masses he presides over—suspended within coffin-shaped vitrines. What had been the very navel of the nightmare—the utter blackness inside the coffin—is now illuminated, and what had been an existential terror of embodiment is now a queasy horror in the face of the abstraction of the body, its special preparation for display. For the camera eye, we repeat, there is no such thing as a sealed room. What is graphic in the age of cinema is what can be exposed to view. "Why is she like this?" asks Werdegast of his former wife's presentation. "Isn't she beautiful?"

replies Poelzig, irrelevantly but tellingly. The graphic in the age of cinema is the vampirism of the image on the body, the knowledge that all that is real, material, or embodied can be made to give way to its presentation as spectacle (see figure 2.2).

Richard Dyer famously argued that early cinema was dedicated above all to the presentation of *whiteness*. Ulmer's luminous, suspended corpses

FIGURE 2.2. Coffin as vitrine. Bela Lugosi, Boris Karloff, and Lucille Lund in *The Black Cat*, directed by Edgar G. Ulmer (Universal Studios, 1934).

present that program with a special purity. Initially, Breen had suggested this effect was inappropriate and should be reconsidered. Ulmer did reconsider it, and decided he liked it a lot: he hired several more actresses to hover in white-robed morbidity in their own glass coffins. That Breen's office did not cry foul at Ulmer's doubling down suggests, at the very least, that visions of mortified white womanhood were not so offensive as all that. Poe's own necrophiliac fantasies, expressed in a series of tales and poems, find a congenial home in early cinema. This is why Ulmer's film, while almost completely ignoring the tale from which it borrows its title, remains remarkably faithful to the Poe brand: "It may be considered one of the most successful attempts to transfer Poe to the screen, even though it transfers only a mood and not a plot," in the words of one historian of horror cinema.

Despite its grisliness and the depravity of Karloff's character, there is a tonal levity in *The Black Cat* that becomes characteristic of much horror cinema, and that looks back to Poe's recipe for excess: "the ludicrous heightened into the grotesque: the fearful coloured into the horrible." Sometimes this curdling effect manifests as a decision to pile it on: having Werdegast flay Poelzig strapped to his own embalming rack. At other times, there is winking to the audience, as when Poelzig shares a joke with Werdegast: "You see, Vitus, even the telephone here is dead!" In the scene of the black mass, a great deal of nonsensical Latin is intoned, beginning with "*cum grano salis*," a phrase repeated later in case we missed it the first time. "Absurdity—campy absurdity—was probably the only way Hollywood could deal with horror." The idea was that if the "more frightening scenes were tempered by lighthearted, even corny, moments," it was less likely that audiences would recoil in disgust or that censors would mobilize in opposition.

Breen had accepted the film with minimal fuss, but reaction elsewhere—in the United Kingdom, Australia, and Europe—was swift: *The Black Cat* was banned or cut in all those places. Tracking the inconsistent, even contradictory, behavior of various censoring agencies adds weight to the argument that censorship—and the concept of the unwatchable that is its raison d'être—is less about the suppression of any title than it is about legitimating the push and pull itself, the discourse about what can be shown and what should be seen. I turn now to another fraught moment in this discourse: midcentury America, era of the Hollywood blacklist and a sudden crackdown on the flood of excessive images in the pulps and comic books.

Juvenile Culture

Is Poe for children? Many people seemed to think so. W. H. Auden lamented that Poe was "doomed to be used in school textbooks as a bait to interest the young in good literature, to be a respectable rival to the pulps." One of those schoolkids was Roger Corman, who went on to produce a successful series of Poe-inspired movies starring Vincent Price in the 1960s: "I had read 'The Fall of the House of Usher' in school, and I asked my parents for the complete works of Edgar Allan Poe for Christmas. They were delighted to give it to me because I could have asked for a shotgun or who-knows-what. And I read all of Poe's stories." The film publicists, for their part, regularly devised campaigns to bring schoolchildren to films bearing the Poe brand. For Ulmer's *The Black Cat*, one suggestion was that kids bring their own felines to the theater. As one historian remarks: "One can only imagine the real horrors that would have been created had well-meaning teachers carted off busloads of impressionable students to see this dark tale of necrophilia, sadism, and torture."

Is a taste for Poe childish? T. S. Eliot thought so. In "From Poe to Valéry," a lecture he delivered at the Library of Congress in 1948, Eliot suggested that the reader who enjoys Poe is recalling an earlier fondness for "poems which enchanted him for a time when he was a boy, and which do somehow stick in the memory." The incantatory effect of these poems "is immediate and undeveloping; it is probably much the same for the sensitive schoolboy and for the ripe mind and cultivated ear." If Poe's work appeals "at a period of life when they [his readers] were just emerging from childhood," this may be because Poe was himself had a "pre-adolescent mentality": "That Poe had a powerful intellect is undeniable: but it seems to me the intellect of a highly-gifted person before puberty."

I ask these questions about Poe and childishness because worries about young readers were prominent in debates about mass culture at midcentury, because Poe is a touchstone in these debates, and because censorship was in the air. Auden suggests that Poe, as "good literature," formed a "respectable rival to the pulps." Gershon Legman, on the other hand, thought Poe was a *source* for the pulps, citing the blood-smeared razor in "The Murders in the Rue Morgue" in *Love & Death: A Study in Censorship* (1949). Both were right.

We have swerved from film, and its medium-specific approach to what can be shown, but we will not leave it behind. And that is because what we find in the period from 1940 to 1960, a period in which "graphic insanity" seized the culture as a whole, is that film joined a variety of other graphic modalities to form a total and interconnected graphic environment. Film noir of the '40s and '50s, for example, was not merely a cinematic idiom; it participated in "a kind of mediascape—a loosely related collection of perversely mysterious motifs or scenarios that circulate through all the information technologies, and whose ancestry can be traced at least as far back as ur-modernistic crime writers like Edgar Allan Poe." Ulmer's directorial debut was *The Black Cat*; eleven years later, he directed the noir classic *Detour* (1945). Jules Dassin—whose films in the late '40s, such as *Brute Force* (1947) and *Naked City* (1948), were masterpieces of noir—also cut his teeth on Poe: his first film was a suspenseful short of *The Tell-Tale Heart* (1941).

Dassin was blacklisted. It is important to remember, however, that the policing of Hollywood was only part of a more general panic about the "mediascape": the pulps were scrutinized by the Committee of Current Pornographic Materials in 1952, and in 1954, Dr. Fredric Wertham published the bestselling *Seduction of the Innocent*, a lengthy and detailed condemnation of comic books. Later that year, Estes Kefauver and the Senate Subcommittee on Juvenile Delinquency held hearings on the comic-book industry.

Besides Wertham, the star of these hearings was Williams Gaines, publisher and editor of Entertainment Comics (EC). EC's New Trend line of comics had come in for special condemnation in the comic-book wars. Kefauver entered into testimony a cover image from *Crime SuspenStories* #22, which showed a woman's decapitated head being held aloft. Asked whether he considered this image in good taste, Gaines famously replied, "Yes, sir, I do—for the cover of a horror comic."

To get a sense of the impact of Gaines and EC, we cannot do better than the description offered in Michael Chabon's hymn to the golden age of comics, *The Amazing Adventures of Kavalier and Clay*: "William Gaines and his E.C. Comics had taken all but one of the standard comic book genres—romance, Western, war stories, crime, the supernatural, et cetera—and invested them with darker emotions, less childish plots, stylish pencils, and moody inks. . . . His comic books had literary pretensions and strove to find readers who would appreciate their irony, their humor, their bizarre and pious brand of liberal morality. They were also shockingly gruesome. Corpses and dismemberments and vivid stabbing abounded. Awful people did terrible things to their horrible loved ones and friends."

The key words here are "literary pretensions" and "less childish plots." Gaines was pushing the envelope with his New Trend line not just in terms of graphic explicitness but also—and this may well have been more threatening to Wertham and Kefauver—in the way these stories and images were honeycombed with a kind of knowingness, an ironic frame over the whole that implied the intellectual superiority of the audience to the material being consumed. The books were sold to children, but they were not childish.

Another headline-grabbing moment from the hearings involved a story titled "The Orphan," published in *Shock SuspenStories*, issue 14. It tells the story of a little girl who, beaten by her alcoholic father and on the verge of being abandoned by her unloving mother and her mother's lover, shoots her father and contrives to frame the lovers for the murder. On the final page, we see the two of them in the electric chair, beneath which, in the very last panel, we see the girl winking at us, saying, "Everything worked out swell" (see plate 6).

This darkly comic tale flummoxed the senators:

SENATOR HANNOCH: As a result of murder and perjury, she emerges as triumphant?

WILLIAM GAINES: That is right.

HANNOCH: Is that the O. Henry finish?

GAINES: Yes.

HANNOCH: In other words, everybody reading that would think that this girl would go to jail. So the O. Henry finish changes that, makes her a wonderful looking girl?

GAINES: No one knows what she did until the last panel.

HANNOCH: You think it does them (the readers) a lot of good to read these things?

GAINES: I don't think it does them a bit of good, but I don't think it does them a bit of harm, either.

There are two things to note about this exchange. The first is that issues of narrative form—the "O. Henry finish"—play an important role. Gaines implies that the surprise ending—the girl is not just a pathetic victim but an avenger—so unsettles the reader's experience of the story's arc, which now must be traversed backward, that it breaks any spell of identification with the girl, either as victim or perpetrator. Narrative irony intervenes. The second point is that Gaines rejects wholesale the view that aesthetic experience is either improving or corrupting: "I don't think it does them a bit of good, but I don't think it does them a bit of harm, either."

When Eliot spoke in the halls of the Library of Congress, one of his central complaints was that in Poe "ideas seem to be *entertained* rather than believed." Literature, and aesthetic culture more generally, is meant to provoke individuals to discover what they truly believe, thinks Eliot. What finally most disturbs him is that Poe's work calls into question the idea that literature is an agent of psychological and moral development at all, that it helps people attain a "consistent view of life." In the exchange with the senators, Gaines frankly disavows Eliot's model—"The Orphan" does neither harm nor good; it does not exalt and mature, nor does it debase and infantilize. And although Poe is not mentioned in the exchange about "The Orphan," he is present anyway, as both the influential fabricator of the brief ironic tales that were the stock in trade of EC-style storytelling *and* as opponent of the idea that literature is meant to be improving, an idea that Poe labeled "the heresy of *The Didactic*."

The artist of the cover image with the woman's severed head was Johnny Craig, celebrated among aficionados for his special flair for the gruesome. In 1950, in the very first issue of *The Haunt of Fear*, and thus of the EC's New Trend line itself, Craig had written and illustrated "The Wall: A Psychological Study" (see plate 7).

The skeleton of the plot is drawn directly from Poe's tale "The Black Cat." A man is tormented by a cat that has engrossed all of his nagging wife's affection. Enraged at the cat—this is straight from Poe—the narrator kills his wife by mistake. He bricks her body up behind a wall—also straight Poe. But here the stories diverge. In Poe's tale, the murderer's deed is betrayed by the cry of the cat from within the niche in which he had secreted his wife's corpse. In "The Wall," however, the narrator continues to be tormented by the cat's cry, which he imagines to be coming from within the tomb. The narrator himself reaches into a hole in his wall, hoping to grab the cat and kill it himself. But his arm gets stuck, he calls for help, and when the police come, the wall falls, revealing his wife's corpse. "Snooky" chooses this moment to reappear on the scene—with a litter of new kittens.

It is odd, though also telling, that scholars and comics specialists fail to see this story's basis in "The Black Cat." They see *Poe* in it, proposing "The Tell-Tale Heart" or "The Cask of Amontillado" as sources, but not the story with the cat. The reason for the mistake, I think, is that walls and "psychological studies" are all over the place in Poe's works—they lie at a deeper narratological level, we might say, than cats. Craig has drawn his murderer pinned against a wall, spotlit, as if the cops have just nabbed the fugitive. He is both inside and outside the wall—he appears pinned against its exterior (we can see a hole leading to darkness on the other side) even as the wall presents and symbolizes his dead end, the fate from which he will not exit.

This image is what is called a "splash page" in comics art, a whole page given over to one illustration, usually containing title information and often attempting to capture a symbolic summary of the coming tale rather than illustrating a unique narrative moment. In his play with the wall, Craig has done just this, visually communicating the slippage between enclosure and disclosure so essential to Poe's narrative art, which I explored in detail in the previous chapter. The image is almost a meta-commentary on comics form: the splash page liberates itself from the grid structure of comics form, but the grid imposes itself, nonetheless, in the shape of the bricks in the wall. Craig's art is both inside and outside the formal constraints, as his protagonist is both inside and outside "the wall."

Poe's narrator describes the story of "The Black Cat" as a "series of mere household events." As often with Poe, the dark humor of this treatment of the domestic sphere activates itself on a timed delay—we must go back after the grisly denouement to get the joke (as readers must go back in "The Orphan"). Craig's "The Wall," I would suggest, is a wry and dark comment on postwar domesticity, on "household events." In Poe's tale, the wife is largely blameless. In Craig's, however, she is a scold (see plate 8).

The cat's imagined crying and visions of a finger-wagging wife merge in this dreamscape: wife and cat become a single force tormenting the poor man. But it's all played with a kind of knowingness. In the center panel, the man's jovial lunacy as he considers how Snooky and Clara will now "be together forever" is meant to bring a smile, while the cat that meets our gaze searchingly on the bottom right seems to say, "You know she and I are the same symbolically, right?" Behind the scolding wife, moreover, is a figure more directly recognizable to the tween readers of *The Haunt of Fear*—a scolding mother. The most significant change Craig introduces to Poe's tale is that the cat triumphs *as a mother*, walking in with her new litter in the final frames.

What I want to underscore is that when Craig looked to launch the visual storytelling specific to EC's New Trend line, he turned to Poe. For the same reasons that Poe was a "stumbling block for the judicious critic" (Eliot), he was attractive to Craig: Poe wrote short, violent, ironic tales that did not distinguish between literature and entertainment. Craig's remediation of Poe is radically simplified, according to the requirements of the format. On the other hand, it is quite sophisticated in its irony. Writing at just this moment (but in a very different context), Northrop Frye described Poe as a "radical abstractionist" with a direct relation to mythic material, "which is one reason his influence on our century" is so direct. This "mythic" tendency toward the abstract, the boiled down—toward that which is striking and graspable but at the same time psychologically mysterious—is another way to describe the graphic in Poe, and it is what the idiom of the comics is especially well-equipped to see and exploit, as Craig's "The Wall" demonstrates. The garish and the opaque form a single presentation.

If this story is for children—and at some level, it clearly is—then it is not for children as the guardians of culture wished to imagine them. The readers of "The Wall" and other stories at EC presented a problem for the powers that be not because they were scarred and traumatized by the graphic violence and immorality (this was the official worry) but because they were not. The reader was a child but not childish—just as readers of Mickey Spillane novels were adult but not mature. What comics pushed into the foreground as no other contemporary medium did was the triumph of a juvenile culture.

One of the most interesting essays published during the comic-book wars is Robert Warshow's "Paul, the Horror Comics, and Dr. Wertham" (1954). Here again Poe plays his ambiguous role. After describing some of EC Comics' most notorious plots, Warshow observes:

> Some of the stories, if one takes them simply in terms of their plots, are not unlike the stories of Poe or other writers of horror tales; the publishers of such comic-books have not failed to point this out. But of course the bareness of the comic-book form makes an enormous difference. Both the humor and the horror in their utter lack of modulation yield too readily to the child's desire to receive his satisfactions immediately, thus tending to subvert the chief elements in the process of growing up, which is to learn to wait; a child's developing appreciation of the complexity of good literature is surely one of the things that contribute to his eventual acceptance of the complexity of life.

That "surely" in the final sentence is whistling in the dark. "Surely" literature helps a child develop into adulthood—doesn't it? Elsewhere in the essay, Warshow admits that if his eleven-year-old son did not have his comic
books, "Paul would be reading things like 'The Pit and the Pendulum' or
The Narrative of A. Gordon Pym—which, to be sure, would be better." Paul
would find his tales of cannibalism somewhere or other, but if he has to
slog through the "complexity" of Poe's prose (which is, one must admit,
often ornate) perhaps Poe could be part of the solution.

But because Poe is a source text for the purveyors of instant gratification,
he is also part of the problem. Rather than moving, slowly, from the fine
brushwork of Poe's language to the effect of the whole, what Warshow
calls the "bareness of the comic-book form" allows eleven-year-old Paul
to take a compelling graphic shortcut. Here again, as with Eliot, a fundamental narrative about the cultivating function of aesthetic experience is
threatened. Warshow concedes that he has read *Mad* magazine (another
production from EC Comics) with "irritated pleasure," responding to
Mad's reduction of "all culture to indiscriminate anarchy" with a kind of
"nagging hilarity." He can't quite shake a sneaking admiration for these
productions. But he concludes, in an almost winning display of bad faith,
with an endorsement of censorship: "I think my position is that I would
be happy if Senator Kefauver and Dr. Wertham could find some way to
make it impossible for Paul to get any comic-books. But I'd rather Paul
didn't get the idea that I had anything to do with it."

When looking at Ulmer's *Black Cat*, we noted that the envelope pushing
inherent in the horror genre was accompanied by a note of levity, of dark
and ironic humor. We can see in EC Comics' New Trend line, as exemplified by Johnny Craig's "The Wall," a version of the same thing, now
compressed to suit the constraints of this new graphic medium. That this
new medium seemed to parody serious book culture—teenage biblio-
philes seeking rare items to complete their collections and so on—only
underscored for its critics how mass culture, and the "graphic insanity" of
its "mediascape," was undermining distinctions between adult and child,
mature and immature. Children were not childish; adults were not serious: the culture as a whole was juvenile, and its trademark was the graphic.

Let us return to the thesis: the graphic is excessive; it is a species of
"insanity"—but it is also normal, the signature of a mediascape that en-
virons cultural production in its totality. Around 1950, we could say, the
"graphic" settled definitively into its modern contradiction as both normal

and excessive, both a baseline experience and a limit concept. It was everywhere, and it was "too much." Even as the handwringers and censors worried about the graphic as excessive, the flowering of design thinking and the kind of graphic utopianism associated with the names Paul Rand, György Kepes, László Moholy-Nagy, and Charles and Ray Eames were normalizing a holistic graphic sensibility. This emboldened design thinking took a total approach to visuality and applied itself to all media and artforms. The unprecedented commercial integration of the mediascape had a corresponding aesthetic sensibility—what we have come to call *midcentury modernism*.

And Poe was useful here as well. In 1953, United Productions of America (UPA) released a remarkable seven-minute animation of "The Tell-Tale Heart," directed by Ted Parmelee, with voice-over narration by James Mason and a highly stylized scenic design by Paul Julian that mixed expressionist and surrealist motifs. Why does UPA decide to make this animation, and why does it turn to Poe? UPA was a successful animation studio, with many government and corporate clients, and it had also scored a hit in entertainment animation with *Gerald McBoing Boing* (1950). But this project answered a specific ambition; namely, to show that "the animated film can be used for any kind of story." *The Tell-Tale Heart* "marks a new era in motion picture making because it is the first dramatic and psychological story ever produced in the medium of animated film," as the production notes have it. Poe recommends himself to UPA, then, because of the serious, psychological nature of his plot. What may have still seemed to many as a medium for children could be shown, through an adaptation of Poe, not to be so.

The dynamic of seeing and being seen so central to Poe's tale is taken up here vigorously. The threat presented by the old man's eye is captured as the exfoliation of a white webbing reaching out from the eye toward the viewer. As in Poe's tale, we are uncomfortably close to the narrator, indeed *inside* him, enduring a stretch of fourteen seconds during which an altogether black screen—the black box in animated form—slowly blossoms into a network of webbing now resembling neural networks, a web that pulses with the sound of a beating heart (see plates 9 and 10).

In the discussion of Redon's treatment of Poe's story in chapter 1, I proposed that an inhuman eye reigns over the whole. The script, voiced by James Mason, agrees: "The eye—everywhere! In everything!" In one unnerving visualization of this point, the policemen lose their heads altogether but not their ability to watch the narrator (see plate 11).

The creators of this animation were engaged in a sophisticated way with the graphic potentials of Poe's tale for the medium of animation. UPA was deeply indebted to design ideas being promulgated elsewhere; indeed, Parmelee and his colleagues understood themselves to be participants in the visual revolution that was underway. UPA's chief, John Hubley, gave copies of Kepes's *Language of Vision* to all new employees. Others saw UPA this way too. In 1955, the studio was the subject of a show at the Museum of Modern Art, a clear sign that animation—even for commercial purposes, which much of UPA's work was—was an acknowledged expressive medium for modern art.

In the film, the walls of the house disappear after the murder and the bedroom—the scene of the crime—rises into empty space. Why? Media historian Dan Bashara argues that UPA's treatment of architecture and space in the film is in implicit dialogue with the "dematerialization" of architecture being championed at just this moment by Richard Neutra and others: "Directly after the protagonist, driven to madness by the presence of the elderly landlord in the cluttered, ramshackle house they share, commits the murder, the claustrophobic house becomes transparent, its floor a freestanding platform floating in a foreboding, cloudy sky. . . . Given mid-century modernism's investment in transparency as a cure for the cramped human sensorium, the madman's release is visually experienced as the disappearance of architecture and the extension of vision into infinity" (see plate 12).

Poe's story, as we have seen, is stretched taut in a contest between vision and opacity, closure and disclosure, and thus provides a ready vehicle for showing precisely the links between psychological states and physical surroundings that concerned the architects and that animation—unconstrained by naturalist representational expectations—could bring to visibility. New ideas of what could be shown emerged from the development of the medium.

The story goes that James Mason was touring the UPA studio, and when he saw the developing work on *The Tell-Tale Heart*, he pitched himself as the voice actor. One can see why he might have been drawn to the project: his narration showcases the distinctive combination of insinuation and polish that made Mason such a memorable villain. (It is in fact one of the greatest sound recordings of Poe's words—and they *are* mostly Poe's words in the animation—that I know). Mason apparently did not worry about the appropriateness of the medium of animation. One suspects he understood that there was such convergence in media formats that an innovative production combining aspects of radio, film, illustration, and comics was cutting edge.

In the United States, the film was understood to be a powerful artistic statement; it was nominated for Best Animated Feature at the Oscars, where it lost to Disney's *Toot, Whistle, Plunk and Boom*. Elsewhere, however, it was received with more uncertainty: the British Board of Film Censors awarded *The Tell-Tale Heart* its first-ever X rating for an animated work. As with Ulmer's *The Black Cat*, what was part of a new graphic idiom in one place was excessive and in need of regulation in another.

What has this foray into comics and animation shown us? That one person's "graphic insanity" was another's new *Language of Vision*—that the graphic is simultaneously normal (the fact of an encompassing mediascape) and extreme: violent and lewd. The authorities wielding the censor's power continue their work, but with less and less coherence, as media forms—comic books for nonchildish children and animated films for elite aesthetes—proliferate and recombine audiences. And we find that Poe's work continues to be available across this wide range of media— the flexible forms of Poe's tales, and their emphasis on sensory extremes, invite transposition to new media that are themselves testing their limits.

The juvenilization overtaking graphic culture was visible in film audiences as well. The series of films based on Poe that Roger Corman produced for American International Pictures (AIP) in the first half of the sixties is transitional, shaped by a midcentury aesthetic but also anticipating aspects of horror cinema from the 1970s to today. A young Martin Scorsese was part of the new youth audience for B movies in the 1950s, and he was a fan of Roger Corman: "We thought [*She Gods of Shark Reef*] was hilarious. We weren't laughing at it. We were laughing with it. . . . Corman's films didn't look as if they were coming out of the studios. They had these preposterous plots and wild acting. And once we were let in on the joke, we embraced it." But then something significant happened: "I was seventeen or eighteen when I saw *House of Usher*. That was a revelation. The use of wide-screen and color. He was serious. And he created an atmosphere. We could see that he was going for something new."

Two things about Scorsese's remarks deserve emphasis: the first is that Corman's B movies, with their nonstudio production values and their "preposterous plots and wild acting," created their own ironic audience, one "in on the joke." This powerful sense of community-in-irony continues to be a signature feature of what some call "paracinema," the motley array of low-budget productions that have violent horror and exploitation films as a core. At the same time, Scorsese suggests that Corman's first Poe-based film was something different, in fact a "revelation": "He was serious."

It's true that the Poe films for AIP represented a turning point in Corman's career. For the first time, he had a slightly larger budget and a longer shooting schedule—three whole weeks! *The Fall of the House of Usher* was the first, and it was a critical and popular success in the summer of 1960, when it sometimes shared a double bill with *Psycho*. *Usher* was clearly on a grander scale than anything Corman had done before, all wide-screen and Eastmancolor. *Usher* carves out a space for modern horror that lies between *Psycho* and *She Gods of Shark Reef*. That space is marked by stylistic features that are neither in dead earnest (*Psycho*) nor a "joke" (*She Gods*), but something in between.

In search of such stylistic features, one might point to the intricate and sometimes confusing plotting of these adaptations of Poe, or—even more—to Vincent Price's slightly overripe performances: the films are not exactly "preposterous plots and wild acting," but they are within hailing distance of that description. The word that sums up the Corman Poe films is *saturation*: following the lead of the color technologies of the day, everything in these films seems slightly more intense than normal.

The basic rule of the graphic in cinematic form is that the black box must be illuminated. Poe's "The Pit and the Pendulum" is fundamentally about constriction: absolute darkness, walls that close in, a pit in the center of the chamber, as if the space were sucked down its own drain. Corman's torture chamber in *The Pit and the Pendulum* (1961) could not be more different. It is a vast space, ornately designed, theatrical—Piranesi meets theme park. Corman's set design is less interested in the obscurities of the pit than in the upthrust platform on which the bound victim awaits the swinging blade. Everything about this torture scene suggests the stage: the sets, the tempo, the histrionic acting.

We have seen that while cinema illuminates the black box according to the needs of the medium, it also displaces the question of not seeing, what I have called the "unwatchable," onto other effects and indeed onto the discourse everywhere accompanying graphic cinema. Corman's *The*

Pit and The Pendulum is pretty tame, all things considered: a few frights, some sick psychology, a rotting corpse. But there is one moment where Corman reasserts the black box with a vengeance, taking back, as it were, all that had been given us to view.

It is the last effect in the film. As the surviving members of the climactic melee mount the stairs out of the subterranean amphitheater, vowing never to open its doors again, the camera wheels to a shot of Barbara Steele locked in the iron maiden, wide-eyed and terrified, knowing now that any hope for release is at an end. The door will shut, darkness will reign over all, and her open eyes will see nothing. Corman does not linger on this: it is a quick shot followed abruptly by the credits (see plate 13). It's as if the door not just of the torture chamber but of the movie itself has just clanged shut.

It is a curiously powerful instance of the play of closure and disclosure we have been tracking. All that had been made so vividly available to our eyes is suddenly snatched away, and we are left, as we watch the credits roll, with the feeling that far from being released from our time spent in the theater—its own black box, of course—we have been left behind there. And we have been reminded that at the core—or perhaps at the very edge—of the cinematic experience of the all-visible lies a terrifying disabling of vision, of its efficacy: the blind spot. It marks you, this glimpse of vision being shut down, and in this sense, it is the most graphic moment in the film—the extreme asserting itself against the normally excessive, which the rest of the film so exuberantly celebrates.

From Body Genres to Torture Porn

Hollywood's Production Code Administration finally gave up the ghost in 1968, and that same year George Romero released *Night of the Living Dead*, arguably inaugurating a new—and newly graphic—approach to horror movies. As an actively censoring body, the Production Code Administration had been essentially irrelevant since the early 1950s when the Supreme Court decided that film was protected speech. But Romero's *Night of the Living Dead*, and what followed, did feel different. His zombie trilogy (*Night* followed by *Dawn of the Dead* [1978] and *Day of the Dead* [1985]) was joined before long by gore and torture films, like *The Last House on the Left* (1972) and *Texas Chainsaw Massacre* (1974), and then the series of slasher franchises, with such familiar psychopaths as

Freddie and Jason—movies in which body counts spiked and ingenious methods of assassination were celebrated. It was the era of "men, women, and chainsaws."

Do remediations of Poe tell us anything new about the graphic in this period? Had the Poe brand not become quaint rather than edgy by this point? I think the answer to these questions is both yes and no. I will conclude this chapter on the graphic and the "unwatchable" by looking at two films: Dario Argento's *Two Evil Eyes* (1990) and James Wan's *Saw* (2004). The first is a self-conscious homage to Poe, while the second makes no such gesture, and one could argue (though I will not) that it has no relation to Poe at all. Both films are unusually—thematically and structurally—focused on questions of watching and the unwatchable.

The mainstreaming of graphically violent film in the 1980s and '90s—not just the slasher franchises but also works by David Cronenberg, Jonathan Demme, Quentin Tarantino, and others—was answered by a kind of mainstreaming in film criticism. Horror flicks were no longer subcinematic: they were one of the three "body genres" that reached past visual and cognitive filters to seize spectators in the viscera—to make them cry (melodrama), to make them aroused (porn), to make them afraid and repulsed (horror). This reorientation toward the "body" of the spectator represents a new chapter in what Martin Jay called "denigration of vision." The psychoanalytically based film theory of the 1960s and '70s—focused relentlessly on how viewers are drawn into a film, "sutured" there, by means of an eye fantasized as sovereign and separate—was no longer adequate for new graphic horror.

"I do not have power over what I see, I do not even have, strictly speaking, the power to see; it is more that I am powerless not to see," writes film theorist Steven Shaviro. Relentlessly focused on special effects, on hacking apart bodies and opening their insides, horror films of the era exacerbated to a nearly unbearable degree the paradox of the unwatchable. To be "powerless not to see" is not to be blind; it is to experience your vision as something taken away from you, as a separable, vulnerable, and limited *function* of embodiment: vision is not your self—it is your body. "In affirming raw sensation, in communicating the violent contents of visual excitation apart from its pacifying forms, and in provoking visceral excitation, film hyperbolically aggravates vision, pushing it to an extreme point of implosion and self-annihilation."

The "unwatchable" is the name for the paradox of the graphic as that unfolds both inside films and outside them, but never in only one of them. It
is not (merely) a formal property or theme, or (merely) a social agency or
general condition. Argento and Wan—in very different ways—illustrate
this fact eloquently.

Like Roger Corman, Dario Argento was a lifelong reader of Poe. Argento
originally hoped to produce an omnibus or anthology, with several directors taking on different works of Poe. He ended up with only George
Romero on the team, so the finished film is a diptych: two evil eyes. Perhaps in compensation for not having more treatments, Argento stuffs his
hour-long recasting of "The Black Cat" with a multitude of references to
Poe. The forensic photographer at the center of the story (played by Harvey Keitel) is named Rod Usher. His neighbor is Mr. Pym. His cat-loving
girlfriend is Annabel; the bartender is Eleonora. Two of the crime scenes
photographed will be familiar to readers of Poe: one contains a body sliced
in half by a pendulum and another involves a body in which the victim's
teeth have been removed.

What is the effect of this allusiveness? Does Argento think his audience
remembers all these details, much less the names of characters in tales and
poems by Poe? In the long run, it doesn't much matter. Even if a viewer
notices only that "Rod Usher" has migrated from his own tale into the
one with the black cat, the effect is secured: the Poe brand is activated as a
grab bag of names, plots, and violent images. And it is these last that most
obsess Argento, who shows considerable ingenuity in extracting horrify-
ing cores from Poe's effects and then rendering them one measure more
explicit, more graphic.

Three quick examples: in Poe's "Pit," the severing of the body is a threat; in
Argento, it is an accomplished fact, and we are treated to a glimpse of the
corpse's interior, as though it were an anatomist's specimen. In "Berenice,"
the extraction of the teeth happens offstage, as it were; Argento shows us
the dental equipment still in the mouth—the extraction has still already
happened, but the details of it are more explicit. In Poe's "The Black Cat,"
the narrator tells us he hanged the cat, and it's kind of hard to picture;
Argento shows the hanged cat at the end of a stick being carried around—
the effect is more gruesome.

Argento's "The Black Cat" is self-consciously belated. The swinging blade
is not a threat—it has done its work, and all Rod Usher can do is shoot

PLATE 1. Doré's "Raven." Illustration by Gustave Doré for *The Raven* (New York: Harper & Brothers, 1884). Courtesy of Lilly Library, Indiana University.

PLATE 2. Radiant maidens. Magic-lantern slide for "The Raven" by Joseph Boggs Beale. Courtesy of the Collection of Terry and Deborah Borton.

PLATE 3. Eye hanging in black space. *Le coeur révélateur*. Lithograph by Odilon Redon, 1883. Charcoal on brown paper, 15 3/4 × 13 1/8 in. Reproduced by permission of Santa Barbara Museum of Art.

PLATE 4. Not to be reproduced. René Magritte, *La reproduction interdite*, 1937. © 2023 C. Herscovici / Artists Rights Society (ARS), New York.

PLATE 5. Poe's *Pym*. René Magritte, *La reproduction interdite* (detail), 1937. © 2023
C. Herscovici / Artists Rights Society (ARS), New York.

PLATE 6. The avenging orphan. Illustration by Jack Kamen for "The Orphan," *Shock SuspenStories*, no. 14 (EC Comics, 1954).

PLATE 7. EC Comics remakes "The Black Cat." Splash page illustration by Johnny Craig for "The Wall," *The Haunt of Fear*, no. 1 (EC Comics, 1950).

PLATE 8. Snooky's revenge. Illustration by Johnny Craig for the "The Wall," *The Haunt of Fear*, no. 1 (EC Comics, 1950).

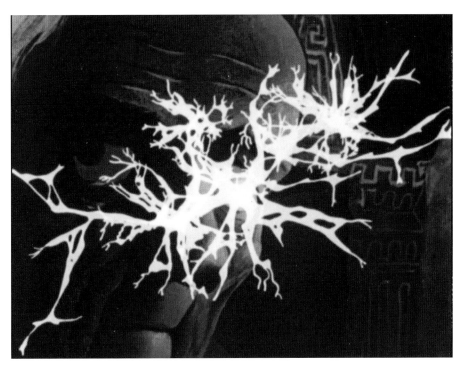

PLATE 9. The old man's eye as white webwork. Image from *The Tell-Tale Heart*, directed by Ted Parmelee (United Productions of America, 1953). Courtesy of Moving Image Archive, Indiana University.

PLATE 10. Inside the murderer. Image from *The Tell-Tale Heart*, directed by Ted Parmelee (United Productions of America, 1953). Courtesy of Moving Image Archive, Indiana University.

PLATE 11. Eyes but no heads. Image from *The Tell-Tale Heart*, directed by Ted Parmelee (United Productions of America, 1953). Courtesy of Moving Image Archive, Indiana University.

PLATE 12. The bedroom à la Richard Neutra. Image from *The Tell-Tale Heart*, directed by Ted Parmelee (United Productions of America, 1953). Courtesy of Moving Image Archive, Indiana University.

PLATE 13. On the threshold of the black box. Barbara Steele in *The Pit and the Pendulum*, directed by Roger Corman (American International Pictures / MGM, 1961).

PLATE 14. Poe's torture chamber, illuminated. Leigh Whannell and Tobin Bell in *Saw*, directed by James Wan (Lionsgate, 2004).

PLATE 15. Ice boat. Pierre Huyghe, *L'expédition scintillante*, 2002. Installation at Kunsthaus Bregenz. Courtesy of the artist and Esther Schipper, Berlin/Paris/Seoul. © The artist / VG Bild-Kunst, Bonn 2023. Photo © Markus Tretter.

PLATE 16. Madeline approaches. Vladimira Michalkova Horakova in Anthony Roth Costanzo's music video of Philip Glass's "How All Living Things Breathe" directed by Rupert Sanders (Universal Music Group, 2018). Reproduced by permission of Anthony Roth Costanzo and Visionaire World.

PLATE 17. Vacant and eyelike. Anthony Roth Costanzo's music video of Philip Glass's "How All Living Things Breathe," directed by Rupert Sanders (Universal Music Group, 2018). Reproduced by permission of Anthony Roth Costanzo and Visionaire World.

PLATE 18. "It's the squeaking of the hideous boots!" Image from Stephen Hillenburg, dir., *SpongeBob SquarePants*, season 1, episode 8, "Squeaky Boots" (Paramount Pictures, 1999).

the crime scene. A forensic photographer is necessarily after the fact, of course. But Usher has artistic ambitions, and Keitel plays him as a deadpan Weegee in a beret. Usher is gathering a collection of his crime scene photos into an art book. The one image Usher does not simply record but *makes* is the cover of the book: a close-up of the black cat screaming because Usher is brutalizing it for this very purpose. The implication is that in seeking to elevate brutality to the level of art, one cannot remain exclusively in forensic mode: one must produce *new* images of brutality as well.

The Black Cat is hardly Argento's best effort, but it shares with his more richly realized grotesqueries a distinctive visual style. I would characterize it as *mannerist,* after the Renaissance mannerists who took inherited visual effects in the direction of artificiality, elegance, and distortion. Watching Argento is not simply seeing the results of this mannerist approach; it is seeing the *process,* the "relentless search for the outer limits of style." We witness the production of the graphic as a kind of discipline, an imaginative torquing of existing materials—hence Poe's usefulness as a toolbox of effects—in such a way that the horror-weary eye can be shocked anew.

"Special effects" in film can take a variety of forms, especially in the era of CGI (computer-generated imagery). But whether it's a tidal wave crashing onto a megalopolis or a close-up of an exploding head, the "special effect" is meant to stand out from the texture of the film, to be separate enough from the demands of narrative logic, for example, to be savored on its own—and to be remembered that way too. Even hyperrealistic special effects, I want to say, are not about realism. They are about shock.

The "special effect" is an avatar of what Theodor Adorno called "shock as a consumer commodity." Sketching a history of the word "sensation"—from Lockean empirical datum to a puzzle for the psychophysicists of the nineteenth century to "shock as a consumer commodity"—Adorno outlines a process of externalization whereby what had seemed most inward—the simple or obscure registrations of personal experience—becomes the most outward, "arouser of the masses," what we call a "media sensation."

Adorno singles out in the stimulus-savoring works of Poe and Baudelaire as early exemplars of the masochism prevalent in contemporary mass society: "Baudelaire's poetry . . . is full of those lightning flashes seen by a closed eye that has received a blow." Like addicts, people seek better and stronger highs from the experiences that damage them. Because nothing is genuinely new, everything must become more intense, more graphic.

But Adorno introduces a caveat: "Concepts like sadism and masochism no longer suffice. In the mass-society of technical dissemination they are mediated by sensationalism, by comet-like, remote, ultimate newness." I take this to mean that we no longer possess even our sadism or masochism as private deformations: they have been outsourced—"mediated"—by a communications cosmos in which we have no choice but to participate, but only from a vast distance, where our psychological investment becomes vanishingly small. Perhaps the moviegoer eagerly seeking out the latest "special effect" or example of "extreme cinema" understands at some level that the sadism and masochism on offer is not his concern, that it is structural to the system of representation and not in need of the identifications of audiences.

These observations about shock and special effects, and especially about what I called the outsourcing of our sadism and masochism, will help me situate my last example of the "graphic," James Wan's *Saw*. The film was released in October of 2004. It was shot in eighteen days, on a budget of $1.2 million. It grossed over $100 million, launched a new franchise, and became an originating instance of what came to be labeled "torture porn." *Saw*, as we say, "caused a sensation." Who would go see it, *should* anyone see it, and was there something wrong with the mass audiences that flocked to it? Who would make a movie like this—and why?

In other words, we have with *Saw* another example of the "curious dialectic" of the unwatchable I have already cited: "One doesn't exhibit the images but talks about them at length; one withholds them but reports what *could have been seen* in them. In this way a curious dialectic is activated involving showing and hiding, seeing and imagining, not viewing and wanting to watch." If you try to locate what is "unwatchable" wholly inside a film, you will be disappointed. The evocation of such an idea is in fact part of the marketing and consumption of "extreme cinema."

But the discourse—the word-of-mouth, the reviews, the marketing— surrounding a graphic film like *Saw* is only one of the contextual elements in play. The very conditions of visibility are social and technological, and they have been since photography and cinematography announced both the "triumph of the eye" and its "grave." Consider this: just a few months before the October release of *Saw*, a series of images from Abu Ghraib prison in Iraq circulated in the press. The torture and the porn—the actions and the memorializing of them in images—were two sides of the same coin, a reality of the world we live in rather than the sick fantasies of a filmmaker. Whatever was inside a film like *Saw* was outside it too.

In Poe's "Pit and the Pendulum," the shadowy figures of the Inquisition are observing the torture of the narrator. We know this because they make adjustments when certain tortures do not work. It has been suggested that *Saw* does, in fact, base itself on Poe's tale of torture: not one, but two, victims are held captive (chained to the wall in the case of *Saw*) in a chamber (a disused and filthy bathroom in the case of *Saw*) while unseen figures observe the victims and redirect their behavior (observation is via a camera eye, while the space is strewn with clues for the victims). The filmmakers—Wan and scriptwriter and actor Leigh Whannell—do not, however, claim Poe as a source.

Perhaps we could say that doesn't matter; that the fundamental plot, setting, and themes of this graphic tale of terror have passed via Poe into the conventions of contemporary storytelling. So be it. But we can make more sense of *Saw* if we view it through the set of features we have been examining to this point. The bathroom in which most of the filmed action takes place is what I called, in looking at Ulmer's *Black Cat*, the black box, illuminated. Smeared and chipped, the white bathroom tile recalls the "rational" grid structure by which Ulmer revised the black box, now gone to seed (see plate 14). The very play with light and dark, the abrupt transitions from one to the other, are part of the "game" of the torturer (Jigsaw by appellation). "Sometimes you see more with your eyes shut" reads one clue, which the victims respond to by killing the lights in the room, revealing a glow-in-the-dark X that indicates the place to search behind the wall.

The most significant innovation introduced by *Saw* to the workings of the graphic is its "aggravation" of vision to the point of "implosion and self-annihilation." Harvey Keitel's character in Argento's "The Black Cat" is punished in the film for his avid visual consumption of violence and, indeed, his implication in the creation of more such violence. In this sense, the story chastises the "pornographic" inclinations of the filmmaker and of the spectators as well—a pretty conventional message in the end. In *Saw*, however, both the violence and the visual consumption of it is, precisely, outsourced. Jigsaw's modus operandi is to get others to do the killing for him—even for the victims to kill themselves, if need be. We see many scenes of watching—the camera trained on the scene in the bathroom (we see grainy footage), video surveillance of a character's house, Adam

(Leigh Whannell, one of the chained prisoners) taking incriminating photographs for hire. But none of these watchers, it turns out, is Jigsaw.

Because Jigsaw is "dead." For the length of the torture in the illuminated black box, a dead body has lain between the two victims, an apparent suicide by gunshot. At the end of the film, this body rises from the pool of its own gore, peels off a face mask, and walks away. It turns out that this is Jigsaw. He consumed none of his elaborate "game" by watching it. He is not outside looking in; he is inside, not looking at all. (Though he *hears* it all—the violence is sonic and atmospheric for him, but I leave that topic to the upcoming chapters). The idea that in the age of mass media we outsource our sadism and masochism is here symbolized by the undead body of the psychopath. Jigsaw, a connoisseur of graphic violence, finds he can best enjoy himself by occupying the stilled and sightless center of the vortex of visibility he sets spinning.

PART II

Atmospheric

The House and Its Atmospheres

Eaten Up by Ambience

You know you are in a room. You are inside and there is an outside. But the windows that confirm this fact are placed too high up to be usable. What's more, the chamber has indistinct edges: the eye struggles to make out the corners of the room or to map the ceiling. This inability to scan the room leaves you feeling closed-in but exposed, claustrophobic and agoraphobic simultaneously.

In his beautiful book *The Poetics of Space*, Gaston Bachelard names the house our "original shell," a primitive image of "protected intimacy." It is against this primal image that we measure the deviance of shelters that are, for one reason or another, wrong. Much is wrong about the House of Usher, as the narrator of Poe's tale tells us: "The windows were long, narrow, and pointed and at so vast a distance from the black oaken floor as to be altogether inaccessible from within. Feeble gleams of encrimsoned light made their way through the trellised panes . . . the eye, however, struggled in vain to reach the remoter angles of the chamber, or the recesses of the vaulted and fretted ceiling."

Poe authored a "philosophy of furniture"; he was, as Bachelard puts it, "a great dreamer of curtains." (Ligeia's return from the land of the dead is first marked by a subtle shudder of the curtains). Rooms and houses signify in Poe's tales—as do windows, curtains, clocks, and fretted ceilings. They all create atmosphere. But where is the atmosphere—inside or outside?

We strive to create the atmospheres in which we can live comfortably, that suit our moods. But here again something has gone badly awry in the House of Usher. Roderick is *not* made comfortable by the atmosphere in his ancestral mansion: "he could wear only garments of certain texture; the odors of all flowers were oppressive; his eyes were tortured by even a faint light; and there were but peculiar sounds and these from stringed instruments, which did not inspire him with horror." Bachelard's child daydreams in the "protective intimacy" of a quiet room, but Usher inhabits his ancestral mansion the way one of Francis Bacon's screaming popes inhabits his chair.

Atmosphere is decor, but it is also weather. Houses are meant to protect us *from* the atmosphere, from storms like the one that consumes the House of Usher at the climax of Poe's tale. But here, again, something is just *off* in the relation between inside and outside. This powerful storm does not pass over the house so much as concentrate on it: "A whirlwind had apparently collected its force *in our vicinity* . . . and the exceeding density of the clouds . . . did not prevent our perceiving the life-like velocity with which they flew careering from all points against each other, *without passing away into the distance.*" I have added the italics to highlight the weird fact that this storm is internal to the vicinity, if not the house itself.

The House of Usher creates its own atmosphere, it seems. Roderick believes that his house is sentient: "The conditions of the sentience had been here fulfilled in the method of collocation of these stones—in the order of their arrangement, as well as in that of the many *fungi* which overspread them, and of the decayed trees which stood around." Such sentience produces an atmosphere indifferent to inside and outside, indifferent even to distinctions between animal, vegetable, and mineral: "About the whole mansion and domain there hung an atmosphere peculiar to themselves and their immediate vicinity—an atmosphere which had no affinity with the air of heaven, but which had reeked up from the decayed trees, and the gray wall, and the silent tarn—a pestilent and mystic vapor, dull, sluggish, faintly discernible, and leaden-hued." We are invited to associate the storm at the end with this "pestilent and mystic vapor."

The Poetics of Space was first published in 1958. In the 1940s and '50s, that era of bombed-out cities and "stateless persons," thinkers began to dwell on dwelling. Bachelard's phenomenological poetics offered one such meditation. Martin Heidegger's "Building Dwelling Thinking" (1954) provided another. The great philologist Leo Spitzer took a third route. In "Milieu and Ambiance: An Essay in Historical Semantics" (1942) and in "Classical and Christian Ideas of World Harmony: Prolegomena to an Interpretation of the Word 'Stimmung'" (1944), Spitzer mapped the intricate and interlocking conceptions by which thinkers from the Greeks to the present imagined the human being's place in the cosmos—sustained in a milieu, encompassed by an ambience, attuned to nature, God, and the universe.

At one time—in the ancient Greek world, or for Dante—knowing where you were in the total surround offered comfort of a kind. In modernity, alas, the human creature's place in a milieu, in an *ambiente*, is more often a symbol of radical disorientation—Pascal's confrontation with the "eternal silence of infinite spaces," to take a well-known example. At its limit, "milieu" in its modern sense names an environmental determination of the human to the point of destruction. The vulnerability and homelessness of modern humanity incites the meditations of Spitzer, Heidegger, and Bachelard; they all look back on experiences of belonging and images of situatedness that are no longer available.

In 1952, Spitzer took a break from his vast researches to write an analysis of "The Fall of the House of Usher." Criticizing Cleanth Brooks and Robert Penn Warren, who had disparaged Poe for failing to render Roderick a suitably "round" character, Spitzer counters that Poe is not presenting a character, he's presenting a *phenomenon*. Roderick "embodies" an idea— "pure passive sentience"—and the story itself shows a man "eaten up by his *ambiente*." Poe's story, Spitzer concludes, "is determinism made poetic, 'atmospheric.'"

"The Fall of the House of Usher" is an emblematically modern tale, according to Spitzer, because both man and house are prey to violent atmosphere, stand in it unprotected, in the mode of "pure passive sentience." And yet both man and house *produce* the violence they suffer: agency and passivity are inseparable.

If Poe's story still feels modern, then, it may be because we now understand modernity itself as a catastrophe of atmosphere.

If that last clause produces a double take, the jolt of a metaphor collapsing into its literal meaning, it is not only because it points to our current crisis of global warming. The concept itself is semantically unstable. When we use the word "atmosphere," we are never entirely sure if we are referring to something literal or something figurative. And therein lies its usefulness: the referential vagueness of "atmosphere" is not a bug but a feature.

In Poe's era, "atmosphere" was understood as a powerful and essential value, in literature, art, and even in social analysis. Nathaniel Hawthorne defended the "atmosphere of strange enchantment" he used in his fictions, "beheld through which the inhabitants have a propriety of their own. This atmosphere is what the American romancer needs." Atmosphere here is integral to the "romancer's" trick of distance: namely, the creation of a world both near and far, "real" and "enchanted," like and strange.

This play with distance is more minutely detailed in Asher B. Durand's "On Landscape Painting" (1855): "When you shall have acquired some proficiency in foreground material," Durand instructs his putative students, "your next step should be the study of the influence of atmosphere—the power which defines and measures space—an intangible agent, visible, yet without that material substance which belongs to imitable objects, in fact, an absolute nothing, yet of mighty influence." An "absolute nothing" that nevertheless "defines and measures space" is not easy to grasp. Durand invokes spatial differences elsewhere in the essay: "Atmosphere . . . is a veil or medium interposed between the eye and all visible objects—its final influence it to obscure and to equalize. It is *felt* in the foreground, *seen* beyond that, and *palpable* in the distance."

This is powerful stuff: a "medium" that manages to "obscure" and "equalize" at one and the same time. Durand edges toward a concept of atmosphere that is not merely literary but that enters a social-semiotic register: "When we come to examine the constitution of society," observed Horace Bushnell in *The New-York Evangelist* in 1850, "we shall find ourselves surrounded by an atmosphere of influences in which every element is in constant vigorous action and re-action." Observations about the "constitution of society" were meant to be attended to in mid-nineteenth-century America. Many in the antebellum era were in fact bowled over by the idea of a medium that surrounded one and all—e pluribus unum!—and that did so in an "obscurely" "equalizing" way. The panoply of such atmospheric influences included telegraphy and communications from the dead (two phenomena so closely associated that the latter was sometimes called "spirit telegraphy"), animal magnetism, mesmeric fluid, ethers and odic forces, all manner of mediums and media.

"Atmosphere" names both a medium (of light, sound, precipitation, temperature), then, and an aesthetic (a play with obscurity that manages distances and verisimilitude). But in being both, it names a third thing, a general condition of *mediatedness*, of systematic interrelation: "every element is in constant vigorous action and re-action," as Bushnell says. Atmospheric mediation, then, is not only meteorological or aesthetic but

semiotic. What we are gathered into, what surrounds us, is an environment of *meaning*.

Back at the House of Usher, it is manifestly the case that "every element
is in constant vigorous action and re-action." Poe's story is not just unusually "atmospheric," however. I would argue that it is *about* "atmosphere."
When Durand sought a metaphor to describe how atmosphere affects
the viewer of a painting, he reached for that of the house, or more specifically a mansion, and a scene of forced hospitality: atmosphere "carries us
into the picture," he writes, "instead of being allowed to be detained in
front of it; [it is] not the door-keeper but the grand usher and master of
ceremonies . . . conducting us all through the vestibules, chambers and
secret recesses of the great mansion, explaining, on the way, the meaning
and purposes of all that is visible, and satisfying us that all is in its proper
place." The narrator of Poe's famous tale, it should be noted, does not find
"all that is visible" in the House of Usher "satisfying" at all. Roderick's role
as "grand usher and master of ceremonies" leaves something to be desired,
to be honest. At the start of the tale, the narrator explicitly wonders why
it was that he could *not* remain "detained in front" of the gloomy mansion
but was forced by energy of atmosphere to pass within.

Durand's elaborate metaphor suggests why the house—going into and out
of it; how the rooms feel—might have been available to Poe not just as a
setting but as the vehicle for a commentary about "atmosphere" as a semiotic, formal, and aesthetic category. As one philosopher of atmosphere
has suggested, "artistic expressions are atmospheres when they are so self-
referential that they induce us to ask what they show (or what their mise-
en-scène is) rather than what they are." In line with such recursiveness, we
could say that Poe's tale is about itself, about art as a medium and a thing
mediated. From the reeking "mystic vapors" of the opening to the climactic
electrical storm, the tale presents the "sentience" of all things as a matter
of *flow*—currents of air and electricity and meaning. The flow might be as
sudden and violent as a storm or as slow and indiscernible as the creeping
spread of fungi, but everything—humans and their buildings too—are in
process of dissolution, are being swept away in the general flow.

When we ask why "The Fall of the House of Usher" has proved so entic-
ing to artists in other media, we must not underestimate this question of
flow: the atmospheric, as Poe projects this aesthetic idea in his tale, names
the volatile conjunction of movement and immobility, of composition
("the collocation of the stones") and its dissolution. Atmosphere puts

the artwork in motion and in so doing envelops the reader—or auditor, or viewer—in a kind of flow. One contemporary commentator says that today we have "art in a gaseous state." Another describes how modern art has increasingly minimized the artwork as object in order to produce an *encounter* with the fluid conditions of its fabrication and consumption: "Traditional art produced art objects. Contemporary art produces information about art events." If, for the sake of argument, we call the House of Usher an art object, then "The Fall of the House of Usher" is "information about an art event."

But atmosphere is never not a vague thing; what exactly is flowing is never entirely discernible. As the French say, it's *flou*—hazy, vague, blurred, indeterminate. At stake in the collapse of Usher's mansion, as much as in Roderick Usher's own destruction in it, is the nature of the artwork in an atmosphere at once hazy and determining. Poe's wide availability across media has everything to do with his presentation of the problem of atmosphere and the form he devised for that presentation: a house internally riven, vaporizing into its own atmosphere, securing neither inside nor outside. In what follows, I look at an unfinished opera, a silent film, an animated short, a conceptual art installation, and a music video—all focused on problems of atmosphere and figures of form, and all making imaginative use of resources provided by Poe.

Flow and Flou

Claude Debussy labored for much of his career to complete an opera based on "The Fall of the House of Usher." One of the few sections to be finished is Roderick's aria about the "sentience" of the house itself. We know from the three versions of the libretto and from letters that the process was driving Debussy crazy. He wrote to a friend that the Usher mansion is "not exactly the house one would choose for calming one's nerves, quite the contrary. . . . One develops there the singular dottiness of listening to the dialogue of the stones; of expecting houses to fall down as a natural, even obligatory, phenomenon."

Why would Debussy want to write an opera based on Poe's tale? Poe was a touchstone figure for French artists of the latter half of the nineteenth century, of course, in part because he conjoined startling sensory effects with an unflustered and methodical approach to his work. Debussy's music, widely understood as "atmospheric," aimed at something similar. His own word for the effect he wished to create was *flou.*

A recent critical biography uses "atmospheric" a dozen times to describe effects of Debussy's music. But what does it mean? In *Pelléas et Mélisande* (1902), "the elements of [Debussy's] language are . . . more or less conventional chords of tonal harmony, but treated as isolated events or colours without past or future, much like Maeterlinck's dramatis personae," writes Stephen Walsh. "These rich chords of the seventh, ninth, eleventh and thirteenth . . . constantly suggest the tonal grammar they are culled from, but hardly ever acknowledge their parentage. What we feel is a certain general presence, something one specifically does not feel, or should not feel, in atonal music, where the tonality is not drowned but strangled at birth."

Debussy's atmosphere is an effect of vagueness. Where are these sonorous chords going? Where do they belong? Are we in any particular key? These questions remain pressing in Debussy's music in a way that they are not in strictly atonal music. Walsh's phrase "general presence" suggests a kind of ghostliness, messages from a world that never presents itself as such—a world in which chords acknowledge their parentage in the tonal grammar, in which they have pasts and futures—in short, the harmonic language of the Western classical tradition. Debussy's atmosphere is the result of a kind of suspense, in effect, in which the musical events he lets us hear are always set against the background of the ghosts of tonal harmony and the principles of compositional development that he eschews.

This question of "general presence" is crucial to the problem of atmosphere. We will return to it. To experience the atmospheric in an artwork is to have a sense of heightened presence. But because atmosphere is so indeterminate, that presence is registered through a scrim, as it were—it is a "general presence," not a particular one. We might say that to experience the atmospheric is to experience the mediation of presence, or the presence of mediation. Or, perhaps best: mediation *as presence*.

Debussy was openly in flight from the norms of Western harmonic language. Like everyone else, he was initially bowled over by Wagner, but he quickly set himself against this fulminating genius, with his "German affectation of profundity and the need to underline everything." Debussy thought that one must submerge tonality (*"il faut noyer le ton"*), not stretch it on the rack as Wagner does. For Debussy, the rules of composition he inherited were like dead stones—inert and constraining. But Roderick's speech implies that one can in fact so arrange the dead stones of the past—because, after all, there is no absolute novelty; we all work in the buildings into which we were born—to reach the *flou*, the hazy yet condensed atmosphere Debussy so prized.

It was not to be. The record of Debussy's struggle with this project during his last ten years of sickness is unhappy. The main stumbling block seems to have been the gloomy and ponderous inheritance of the form of opera itself. The "all-too-physical, all-too-tangible practicalities of the operatic stage," suggests Walsh, simply blocked access to what was so tantalizingly *flou* in Poe's tale. Eventually, the Usher opera became more "an obsession, perhaps to some extent a psychological retreat, than a practical creative project."

In 1911, Debussy wrote his friend and orchestrator André Caplet: "It all seems to me as dreary as a vault. For every one bar that is almost free, there are twenty that suffocate under the weight of a deaf tradition whose flabby and hypocritical influence I admit, in spite of all my efforts." Here Debussy is the captive in the vault—Madeline or Roderick, it doesn't matter—and the struggle for freedom, waged "bar" by "bar," is failing in the face of the asphyxiating "influence"—a kind of poisoned atmosphere—of a "flabby and hypocritical" tradition.

Poe's tale offers a great deal to Debussy, in fact more than he can use. Much is at stake for Debussy in the idea of "atmosphere," as that aesthetic ideal is suggested by Poe. There are considerations of medium—music itself as the supreme medium of the *flou*—but also genre—opera, where requirements of character and staging may weigh too heavily. Ultimately, tradition itself is in play, the vexed relationship between the creative artist and what he has been bequeathed. If Roderick's ideas about atmosphere represent the possibility of freedom through new "methods" of "collocation," the story itself represents an inescapable doom. Just as surely as in Poe's tale, Debussy's *House of Usher* collapsed on him, and what we have are merely pieces of unfinished stone lying in a heap. He died in 1918.

La Lumière Cendrée

The question of how atmosphere links presence and mediation takes on a new urgency and complexity with the advent of cinema. Already in 1913, as Debussy fiddled and fussed with what seemed to him the archaic burden of the form of opera, Georg Lukács published a short essay titled "Thoughts on the Aesthetic of Cinema." His central point is that cinema and theater operate according to fundamentally opposed aesthetic logics. For Lukács, theater is essentially about presence—the presence of live human beings on stage and in the audience. The ontological and phenomenological situation of theater brings with it a confrontation with finitude, with shared mortality. On the other hand, the "absence of this 'presence' is the essential characteristic of the 'cinema,'" writes Lukács, "not because films are imperfect, not because the characters today must still move silently, but rather because they are only movements and deeds of people, but *not people*."

What we see on film are "movements and deeds of people" who had once been present but are so no longer. Their presence comes to us—as it does in any photograph—in the form of its *having-been*. So, while it is true that what we see on the celluloid is *not people*—it's celluloid—people and their presence are not vacated entirely from what we witness. We experience their presence as something that once was but that now comes to us only as mediation.

Anticipating much of the writing about cinema over the succeeding fifteen years, Lukács says that the "temporality and flow of the cinema is movement in itself, the eternal transience, the never-resting change of things." Cinema is given over to "possibility restricted by nothing," and thus to "the fantastic," unlike drama's tragic focus on finitude and fate. A new relation to the natural world and to embodiment emerges with cinema: "The animate in nature here acquires artistic form for the first time: the rushing of the water, the wind in the trees. . . . Man has lost his soul yet gains his body in return." This new artform, fantastic and flowing, has not yet found its proper genius, says Lukács. But "a Poe of our days . . . would find an instrument ready for his scenic yearning."

In 1928 a film came along that realized Lukács's vision of a cinematic artwork that self-consciously exploited the medium's essential affinities for the fantastic and the flowing: *La chute de la maison Usher*, directed by Jean Epstein, a key player in the French avant-garde of the twenties. Epstein's decision to make a film based on a Poe story was both unsurprising and a bit risky. Unsurprising because the French filmmakers in his circle were, as several historians of film have noted, essentially extending a symbolist aesthetic (and its obsession with Poe) into cinema. (One emblem of this continuity: Maurice Maeterlinck, the Belgian playwright and poet whose *Pelléas and Mélisande* was the basis for Debussy's landmark opera of the same title, was apparently meeting with Epstein and his production assistant Luis Buñuel during the filming of *La chute*).

A French redo of Poe is, then, never all that surprising. But, at the same time, the "impressionists," for whom Epstein was something of a spokesman, were insistent about the medium specificity of film, and thus set their face against both theater and literature: "The Impressionists' search for cinematic specificity was extended to an elimination of all materials common to literature or theatre and film," writes David Bordwell. "Cinema should not use language; thus ensued the long debate about the propriety of dialogue titles. Cinema, it was urged, should not tell stories."

Epstein was caustic about films he thought were basically theater: "If you must say about a film that it has beautiful sets, I think it would be better not to speak about it at all; the film is bad." Hence his contempt for *The Cabinet of Dr. Caligari*. (One imagines Epstein would have felt the same way about James Sibley Watson and Melville Weber's short version of Poe's tale, released the same year as *La chute*—all expressionist angles and deranged scenery, a modernist pastiche).

Poe's work, however, and "Usher" in particular, offered several provocations to Epstein's developing theories, to the extent that he was willing to risk making what might look like a tired "adaptation" from a literary source. In the first place, Poe's presentation of what Spitzer called "pure passive sentience" drew Epstein, who was exploring what he called "coenesthesis," a kind of affective synesthesia, in which sense modalities are merged in the depths of the body. At the same time, Poe's work posed questions of medium specificity that were of urgent concern to Epstein.

Epstein's film is nothing if not atmospheric: clouds scud, waves lap, curtains rustle and billow. For Epstein, cinema's capacity to present "the rushing of the water, the wind in the trees" is central to his artistic goal—a theme as much as an effect. In his dissertation on the impressionists, David Bordwell analyzes a particularly complex sequence in *La chute*, in which Epstein cuts between shots of Roderick strumming his guitar and the waters and wind in agitated movement outside the house. Bordwell's point is that the editing obeys a complex and precise rhythmic design, comparable to how a musical composition might structure its temporal unfolding.

But Bordwell sees something more, something atmospheric: "Apart from the specific content of the interspersed shots—which makes them not only atmospherically evocative but dramatically and thematically significant in the film as a whole—the pattern of the editing follows a strict tempo." The shots of wind and waves are "dramatically" significant because they foreshadow the storm at the end; they are thematically significant because *La chute* makes atmosphere a theme, not just an effect. And yet Bordwell, who is not prone to imprecision in his criticism, sees something more: an "evocative" something, beyond theme and plot.

Trying to locate this atmospheric extra beyond theme and plot takes us once again to the question of medium and mediation. As so many have done, Epstein produces something of a mash-up, dropping Poe's story "The Oval Portrait" (1842) into the middle of his treatment of "The Fall of the House of Usher." The theme of "The Oval Portrait" is the theft of life by art: "The painter had grown wild with the ardor of his work, and turned his eyes from the canvas rarely, even to regard the countenance of his wife. And he *would* not see that the tints which he spread upon the canvas were drawn from the cheeks of her who sate beside him."

Epstein borrows this scene, and this theme, as the focus of Roderick's relationship to Madeline (who becomes his wife rather than sister). There is an extraordinary sequence near the middle of the film in which Madeline, who is being painted by Roderick, seems to fade away before our eyes. We are shown, in a beautiful slow-motion sequence, Madeline spreading her arms like useless wings and collapsing to the floor. Roderick looks back and forth between his wife and his canvas all this time, apparently not seeing what we see.

The artist in Poe's story "*would* not see," but Epstein's Roderick *cannot* see. Epstein incorporates "The Oval Portrait" so that he can make a point about media. Roderick literally cannot see what we see because he is only in a film; he is not watching one. For Roderick, and the painterly world he inhabits—and this is the "moral" of "The Oval Portrait"—life and representation are in a zero-sum relation. If, as both Poe's painter and Epstein's Roderick exclaim, it is "life itself" transferred to the canvas, the body from which such life is transferred is now extinct. This either-or conception means that Roderick is blind to the states that flow between the poles, cannot see life leaching away, slowly crumpling. He cannot see, in other words, a process that is neither life nor death but something in between.

Making free use of the optical effects so dear to the impressionists, Epstein offers us several versions of this "in between." Madeline's body blurs and bifurcates, two heads wagging at us, followed by a slower process in which, through superimposition, Epstein shows Madeline fading toward the mortified image of the photographic negative, which itself tends toward the immobility of sculpture (see figures 3.1 and 3.2).

FIGURE 3.1. Two-headed Madeline. Image from *La chute de la maison Usher*, directed by Jean Epstein (France, 1928).

FIGURE 3.2. Madeline's Head (*la lumière cendrée*). Image from *La chute de la maison Usher*, directed by Jean Epstein (France, 1928).

In a comment on Poe published at this time, Epstein writes that, in Poe, "Life and death have the same substance, the same fragility. All the dead are so only barely" (or lightly; Epstein's word is "*légèrement*"). "Madeline and Roderick feel that they are going to die the way we feel sleep overtaking us." Criticizing Baudelaire's agitated translation, Epstein insists, despite the manifest violence of the text, that there is no real horror in the tale—"*Il n'y a rien d'horrible*"—only a kind of ashen light, "*la lumière cendrée.*" This ashen light is what Epstein tries to capture in the scene of Madeline's death.

The atmospheric in Epstein's film thus encompasses both meteorological and media phenomena. At one point in the film, Roderick consults a book on magnetism: "It is clear that Epstein is pointing to cinema itself as a new kind of materiality that transcends the four elements and thus approximates ether," writes one contemporary critic. Epstein argued throughout his career that film has the capacity to grant access to a cosmic reality that lies beneath and beyond our limited perceptual apparatus. In *The Intelligence of a Machine* (1946), Epstein suggests that one effect of such access is that human being itself becomes "gaseous": "Man acquires the density of a cloud, a consistency of vapor; he has become a purely gaseous animal, with feline grace and ape-like dexterity. All the partitioned systems of nature are disarticulated. Only one realm remains: life."

Lukács said that what we see on the screen "are only movements and deeds of people, but *not people*." It's a strange thought, as we have already seen: movements of people separated from people themselves. A fundamental abstraction takes place in what Epstein called "*photogénie*." We tend to use "photogenic" to mean "looks good in a picture," but as Bordwell glosses Epstein's use, its meaning becomes stranger: Epstein's "*photogénie*" is an "attempt to account for the mysteriously alienating quality of cinema's relation to reality." The impressionists sometimes called the effect of "*photogénie*" an encounter with the soul of an object, a face, a location. But Lukács had it right: in cinema, "man has lost his soul yet gains his body in return." This body, which is no longer distinct from its environment, is gaseous, vague, flowing, with the "consistency of vapor": atmospheric.

There is a final facet to the work of abstraction in the cinematic medium. Gilles Deleuze, whose thinking about film was powerfully influenced by Epstein, latched onto a passage from Epstein's *Lyrosophie* (1923) to argue that in film affects become separated from humans while also becoming a species of thing: "*affect-chose*" is Deleuze's term. Here is what

Epstein says: "On screen you see what is not and cannot be on the screen. Moreover, you see this unreality specifically and feelingly, with all the particularities of real life. A movie shows you a man who betrays. You know full well first that there is no such man, and secondly that there is no such betrayal. Yet the movie . . . created, through the ghost of a thing, a feeling; and since this feeling cannot live without the thing for which it was made, and since this feeling too obeys the law of preservation, the false thing will come alive for you. Or rather there will come to life a thing-feeling, and you will believe in more than a traitor—you will believe in a betrayal."

Spitzer had noticed how the project of presenting atmosphere in Poe's tale entailed taking an input of sensory data—for Roderick, data of such impinging intensity that he can barely survive it—and transforming it into abstract "patterns of intellectual design." Epstein, then Deleuze in his wake, push this point even further: film, in their view, had unique powers of abstraction, able to project a "thing-feeling" (Epstein) or "affect-thing" (Deleuze). Film trades in the movements and indeed feelings of people but not the people themselves: it delivers abstract and intellectual images that are nevertheless affective. The natural habitat of the "affect-thing" is the atmosphere created by film.

Atmosphere, Art, Eversion

For Jean Epstein, the "intelligence of the machine" of cinema is its ability to register and record the reality of an animation (an animation inclusive of death) otherwise inaccessible to humans. The machine peers into a world of things and finds hidden movement within. For Czech surrealist filmmaker Jan Švankmajer, it is not a question of what lies within—it is rather a matter of what lies on the surface. The horror of Poe's tale, for an artist of Švankmajer's sensibility, is not that hidden forces—Madeline back from the dead—emerge from within but rather that the house becomes pure surface, nothing *but* the fungi spreading on the walls, as it were. The house does not implode so much as turn itself inside out, like a glove. The house *everts*, vomiting its contents so comprehensively that we are left only with flesh, crawling.

For Švankmajer, the obligation of a filmmaker is to access the primitive life of beings and objects—a life lived on the surface, a life of touch. In 1973, the Czech authorities told Švankmajer that he was not to make any more movies. For the next six years, he undertook a series of peculiar experiments in the tactile imagination, which he documented in his book, *Touch-*

ing and Imagining: An Introduction to Tactile Art. In 1979, he was allowed to make movies again, but only if he restricted his sources to canonical literature. Švankmajer turned to Poe, making a fifteen-minute treatment of "The Fall of the House of Usher" (1980), followed shortly after by an impressively claustrophobic take on "The Pit and the Pendulum" (1983). More recently, he has returned to Poe for *Lunacy* (2005), a combination of Sade and Poe's madhouse tale, "The System of Doctor Tarr and Professor Fether."

Poe's literary status met the requirement imposed by the authorities. But Poe had also long been a touchstone figure for Švankmajer. In a familiar story, Švankmajer read Poe when young and could never shake it: "There are obsessions that we pick up here and there along life's road, which we then sometimes drag about for the rest of our life." Švankmajer found Poe's stories "crammed with descriptions of the tactile" (recall that wearing most clothes is agonizing for Roderick Usher). And Poe had succeeded in doing what Švankmajer himself aimed at. "For the reader," Švankmajer observed, "these are feelings which have been conveyed to him, he has not experienced them for himself, but tactile imagination is capable of transforming these feelings and making them considerably intensive." He remarked in an interview in 2004, "Though a supremely audiovisual medium, I don't think film is incapable of transferring tactile sensations to the viewer"—and he points to his *Usher* as an attempt to do just this.

Švankmajer's *The Fall of the House of Usher* (1980) is fifteen minutes of stop-motion photography, Claymation, and disorienting camerawork, with Poe's story in voice-over. There are no human beings (other than the voice). The walls chip and decay before our eyes, covering themselves in fast-acting fungi; the trees send forth tentacular roots to do battle with each other. Mud erupts into grotesque protuberances and open lips, and tree trunks sprout growths that look like eyes, or anuses (see figures 3.3 and 3.4).

There is a remarkable sequence in Epstein's *La chute* that follows the itinerary of Madeline's coffin, the camera slung so low that we cannot help feeling that we are being given a coffin's-eye view. In Švankmajer's film, this uncanny dead-alive effect takes the form of Madeline's coffin propelling itself with no human assistance. The effect in Epstein is passing, but in Švankmajer we cannot help feeling that the camera itself is *consistently* dead-alive. Crawling across the surface of the chair that stands in for Rod-

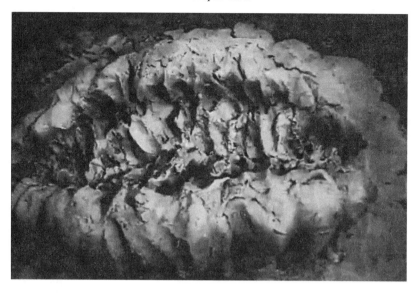

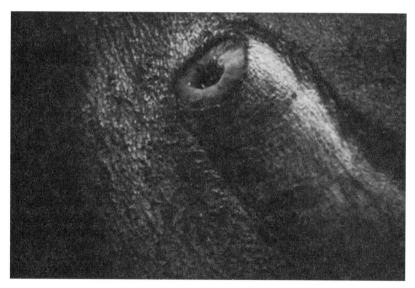

FIGURES 3.3 AND 3.4. Nature's orifices. Image from *The Fall of the House of Usher*, directed by Jan Švankmajer (KimStim Inc., 1980).

erick, Švankmajer's camera seems to lick each furrow and bulge of the chair's patina. Seemingly fascinated by the design of the chair's back, the camera sways back and forth between the two humanlike shapes made by the cutouts, as if allegorizing the gravitational attraction between Roderick and Madeline.

For Švankmajer, gesture leaves an imprint on things, and things leave an imprint on their perceivers. Gestural acts leave, in the very texture of the object acted on, a "fossilized emotion": "If we are prepared to believe the old hermetic books, strong emotion leaves an indelible impression on objects touched, which are then capable of transferring these emotions to sensible perceivers, and even of making them visible." In his film, the gestures made directly present through techniques of animation are just one facet of the life of things; just as important are the textural fossilizations—peeling paint, organic decay, patina, slime—that lie on the surface of all things, both natural and artificial. This is how Švankmajer enlists imagination in the task of conveying the tactile through the filmic medium, just as he insists Poe can through the literary medium.

It is not finally the case that there are no humans in this film. There is the narrator's voice, to begin with, but more important is the camera eye itself, which seems to be at once human, animal, and machinic—dead and alive. Švankmajer's extreme close-ups of textural details present the world as simultaneously alive and "fossilized." This is why an ordinary chair, empty as it is of any present occupant, retains the traces of its human use, and why seeing it fling itself in terror from an upper story window can be so disturbing (see figure 3.5).

I suggested that Švankmajer everts Poe's house, turns it inside out, to get everything to the level of the surface. The unstable relation between inside and outside already present in Poe's depiction of the Usher mansion is here taken to a limit, less the drowning of the interior than its transformation to an epidermal flow—skin crawling. Atmosphere here is a topological oddity, the tactile registration on a surface without depth.

Atmosphere and the Deformation of the Same

Beside a lake in Bregenz, Austria, stands a glowing glass cube. The Kunsthaus Bregenz is the much-admired building of Swiss architect Peter Zumthor, whose general approach can be gleaned from the title of his 2006 book, *Atmospheres: Architectural Environments, Surrounding Objects.* It was to this building, in 2002, that French conceptual artist Pierre Huyghe brought his installation *L'expédition scintillante* (see plate 15).

The work commandeered the entire Kunsthaus. Viewers entered a ground floor space made chilly and wet by weather events introduced periodically from the ceiling: some fog, later an episode of gentle rain, and then snow

FIGURE 3.5. A chair throwing itself out the window. Image from *The Fall of the House of Usher*, directed by Jan Švankmajer (KimStim Inc., 1980).

that lingered in little piles. A ship intricately carved from ice lay canted over in the middle of the room, beginning to melt—or if you came later to the exhibition, entirely gone, just a wet patch on the floor. Selections from John Cage's "Radio Music" (1956) were broadcast from a speaker on the floor.

On the second floor, a large "music box" dominated the center of the space and projected a shifting array of pink and orange lights and curling smoke, accompanied by Debussy's orchestration of Satie's *Gymnopédies*: "At the end of each cycle . . . the lights were brought up, the fog ceased, and the room was bathed in a warm pink glow that emanated from what Huyghe referred to as the 'sunrise/sunset ceiling.'"

The top floor featured a rectangular ice rink with black ice, with specially produced books purporting to tell the story of the exhibition just traversed by the viewer. These books featured, among other things, reproductions of the title pages of Poe's *The Narrative of Arthur Gordon Pym of Nantucket* (1838) in Baudelaire's translation and of Jules Verne's *Le sphinx des glaces* (1897), a sequel to Poe's tale. Every so often, a lone ice skater would appear, and as she moved around the rink, she would comment on the reinscriptions of Poe, Baudelaire, and Verne.

This is all puzzling, to say the least. I suggested that Švankmajer's tactile filmmaking turned the House of Usher inside out, like a glove, in order to get everything on the surface. Such a maneuver suggests that there is no "inside" of the house, and that inside and outside are two aspects of a single topological surface. The example often given of topological transformation is a rubberized disc that might function as a coaster one moment but can be reshaped into a vessel with no break of its surface. Huyghe was committed at this point in his work to a topological model of transformation. In an interview published in 2004, he suggested what was at stake: "It's a way to translate an experience without representing it. The experience will be equivalent and still it will be different. When you translate something, you always lose something that was in the original. In a topological situation, by contrast, you lose nothing; it is a deformation of the same."

This idea of "the deformation of the same" governs Huyghe's work at several levels. Let us take the weather events of the ground floor. Huyghe marked every description of weather in Poe's *Pym* and then programmed his hidden weather machines to produce the rain, fog, and snow as they had been experienced by Poe's fictional characters. But, of course, Poe's characters *are* fictional, as is his weather—whereas visitors to Huyghe's installation had to negotiate real snow and fog. "The experience will be equivalent and still it will be different."

In Huysmans's *À rebours*, the decadent hero, Des Esseintes, dedicates an entire room to maritime fantasy, complete with porthole windows and the smell of tar piped in. The sole book in the room is a copy of Poe's *Pym*, as I noted in discussing Magritte's *La reproduction interdite*. Des Esseintes's room is an "installation" just as much as Huyghe's, and it is of course possible that Huyghe is alluding to it in his artwork. For Des Esseintes, the room is testimony to the superiority of the artificial over the natural—of the atmospheric qualities of decor over those of wind and weather.

Huyghe and Des Esseintes share the pleasure in producing atmospheric effects indoors. But Huyghe's fascination with topological transformation takes things a few steps further. Poe's adventure novel is, among other things, a metafictional experiment. Arthur Gordon Pym is said to have entrusted his tale to the editor at *The Southern Literary Messenger*—a certain Edgar Allan Poe—asking him to dress up the story in literary language, since a bare recital of fact would produce only incredulity. The tale itself is filled with realistic details: ship's log entries, latitude and longitude, the weather reports that so fascinated Huyghe, and a weirdly long excursus on proper techniques of stowage.

These apparently realistic details can only seem, given Pym's charge to Poe, frankly literary attempts to produce belief with the means of fiction. The atmospheric conditions recorded by Pym (and supplied by Poe) are thus indeterminately factual and fictional. Perhaps the best way to express it is to say that the weather, as thematized in *Pym*, stands for the topological continuity between fact and fiction. And this is also why Huyghe's weather in *L'expédition scintillante*—"real" weather experienced as fabricated (as "art") and drawn from a fictional source that plays with the continuity between fact and fiction—is simply another topological transformation, a "way to translate an experience without representing it."

And here is where Huyghe departs from Des Esseintes. At one point in *À rebours*, Des Esseintes considers a trip to London but gives it up—why travel when you can make your own weather? Des Esseintes considers artificial "atmospheric" experiences to be *replacements* for any experience in nature. No such competition exists in Huyghe's work. In fact, *L'expédition scintillante* was presented as, and understood to be, a plan—a proposal for a future work that would involve an actual trip to the Antarctic, something that came to pass a few years later as *A Journey That Wasn't* (2005). The skater in *L'expédition*, as well as the literary remains and booklets on the third floor, expose the sources of the present installation, summarize the itinerary of the visitor, and project a plan for an as-yet-uncompleted project all in one go. Huyghe plans to travel, even as Des Esseintes gives up.

The essential instabilities I have been noting that characterize the idea of atmosphere—inside as well as outside, cause as well as effect, mediatic as well as meteorological—gather themselves in *L'expédition*, as that has been incited by Poe. Huyghe's presiding commitment, we could say, is to the ephemerality of the artwork in the face of atmospheric flow, its temporal irreversibility. The ice ship melts; the weather changes; Poe's tale is torqued across 144 years to appear in Austria, a "deformation of the same." And it is all simultaneously a précis and a pitch. To cite Boris Groys again: "Traditional art produced art objects. Contemporary art produces information about art events." Not a well-wrought urn but the collapse of a shelter into its surround, weather on a featureless Antarctic plain.

Aura and Aria

I have been exploring the aesthetics of atmosphere as it has incited an array of artists to think about the medium in which they create. I have suggested that Poe's "The Fall of the House of Usher" has been a paradigmatically "atmospheric" text for these artists and thus an invitation, or provocation, to ask what atmosphere can do for their medium, or what their medium can do with the idea of atmosphere. The media involved have been quite various, and purposefully so: opera, silent film, stop-motion animation, conceptual art. With the exception of this last example, Pierre Huyghe's complex engagement with Poe's *Pym*, these have all been treatments or interpretations of "The Fall of the House of Usher."

I do not think we will be able to assemble a list of traits, a checklist or recipe, for effective atmosphere from looking at Poe's story or any of its many transformations in other media, despite the formal continuities I have been following. This undefinability is in the nature of atmosphere as a value: the term exists, aesthetically speaking, to name an encounter with an aesthetic object that cannot be reduced to criteria or formula. It exists to be vague, in other words; it names vagueness. What Huyghe's work entertains is the idea that, at its most extreme, the atmospheric cancels the aesthetic object altogether in favor of an aesthetic experience in a surround: the aesthetic object is an expedient and thus expendable. The ice boat melts.

To the extent that the "atmospheric" is grounded in meteorological phenomena, it is about flow and ungraspable change. Leo Spitzer had demonstrated the multiple ways in which humanity had, despite this flow and fugitiveness, contrived to feel at home in the cosmos, and he also pointed to Poe's "Usher" as exemplifying the modern collapse of that comfort, of the arrival of atmosphere as threat, of a world in which humanity is not at home. Poe's tale allegorizes this catastrophic change: despite being attached to the House of Usher—so attached that he never leaves it; perhaps none of the Ushers ever have left it—Roderick is existentially homeless, and the collapse of the house is just the final confirmation of this.

And the house itself, the feel of being in it, allegorizes—aesthetically, as a matter of atmospheric decor—art's representation of this experience of uneasy dwelling, this being in but not belonging. When the house collapses, the artwork manifests its expendability: it was an occasion not an object.

I want now to circle back to opera to conclude this long itinerary through the varieties of Usherian atmospherics. But not quite to opera, per se. Rather, I will discuss a music video that is part of a multimedia project under the creative control of the contemporary countertenor Anthony Roth Costanzo. "Glass/Handel" was a CD released in 2018 featuring Costanzo singing seven arias by Handel and five by Philip Glass. Many of these performances were also recast into short videos, directed by James Merchant, Mark Romanek, Maurizio Cattelan, and others. Costanzo also created—or curated—a live iteration of "Glass Handel" (he removed the slash for the live event).

This performance in New York's Cathedral of St. John the Divine might be called a disassembled *Gesamtkunstwerk*: where Wagner famously aimed to marshal all the arts to create an overwhelming, immersive experience for an audience sitting immobile in the dark, Costanzo has created "stations" to which audience members are randomly wheeled by staff, stations at which the music takes on different roles—now the soundtrack to a video, music for dance, the focus of a lavishly costumed aria performance, or the provocation to the real-time creation of a painting.

Debussy had struggled to make his engagement with "The House of Usher" fit the generic conventions of opera. The expectations regarding staging and plotting, how the audience participates—all this was cumbersome and prevented Debussy from reaching the *flou*, the musical atmospherics adequate to Poe's tale. A century later, Costanzo is still wrestling with how to make opera more fluid, though it is an open question whether wheeling spectators to different places rather than keeping them in their seats for four hours is any less controlling.

I will focus on only one aspect of Costanzo's project—the use of "music videos"—and on one video, the one created to accompany Costanzo's performance of "How All Living Things Breathe," an aria from Philip Glass's opera *The Fall of the House of Usher* (1988). I say "created to accompany" in order to highlight an ambiguity basic to the genre of the music video.

Because the music precedes the making of the video, we are invited to resist thinking of the music as a soundtrack of the kind we encounter in a film. And although the videos very often feature the artist performing (or pretending to perform) at least parts of the recorded music, or cast such performances into brief narratives, often what the videos show and what the music describes are quite distant from each other. When this happens, perhaps we do best to think of the music video as an attempt to capture a mood or atmosphere implied by but exceeding the purely musical content.

"How All Living Things Breathe" gives voice to Roderick's speech about the "conditions of the sentience" of the house itself. It is the part of Poe's story Debussy called "the dialogue of the stones." It is, I have argued, also where Poe thematizes the issue of atmosphere that elsewhere exists as setting (decor) or plot (electrical storm). But Glass and his librettist Arthur Yorinks change "sentience" to "breathe," a change of emphasis appropriate for vocalizing. In Poe, atmosphere is received, as it were, passively (and for Roderick painfully): the uncanny life of all things is a matter of passive "sentience." Changing the index of vitality from sentience to breath has the effect of highlighting opera's participation in this universal spiritual life. As Costanzo has said, "The human voice is very primal." There is an "intimacy" of "the sound from one human body traveling through air and entering another human body."

An aria is a solo vocal performance. It is "an air." It does not merely endure a surrounding atmosphere, it participates in it, creates a current in it. It is both an assertion of the individual—as the soloist steps forward from the orchestra or the chorus—and a kind of forfeit of that individuality, as the sound travels from one human body, leaves it behind, and enters the sonorous envelope. Arias have a kind of strange combination of intimacy and distance. In this respect, we might also say they exemplify "aura" (which also means breath) as famously defined by Walter Benjamin: "a unique phenomenon of a distance, no matter how close it may be."

The intimacy and uncanniness of the solo operatic voice has been described in many ways. To take just one example, Stanley Cavell points to the "new conception [opera] introduces of the relation between voice and body, a relation in which not this character and this actor are embodied in each other but in which this voice is located in—one might say, disembodied within—this figure, this double, this person, this persona, this singer, whose voice is essentially unaffected by the role." Opera adds something new to the age-old dialectic between actor and role, between body and character: it adds voice, somehow both an expression of overwhelming physical effort and an agent of disembodiment.

The voice in opera has often been read in starkly gendered terms. In her feminist philosophy of voice, Adriana Cavarero cites Hélène Cixous: "What sings in a 'man' is not he, but she." Voice itself, insofar as it is overflows speech, is feminine. The role of Roderick Usher in Glass's opera is sung by a tenor. But Costanzo is a countertenor or, as he says, "a boy who sings like a girl." By recasting Glass's aria for countertenor, Costanzo makes a point about the operatic voice itself, its tendency to detach itself from the body from which it emerges.

The video accompanying Costanzo's performance of "How All Living Things Breathe" looks to Poe's tale as much as Glass's opera. In the video, directed by Rupert Sanders, we do not see Costanzo, we only hear his voice. What we see is a figure entering a large space—a warehouse, perhaps—who walks slowly and steadily toward us. From a distance, the bald figure seems ambiguous. But it becomes clear that this fragile form is in fact a woman (Vladimira Michalkova Horakova), who may be bald on top but has a profusion of hair cascading around her shoulders (see plate 16). This gender ambiguity is, we might surmise, a way of playing visually with the "freak nature" (Costanzo's phrase) of "a boy who sings like a girl." It adds a visual amplification of the aria's projection of a disembodiment harbored within the hyperembodied operatic voice.

But this gender ambiguity also taps the symbolic core of Poe's tale. In "The Fall of the House of Usher," Roderick waits expectantly for his (twin) sister's return from the dead. Her opening the door to the sitting room is the beginning of the end. She totters forward, falls on Roderick, they die together, the narrator flees, and the house, fractured all along by a structural flaw, collapses into the tarn. It is as if the house's self-divided nature could only remain structurally sound as long as Roderick and Madeline—two aspects of the same soul—remained divided: by sex, by death. When they collapse into one another, the house itself collapses: the fissure, in a sense, held it up all along.

The play between fusion and fission in Poe's tale structures the video as well. In the beginning, there is an opening: a line of light slices through the black screen as the massive doors of the warehouse slide open. The figure enters the space, which now expands. We are inside but also outside:

there are rain puddles on the floor. Just as in Poe's description of Roder-ick's house, the space is somehow both claustrophobic and larger than we can make out. As the figure walks slowly toward us, shadowy presences edge in from the sides. We discover that they are warriors of one kind or another—a samurai, a man in chainmail. Following closely behind the walking figure is another engine of war—a tank, incongruously painted pink, perhaps another gesture toward gender fusion. Eventually a samurai leaps forward and slices the main figure in half, as the tank looms closer and closer, coming to a stop only when it fills the screen. What has been joined is sundered (see plate 17).

Poe's tale thematizes atmosphere as both condition and product of a fig-ure of form—namely, a space that shelters and exposes, closes and opens again, lives and perhaps even breathes. Sanders and Costanzo's video is an exercise in what atmosphere can be in a work that combines operatic voice and music video. Its formal clarity is striking: an inside-outside space becomes fissured by an open door; a space that first seems empty turns out not to be; things that start out in the distance end up being oppressively near, as the pink tank seems to roll up space itself behind its slow advance, and we are left face to face with it and its "vacant eye-like" features.

Estrangements of Voice

The Pythian Cosmos

A frantic jabbering. Who is speaking and in what language? Is it Italian or, perhaps, Spanish? Now it sounds Russian. It is *some* language, but not a known tongue.

A human being on his deathbed is saying something: "The voice seemed to reach our ears . . . from a vast distance, or from some deep cavern within the earth." The man dies "amid ejaculations of 'dead! dead!' absolutely *bursting* from the tongue and not from the lips of the sufferer." This ejaculatory tongue, somehow producing articulated words without aid of lips or palate, is also not a known tongue.

If we can, we identify articulated noises as human language. But we are often wrong. The agitated cries of an orangutan are interpreted as Italian or Spanish ("The Murders in the Rue Morgue"). The "gelatinous" voice emanating from a dead man's mouth is no longer human, yet we take it to be so ("The Facts in the Case of M. Valdemar"). We try desperately to tune the ambient sounds to a human frequency.

The idea that the cosmos is sonic is an ancient one. Pythagoras extrapolated the ratios between musical intervals into a structuring principle of the universe, arriving at the idea of a "music of the spheres." Even more ancient is the Pythia, otherwise known as the Oracle at Delphi, who translated emanations from fissures in the earth into human, if obscure, speech. The cosmos in which the speech of the dying man, Valdemar, reaches us "from some deep cavern within the earth" is Pythian, not Pythagorean.

After he published his philological investigation into the concepts of "Milieu and Ambiance," Leo Spitzer wrote a companion piece, "Classical and Christian Ideas of World Harmony: Prolegomena to an Interpretation of the Word 'Stimmung'" (1944). Here, concord and *harmonia* structure and stabilize human being in the divine and natural order, much as the Greek concept of *periekhon* and its avatars had, in the earlier essay, offered the comfort of a cosmic holding environment.

Spitzer's researches ended in the seventeenth century. He offers only "prolegomena" to the contemporary and widespread use of his key word, "Stimmung." He wishes to recall the term, today usually indicating mood, to its sonic roots. But as with his elaborate excavation of modern terms "milieu" and "ambience," this older root idea of "Stimmung" as attunement to a world harmony is well behind us. Already in Heidegger's early phenomenological treatments of anxiety and boredom, for example, these moods ("Stimmungen") do not disclose a harmonious cosmos of the Pythagorean sort. On the contrary, Heidegger's descriptive brilliance affords a view of a "dissonant attunement," or perhaps even an "attunement to the *nothing*."

Poe's sonically saturated cosmos is Pythian, both ancient and very modern. In the nineteenth century, sonic material was reconceived in terms of waves and their frequencies. This is not so much an ordered cosmos as a metamorphic one, fugitive, undulatory. In this Pythian cosmos, the human voice forming articulated words is just one modulation on a sonic continuum that extends to animal, natural, and machinic dimensions. "The phonograph does not hear as ears do that have been trained immediately to filter voices, words, and sounds out of noise; it registers acoustic events as such. Articulateness becomes a second-order exception to a spectrum of noise."

But, of course, nobody was waiting for the phonograph to teach them about "acoustic events as such," or about "noise." The year before Poe died, the Fox sisters received communications from the spirit world in the form of rapping sounds. The events in Hydesville, New York, were a famous inflection point in spiritualist practices, but there had been a lot of chatter in the realms beyond for quite a while. Emmanuel Swedenborg, whose mystical writings were influential in antebellum America, located the voices of certain kinds of spirits at precise locations around their bodies: those who in life had been logicians and metaphysicians, for example, spoke from deep within the body and were barely audible even though they shouted. The realms beyond were also the realms within.

What can be received, tuned in, can also be broadcast or projected. In the remarkable *Ninth Bridgewater Treatise* (1837), Charles Babbage suggested that the universe is one vast recording device. No sound or word is ever lost: "The pulsations of the air, once set in motion by the human voice, cease not to exist with the sounds to which they give rise. . . . The air itself is one vast library, on whose pages are for ever written all that man has ever said or woman whispered."

"If there is a modern age," write Gilles Deleuze and Félix Guattari, it is "the age of the cosmic." This statement is made in the context of an account of modern aesthetics. Their idea is that artists turn from creating or expressing things (the artist as demiurge) to recording and reporting encounters at the edge of chaos. The artist is in the business not of producing but of harnessing energies, capturing, modulating, tuning in. It is all about technique: "There is no imagination outside of technique. The modern figure is not the child or the lunatic, still less the artist, but the cosmic artisan."

The primary examples Deleuze and Guattari offer of the "cosmic artisan" are musicians: Debussy, Varèse, La Monte Young, Cage. They might have turned to Poe, whose "Philosophy of Composition" offers a definitive presentation of the "cosmic artisan," one so thoroughly absorbed in the French critical tradition that it probably underlies their discussion. But the sonic dimension is privileged in their titanic dramaturgy: "Sound invades us, impels us, drags us, transpierces us. It takes leaves of the earth, as much in order to drop us into a black hole as to open us up to a cosmos. It makes us want to die."

It is a strange thing to say: "It makes us want to die." But perhaps it looks like this: a man mourning his lost love is subject to a rude and incomprehensible sonic intrusion. It is a bird that iterates a single word—"Nevermore." The man elaborates a series of questions—about death, about a longing for death—that elicits the inevitable reply, each time ratcheting up his agony. He passes into death but still speaks to us about the bird that likewise "still is sitting, still is sitting."

The sonic intrusion is incomprehensible not because the English word "nevermore" cannot be understood but because the voice speaking the word is neither human nor animal, but both. And in being both, it is machinic, a kind of recording. And in being all three, it is cosmic. The bird embodies a phenomenon central to the Pythian cosmos, one that only grows more perspicuous with the advent of sound recording: "voices absent to themselves."

"Art begins with the animal," announce Deleuze and Guattari, "at least with the animal that carves out a territory and constructs a house." The epitome of this artistic animal is the bird that sings and returns again and again to its song—its "refrain." Carving out a territory is here a sonic operation, but it is also always linked to a place—a staging area, a "house." The bowerbird has a song and a bower, both. Deleuze and Guattari were not writing in the era of earbuds and Spotify, but their desire to extend their understanding of sonic territory from birdsong to modern sound technologies is clear: "Radios and television sets are like sound walls around every household and mark territories."

Refrain and house: the bird's croaked "nevermore" and the man's room. We might think these oppose each other, but in fact they form a single compound, the man tying himself, fixating himself, to the bird's refrain. Together, bird and man, refrain and house, sound and structure, create something that endures—a work of art, what Deleuze and Guattari call a "being of sensation": "The being of sensation is not the flesh but the compound of nonhuman forces of the cosmos, of man's nonhuman becomings, and of the ambiguous house that exchanges and adjusts them, makes them whirl around like winds." (The House of Usher, with its self-generated storm, is another such being.)

Let me draw out three propositions from this discussion that can help guide us in what follows. The first is that sound and voice in modernity are cosmic and atmospheric—invasive, immersive, permeating. This cosmos is Pythian, not Pythagorean. It is not an eternal structure, a ratio, but a metamorphic continuum along which the puny human voice shuttles outward to animal, natural, and machinic dimensions—hence a bird speaking English.

Second proposition: there is something phenomenologically odd, even paradoxical, about sound and voice in this dispensation—although sound is inescapably (because immersively) *present*, a distance inhabits the core of it, such that noises and voices can be "absent to themselves."

A third proposition is that our access to such sonic intrusions depends on *structures*, an "ambiguous house" that tunes in the frequencies, "exchanges and adjusts them, makes them whirl around like winds." There is no hearing without a house, which is to say without a medium and a form.

This last proposition can be unfolded further: because it is atmospheric and cosmic, sound pervades and permeates. But it is not uniform in its effect. Obstacles and blockages arise, and there, sound is an *incursion*: a speaking raven blows in, and what follows is an attempt to create structure around this incursion. Openings and escapes also arise, and when that happens, sound *explodes*: the structures that have been built collapse when the cry of the cat, the beating heart, the tinkling bell announce an escape. In both cases, incursions and explosions, *the encounter with sonic atmosphere always takes place in relation to form or medium*. What attracts later artists and artisans in nonliterary media to Poe's works is not only the weird, violent, or otherworldly effects in his work. It is equally—and at the same time—the formal devices that capture, amplify, or release those effects.

Technique and technology thus take precedence in modernity, where any encounter with "imagination" must pass via the tinkering of the "cosmic artisan." It is all a question of thresholds. Roderick Usher cocks an ear and cries to his obtuse friend, "Not hear it?—yes, I hear it, and *have* heard it." The murderer in "The Tell-Tale Heart" confides to us: "I heard all things in the heaven and in the earth. I heard many things in hell." The Fox sisters post themselves close to the threshold between the living and the dead; like Poe's maniacs, they tune in to messages from beyond more efficiently than others. In the decades after Poe's death, scientists like Helmholtz and inventors like Edison focused on the question of thresholds, how to capture sound and through a process of inscription make it permanent. People welcomed improved technologies for talking to the dead.

Earworm

In *Seven Types of Ambiguity*, William Empson takes up the topic of "atmosphere" in poetry, something he considers a "deduction from the belief in Pure Sound." He is initially skeptical: "Critics often say or imply casually that some poetic effect conveys a direct 'physical' quality, something mysteriously intimate, something which it is strange a poet could convey, something like a sensation which is not attached to any of the senses."

The idea of a "sensation not attached to any of the senses" is confusing, but Empson soldiers on, proposing a terminological "distinction between 'sensation' and 'feeling.'" This latter category, Empson muses, perhaps points to a domain beyond any "assembly of grammatical meanings," in which what prevails is "a 'mood,' an 'atmosphere.'"

If feeling, mood, and atmosphere are species of sensations unattached to the senses, they suggest a self-distancing of our corporeal condition, an embodiment beyond body, what Deleuze and Guattari had called a "being of sensation [that] is not the flesh but the compound of nonhuman forces of the cosmos." In a surprising and brilliant turn, Empson temporalizes this self-distancing and calls it memory: "Probably it is in this way, as a sort of taste in the head, that one remembers one's own past experiences, including the experience of reading a particular poet." Memory itself—the "taste in the head"—is conveyed by feeling: it is a mood, atmospheric. It is a spectral embodiment, present and absent at once.

This all may be true, says Empson, but is it useful in understanding poetry? "You may say, then, that any grammatical analysis of poetry, since it must ignore atmosphere, is trivial." Being the master of grammatical analysis that he is, however, Empson begs to differ, offering this parting shot: "This belief may in part explain the badness of much nineteenth-century poetry, and how it came to be written by critically sensitive people."

Sing-song, rhymey-chimey. Emerson called Poe "the jingle man." Though Empson does not say this here, more than a few people have thought that Poe epitomized the "badness of much nineteenth-century poetry." T. S. Eliot, for one. Poe wrote a "few short poems," Eliot confesses, "which enchanted him for a time when he was a boy, and which do somehow stick in the memory." That awkward wording—"do somehow stick"—signals an admission made against resistance. *Should* poetry be memorable in this way, via sonic atmosphere floating free of the "assembly of grammatical meanings"? A more fearful question: Is it memorable in any other way?

The world we live in is replete with jingles, sonic shards that "do somehow stick" in the memory, that live on, as atmosphere. When jingles work, some very simple memory follows the sound—a brand name, for example. The earworm is a cousin of the jingle, a repetitive musical "hook" that comes unbidden, again and again, whether you liked it on first hearing or very much did not. Being plagued by an earworm is to have an Empsonian "sensation unattached to any of the senses." It is like having a recording device lodged in your brain that you cannot control. The intrusiveness of the earworm is an effect of intimacy and alienation, closeness and distance, simultaneously.

In 1891, Francis and James Criswell filed a patent application for a "new and useful Improvement in phonographs." This is a phonograph that repeats itself indefinitely: "We have constructed the record-cylinder with mechanism whereby when it has made its full lateral travel it is returned automatically to its starting-point and its revolution and progressive lateral motion continued indefinitely in accordance with the length of run or motion of the motor." The key words here are "automatically" and "indefinitely." The "Improvement" on which the patent claim rests has to do with this automaticity.

But what did the "Improvement" look like? What was it for? "One of the inventors of this invention has adopted for use in advertising his manufacture of a proprietary remedy for corns a stuffed crow, or representation of a crow and to add to the attractiveness of such advertising device we have combined therewith a phonograph" (see figure 4.1). And what, you may ask, repeated itself automatically and indefinitely from within this crow? An advertisement, a hook, possibly even a jingle. Maybe it said or croaked: "With 'Criswell's Corns-Away!' you'll have painful feet—*Nevermore!*"

It's perfectly possible, of course, that the Criswells used a crow because everyone knows that crows repeat what they have learned to imitate. In a sense, then, the crow advertises the mechanicity of their device, the mechanicity of advertising itself, and the "proprietary remedy for corns" all at once. Ultimately, the Criswells want a little mechanical crow lodged in our own heads talking to us "indefinitely" about "Corns-Away!" But in 1891, Poe's "The Raven" was so widely known, and so widely memorized, that it

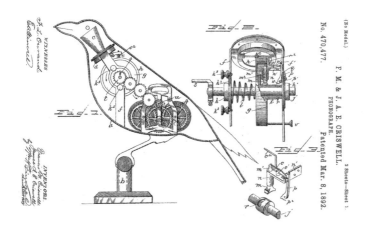

FIGURE 4.1. Phonographic crow. James and Francis Criswell. US Patent 470,477. March 8, 1892.

is not far-fetched to think that the Criswells borrowed some of the poem's notoriety and memorability to add punch to their advertising. However we interpret this patent application, the idea that sonic atmosphere— jingle or hook—can be human, animal, and machinic simultaneously is essential to its meaning.

The Work of Art in the Age of Its Supernatural Reproducibility

On November 2, 1863, the poet and spiritualist Lizzie Doten delivered a lecture titled "The Mysteries of Godliness." Offering a detailed itinerary of Poe's movements in the afterlife, the lecture prefaced Doten's recitation of "Farewell to Earth," a poem communicated to her by the spirit of Poe. Doten assures us that this is Poe's final word: "This night he gives his 'Farewell to Earth.' . . . He can still minister, as an Everlasting Truth and living power, to the needs of Humanity; but as Poe, the individual, he is willing to be forgotten. His personality, as far as human recognition is concerned, can end here."

Except for some scattered illustrations, the first remediations of Poe's work took the form of spiritual dictations. The field was crowded: "Lizzie Doten was one of two hundred or so women who made a living as a trance speaker . . . before the Civil War." Those who received poems were fewer, but even here competition was fierce, since Poe had become one of the "most popular spirit visitors to mediums." Doten's bold claim that "Farewell to Earth" is Poe's valedictory message makes more sense in this context: she is essentially calling a halt to the use of Poe's name. He may still operate as a "living power" but "Poe, the individual . . . is willing to be forgotten." There will be no additions to Poe's corpus through posthumous communication after "this night." Doten got the last one.

How do we know "Farewell to Earth" is a poem by Poe? Well, it *sounds* like Poe:

> Ye, who grope in darkness blindly,
> Ye, who seek a refuge kindly,
> Ye upon whose hearts the ravens—ghostly ravens—perch and prey,
> Listen! For the bells are ringing,
> Tuneful as the angels singing,
> Ringing in the glorious morning of your spirit's marriage-day,
> When the soul, no longer fettered to the feeble form of clay,
> To a high, harmonious union, soars, elate with hope away.

We see in these lines not only the replication of formal structures—the metric and stanzaic signatures of "The Raven," for example—but also Poe's props—the ravens, the bells. Possessed by Poe, Doten takes possession of Poe's poetry, occupies it, as it were, so that she can rewrite it, in his idiom, from within.

When we claim a poem *sounds* like Poe, we can mean several things: a characteristic way with rhythm and rhyme, a predilection for certain themes or props, a prevailing mood. But *if* we say it "sounds like" Poe—rather than "looks like" or "reads like" Poe—we prioritize sound. The themes and props are subordinate to a more fundamental sonic atmosphere.

On the title page of her book, Doten includes an epigraph, which she attributes to Poe: "And my soul from out that shadow shall be lifted evermore." Removing one tiny "n" from the famous refrain of "The Raven," so that "nevermore" becomes "evermore," leaves Poe's music intact while flooding his darkness with the refulgence of spiritual salvation. I say Poe's music is "intact" because he tells us, in "The Philosophy of Composition," that the nugget of his poem, its sonic core, is the phoneme "—*or*." Having chosen this phoneme for reasons he explains, he moves next to his refrain word: "Nevermore," a word "embodying this sound," a word "impossible to overlook."

But perhaps other words are also "impossible to overlook." In rewriting the final lines of Poe's poem with "evermore" instead of "nevermore," Doten stays faithful to Poe's sonic signature while reversing the semantic charge. You can go pretty far in changing Poe as long as you stay true to the sonic core; the "—*or*" announces itself, as Poe says it would, as the essential grain of sound around which the pearl of the poem grows. When *The Simpsons* "do" "The Raven," Homer reads Poe's poem as written, except for the refrain, which is crowed by a bird-Bart: "Eat my shorts!" The one place they change is the place of no change—the refrain; but within this change the signature phoneme "—*or*" still is sitting, unchanged.

Poe was—and is—easily and often parodied. But those productions—many quite ingenious—are not what we're looking at here. Nobody thinks the parodies are by Poe, but the poems in Doten's book are signed, as it were, with Poe's name. At the same time, spiritual dictation was not the *only* way to circulate new poems by Poe. In 1877, Hoosier poet James Whitcomb Riley, frustrated by his lack of recognition as a poet, fabricated a "lost" poem by Poe. The original of "Leonainie," inscribed in the flyleaf of a dictionary, is in Indiana University's Lilly Library (see figure 4.2).

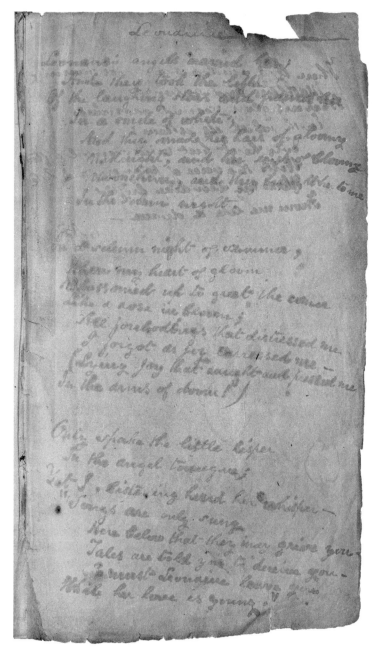

FIGURE 4.2. James Whitcomb Riley's "Leonainie," inscribed in the back flyleaf of a dictionary and passed off as a poem by Poe. Lilly Library Riley MSS, LMC 1884. Courtesy of Lilly Library, Indiana University.

The ink, diluted to begin with to suggest age, has faded still more. But one can make it out. Here is the final stanza:

> Only spake the little lisper
> In the angel tongue;
> Yet I, listening, heard her whisper—
> "Songs are only sung
> Here below that they may grieve you—
> Tales are told you to deceive you—
> So must Leonainie leave you
> While her love is young."

This poem seems less literal-minded as a replication of Poe than Doten's "Farewell to Earth." There are no bells or ravens, but we *can* check the box labeled "untimely death of beloved female" (*very* untimely if she really is a "little lisper"). The peculiar name "Leonainie" also recalls Poe's Lenore, Annie, and Annabel Lee, all in one go. The home truths delivered by this "angel tongue"—namely, that "Songs are only sung / Here below that they may grieve you"—seems more in line with Poe's fascination with the "human thirst for self-torture," with *poems as pain*, than Doten's bromides.

Riley's hoax was a huge success, until it wasn't. He eventually confessed, was fired from the Indiana newspaper where he was working, and moved on to fame as the down-home poet celebrating "the frost on the punkin." But Riley had disturbed the energy field named "Poe," and he never fully extricated himself from it. Alfred Russel Wallace, the great British man of science who shares credit with Darwin for the theory of natural selection and who was a committed spiritualist, happened to read "Leonainie" in the 1890s and never forgot it. Riley had long since confessed to the hoax, but Wallace did not know this and was open, in any case, to a spiritual provenance for the poem. The poems ascribed to Poe in Doten's *Poems from the Inner Life*, for example, were in Wallace's estimation "finer and deeper & grander poems than any written by him [Poe] in the earth-life."

Wallace was eventually informed that Riley had confessed to fabricating the poem, but even then he didn't believe it: "Till we have the alleged *proof* that Riley wrote 'Leonainie,' it seems to me quite as probable that *he* found it, and on the suggestion of a friend made use of it to gain a reputation." In other words, Wallace thinks it quite possible that Riley faked a fake. Given Wallace's odd combination of a dogged focus on textual facts and an openness to supernatural creation, there was no way out for Riley. "There is nothing for me to do but acknowledge that I wrote it," Riley later told the *Indianapolis Sentinel*, "but that does not stand, as I once denied being the author. I wrote it but I did not. I did not write it but I did, and I am a liar any way you put it."

What conclusion can we draw from these two efforts to introduce new poems by Poe into the world? Perhaps we can say that the link between *sound* and name is stronger, more fundamental, than that between *text* and name. If it sounds like Poe, it might well be taken as by Poe. The sonic atmospherics of Poe's poetry, especially when understood as having spiritual provenance, effect a strange disturbance to authorial identity. Doten's poems can pass as Poe's. And so can Riley's "Leonainie" for someone like Wallace, even in the teeth of overt denial. "I wrote it but I did not. I did not write it but I did." What "sounds like Poe" links a sonic atmosphere with Poe's name: neither biographical nor textual evidence can trump this link. Perhaps what sounds like Poe is an emanation of the Poe brand rather than an effect controlled by any author of any text.

Here is a coda to this suite of reflections on "The Work of Art in the Age of its Supernatural Reproducibility." Sometime in the late 1890s, or perhaps the first few years of the twentieth century, Charles Sanders Peirce sat down at his writing desk, wrote the words "Art Chirography" across the top of a sheet of paper, and began a peculiar experiment that he extended over five separate trials (see figure 4.3).

The opening words of Poe's "The Raven" are here visualized as if they were in a state of agitation or metamorphosis. The tails of the *p*'s slide down the page as if dripping or dissolving, while the upstrokes of other letters rise like smoke. End-line downstrokes are regularly swept back across the page as if an invisible wind propelled them. The poem itself seems to emerge from a vortical *O*, and some extensions curve and arch toward each other as if drawn by a force of attraction.

By the time Peirce sat down to his "Art Chirography," he had had this particular poem in his head for decades: "Edgar A Poe's Poem, 'The Raven' was recited by Charles S. Peirce, in a most superior manner," reported *The Cambridge Chronicle* for August 5, 1854, describing the Cambridge High School Annual Exhibition. "For effective reading and speaking, probably this young man stands at the head of the school." As late as 1912, childhood friend Mary Huntington vividly recalled Peirce's dramatic readings that occurred a half century before: "You were famous . . . for your powers of

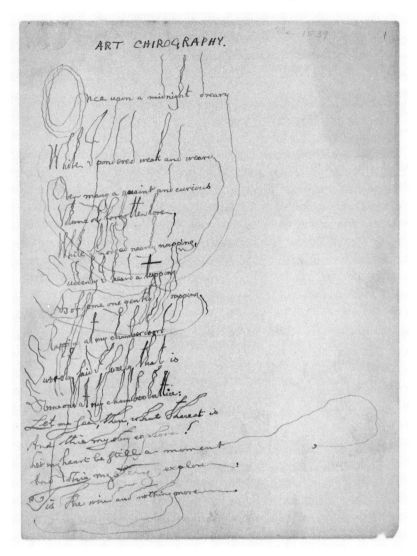

FIGURE 4.3. "Art chirography." Charles Sanders Peirce transcription of "The Raven." MS Am 1632 (1539), Charles Sanders Peirce papers, Houghton Library, Harvard University, Cambridge.

elocution and often a charmed circle of family and friends would listen to your declamation of Edgar Poe's 'Raven' and other blood-curdling poems."

All of which is to say that Peirce very likely began this odd transcription from memory. "The Raven" is available as an aural/oral object to him. It has been suggested, in fact, that Peirce's experiment is an investigation into the "phonic-semantic knot." But that doesn't seem quite right: commas get the same drippy treatment as vowels and consonants. I think we need to understand Peirce as taking the *whole* of Poe's poem, the phenomenality of it, as the object of his treatment. We might conclude that Poe's poem emanates an energy that deforms and attenuates the marks that make up its text. Alternatively, we could conclude that the poem is swept up in, and penetrated by, an energy from without.

One way to embrace this ambiguity is to say that Poe's poem is interesting to Peirce less for the text itself than for the "atmosphere" it mediates. Poe's poem made its way into the hearts and minds and memories of nineteenth-century people as a media event—as having "made a sensation," in the locution taking off during Poe's lifetime, one he used and understood well. And this "sensation," being in part a sound memory, is what Empson suggests it might be: a "sensation not attached to any of the senses."

Peirce's repeated trials in his loopy transcriptions of "The Raven" are attempts to find the right technique with which to "tune in" a poem that exists, as it were, "in the ether"—in a zone of sensation and extended memory beyond any one human being's capacity to encompass. Peirce does not so much remediate Poe's poem as its atmosphere.

The Presence of Absence

With the advent of sound recording and, later, radio, encounters with the Pythian cosmos take a new turn but retain a firm grip on the unearthly. These media remain "haunted" by atmospheric voices unattached to visible bodies. Because of its immateriality (no telegraph wires, no surface of inscription), radio especially incited fantasies of mind transfer, of communications with the dead or with extraterrestrial beings. The panicked response to Orson Welles's broadcast of *The War of the Worlds* (1938) merely confirmed a mass predilection to treat radio as a privileged medium for contact with extramundane forces.

At the heart of the experience of listening to radio was a paradox. Writing under the aegis of the Princeton Radio Project, Theodor Adorno puzzled it out this way: "The radio voice, like the human voice or face, is 'present.' At the same time, it suggests something 'behind' it." This radio voice is very near, even intimate—hence the advent of "crooning" in the late 1920s—but it is also unimaginably distant. "The strangeness of the phenomenon expresses itself in the somewhat vague and half-conscious awareness of being at home with it and yet quite far away."

The domestication of radio—"being at home with it"—carries forward this paradox. We get used to having spooks in the house. "In fact the 'shock' of radio ubiquity is apt to vanish or recede into the background as soon as the listener gets accustomed to the tool." Adorno's phrase "radio ubiquity" refers both to the radio signal and the absorption of the medium into daily living. In both ways, radio is eminently atmospheric. Writing in 1948, André Bazin confirms the point: "The cultural interest of radio . . . is that it allows modern man to live in an atmosphere of sound comparable to the warm atmosphere created by central heating."

We can call this phenomenon the domestication of the presence of absence. Such a development may also help make sense of the popularity of paranormal themes in radiobroadcasting. On August 3, 1941, the radio show *Inner Sanctum* featured Boris Karloff in a treatment of "The Tell-Tale Heart," with a script by Robert Newman. Karloff plays Simon, who tells us early on that he had been deaf for two years but has regained his hearing. Indeed, his recovered hearing recalls the preternatural sensitivity of Poe's narrator: Simon hears the grass growing, sap rising, fish breathing, and so on. He meets Oliver, who has a similar story to tell, except that it is his blindness that has miraculously disappeared, allowing him to see missing cows from miles away.

The half-hour radio play has been called "pure nonsense" by one contemporary critic, so ridiculous that Poe "would have spun in his grave had he heard it." But that seems extreme. The story retains from Poe the fundamental conflict between one who sees and one who hears, after all, a conflict ending in attempted murder. There is also an extended confession scene, as in Poe's tale. And Karloff's softly spoken account of his need to murder, ornamented with his trademark lisp, captures the way Poe's narrative structure—a crazy person buttonholing us with his "reasonableness"—itself produces an uncomfortable combination of intimacy and alienation. This radio play is recognizably part of the Poe brand.

Each episode of *Inner Sanctum* began with the sound of a creaking door inviting us into a privileged and confined space. Radio itself is borderless, unplaceable and distant, but our experience of it is domestic and intimate. As we sit in our own inner sanctums, we somehow have access to voices reaching us across the void. We are in fact like Simon, or like Poe's narrator, who "heard all things in the heaven and in the earth" and "many things in hell." Our own experience of the medium, we could say, is allegorized in the episode.

The grandiosity of our aural power, and the uncanniness inherent in supernatural hearing, are allegorized in the show, then. But so is its banality. And here is where a species of self-deflating irony, so pervasive in the twentieth-century horror mode, testifies to the medium's domestication. It turns out that both Simon and Oliver had escaped from their confinement at a psychiatric institute. They are both quite mad, and their boasts to have overcome their deafness and blindness are sheer fantasy. The truth is, we were warned. Simon's hearing is so acute, we were told, that he heard "things that don't even exist." *Caveat auditor*!

Inner Sanctum featured a host who, like the "Crypt-Keeper" in EC Comics' *Tales from the Crypt*, announced the show's intent to terrify in such a patently over-the-top manner that its irony was inescapable. This host also dealt with the sponsor, which in the case of the Karloff episode was Carter's Little Liver Pills and its promise to deliver "the *glorious* feeling that goes with regularity." For reasons that are unclear in the episode, Simon buries the body of Oliver beneath the floor of an old mill. As he becomes tormented by the beating heart, and perhaps to cover the sound from both himself and the policeman, he pulls the lever releasing the flow of water from the mill. What is the meaning of this giant flushing sound at the climax of the story? Some listeners surely will have detected a reference to the show's sponsor and its promise of a "*glorious* feeling" awaiting them in that most private of inner sanctums.

Poe's innovations with narrative voice, the insistent appeal to a reader from an "imaginary space" inaccessible to that same reader, have received a good bit of attention. Sound media have several different ways of exploring this ambiguous voice, so near and so far, so intimate and so alien. I mentioned Karloff's earnest explanations of his need to murder, and some of the most memorable sound recordings of Poe's works—by Vincent Price and Basil Rathbone, or James Mason's liquid voice-over to the UPA animation discussed in an earlier chapter—manage this with subtle voice acting. But even the most mild-mannered actor often leaves a sonic signature of the alien that has no motivation in Poe's text—Karloff's delicate lisp is an example.

The idea that voice is sonic stuff and not a mere vehicle for meaning is essential to the Pythian cosmos and goes back to the earliest days of sound recording. Early exhibitions of the phonograph provoked creative descriptions of what such reproduced voices sounded like: "little explosions and an enormous buzzing" or words that come "struggling up from the underworld." The alienating effect of voices unattached to visible bodies may well have influenced the choice of texts in these early exhibitions. Poe's "Annabel Lee," for example, with its plangent tale of love and loss, was a regular in exhibitions as early as 1878, the machine and the poem equally "evoking an entire discourse of the uncanny associated with Poe's writing."

Audiences may have found the phonograph uncanny, but they were far from overawed by it. They understood they were dealing with a machine that processed sonic material as such: early exhibitions were as interested in "whistling and singing and sighing and groans—in fact, every utterance of which the human voice is capable" as they were in speech. And exhibitors and their audiences were also interested in what the mechanism could do to this material, beyond merely reproduce it: rolls were played faster or slower, and even backward. "Far from disguising the fact of mediation, demonstrations flaunted it." The machine that recorded could also be the machine that distorted, leading to an embrace of technological mediation as a source of the artificial and the weird. As with my interpretation of the *Inner Sanctum* episode, the affordances of the medium are not simply accepted passively but become a tacit *theme* of the favored content.

In the early 1930s, Robert Irwin, the director of the American Foundation for the Blind, collaborated with RCA records to develop a record disc that played longer than the eleven minutes per side of a 78 rpm record. The result was the LP, made from a new material called "vinylite." The first test recordings for the new format were a chapter from Hellen Keller's *Midstream* and a recording of Poe's "The Raven."

Why does Irwin turn to Poe? Apparently, he had come across an unusual "picture disc" produced by RCA Victor in 1932, featuring the recording of Arcady Dubensky's composition for voice and orchestra, "The Raven," as played by the Philadelphia Orchestra under the direction of Leopold Stokowski. The 78 rpm disc was made from clear material, allowing an image to be laminated into each side: the text of Poe's poem and one of Gustave Doré's 1883 illustrations. These RCA Victor "picture discs" sold poorly, possibly because the inclusion of the image added noise in the playback.

Whatever its defects, this strange object testifies to Poe's visibility as a multimedia artist: word, image, sound all together.

Perhaps it was just this experimental profile that caught Irwin's eye. He was himself testing new boundaries, and Stokowski's profile as a champion of music over the radio was in the same mold. Irwin seemed to think that the Dubensky recording, with its combination of speech and atmospheric orchestral effects, might appeal to blind Americans eager for reading material.

He was wrong about that. As the American Foundation for the Blind's auditors made clear, and as has been subsequently confirmed again and again by consumers of audiobooks, the preference was for minimal theatricality. Consumers of talking books do not want a night at the theater; they want someone reading a book aloud, to which they can add tonalities of their own imagining.

But Poe's works and words retain an enduringly estranging power, and there is a significant strand of sound recordings of them that are no longer recitation but not yet music. Benjamin DeLoache, who declaims "The Raven" amid Dubensky's brooding atmospherics, is an example. The impression here is that words and music are neither aligned nor wholly separable. This is neither song nor recitation. Perhaps it is closest to sprechstimme, that modernist mutation of operatic recitative.

Such performances can at times tap into the fascination with voice as pure sonic material displayed in the early exhibitions. A version of "The Raven" recorded in 1913 features piano accompaniment that waffles uncertainly between tentative tinkling and music hall bounciness. But it fades into irrelevance beside Percy Hemus's robust recitation with its relentlessly rolled r's: "Ah! Distinctly I rememberrrrr, it was in the bleak Decemberrrr, / And each separate dying emberrrrrwrrrrought its ghost upon the floor."

I want to conclude this consideration of voice in sound media and as an atmospheric phenomenon with a glance at a more recent production. In the mid-1990s, the New York producer and impresario Hal Willner produced a stage show that brought actors and musicians together in an homage to Poe. This show became a recording—*Closed on Account of Rabies*— and also inspired Lou Reed, who had been part of Willner's show, to join forces first with Robert Wilson on a stage show and then to produce his own recording, *The Raven*. Willner had produced many spoken-word and musical tribute albums—to William S. Burroughs and Allen Ginsberg, to the music of Thelonious Monk, Nino Rota, and Kurt Weill. But this one was different: "On my previous concept albums, the artists had tended, in effect, to bring the composer into their world. The opposite happened with the Conqueror Poe, the feverish atmosphere of whose work enveloped every reader."

Can we *hear* that "feverish atmosphere"? There are several techniques on display. Christopher Walken's superb rendition of "The Raven," for example, uses tempo and volume to downplay some of the more florid sonic effects of Poe's original, but the soundscape in which he tells the story is "sprayed with lurid feedback," at times almost drowning Walken's voice. The effect is of a voice at once familiar and in danger of being torn away from us, overcome by a storm of sound. Almost every performance on *Closed on Account of Rabies* achieves an unnerving intimacy with the listener through a simple device: the speaker is extremely closely miked, making every click of the tongue pop like a gun going off. But there is also considerable reverb everywhere, suggesting an empty space of uncertain dimensions opening behind the voice.

The voice as denizen of the Pythian cosmos is perhaps best exemplified by the forty-minute recitation of "The Black Cat" by Diamanda Galás. Willner's inclusion of this artist speaks to his interest in vocal extremity and experimentation, since by the mid-1990s Galás had completed her three-part *Masque of the Red Death*, which borrows Poe's title only to connect a set of assaultive sonic environments focusing the horrors of the AIDS crisis, a "startling barrage of advanced vocal techniques intensified by electronic dynamics." While her performance of "The Black Cat" is conventional in comparison, it is nevertheless simply impossible to escape Galás's voice in order to concentrate on Poe's text. Galás moans, articulates her final consonants mercilessly, and most of all she *whispers*, and whispers most, and most urgently, at the moments of extremest terror. The simultaneous intimacy and alienation of the voice in the Pythian cosmos can surely have no more direct an expression than this.

Incursion, Immersion, Explosion

The sonic atmosphere must be captured, tuned in. What we *hear* of the sonic cosmos is the result of an encounter with form or medium. As Deleuze and Guattari put it, the refrain must be coupled with the "ambiguous house"—a structure dedicated not so much to stability and permanence as to the passage of "nonhuman forces of the cosmos" through it, forces that "whirl around like winds."

A great deal of musical experimentation since the latter half of the nineteenth century has concerned itself with this task of corralling externalities. Musical form becomes preoccupied with managing sonic incursions, up to and including "noise." This is why the "cosmic artisan" is paradigmatically the musician. "Mood, atmosphere . . . what do those words mean?" asks one historian of ambient music. "What Varèse sought to develop was the superior capacity of all kinds of music to capture emergence in complex phenomena; transient, non-articulated feelings; or what Gaston Bachelard called the Poetics of Space, whether the ambience of a room, the ribbon of a road or the boundless envelopment of oceanic space."

To "capture emergence" is to commit oneself to transience over structure, as if your house was not meant to protect you from atmospheric conditions but rather to serve as host to those conditions. "What I want to achieve through my music is to create a 'tunnel of sound,'" says contemporary composer Toshio Hosokawa, "a musical, aural bridge between dream and reality, madness and sanity, the world of the living and that of the dead. By going through this tunnel, people will be able to lighten their grief, or at least, to find a small light in the darkness." Hosokawa's ambiguous house is a tunnel.

Hosokawa is known for combining European avant-garde compositional practices with techniques drawn from Japanese culture. Thus, when he first considered a piece based on "The Raven," he had an ancient form ready to hand: "When I read 'The Raven' by Edgar Allan Poe, it reminded me of the Japanese Noh play. A view of the world in the Noh is not anthropocentric. Some of the main characters in the Noh are animals and plants, and some are unearthly spirits. Poe describes the process of the collapse of the modern rational world, as a consequence of an invasion of the world by a weird animal 'raven' which lives in the other world. I considered this poem as a story of Noh and expressed it in the form of monodrama with mezzo-soprano and ensemble."

The Raven was premiered in 2012; it was the first composition Hosokawa completed after the Fukushima disaster. Poe's poem follows a familiar form for Hosokawa, the "invasion of the world" by an "unearthly spirit." But a different incursion is also in play for him, the catastrophic convergence of natural and human powers—a tidal wave destroying a nuclear reactor. It begins to be clear how Poe's poem might strike Hosokawa as not just a Noh-like meditation on grief and the other world but as something more: "the collapse of the modern rational world."

One choice Hosokawa makes will be familiar after the recent consideration of sound recording: the voice enunciating Poe's words veers wildly from "intoned speech to quasi-sung declamation to lyrically alluring flights to bursts of soaring intensity." We might describe the mezzo-soprano as herself a "tunnel of sound," human speech undergoing a constant torquing in its passage through her vocal apparatus. Hosokawa's piece is through-composed: we do not perambulate through a structure, perhaps noticing the same room from different vantages as we take our tour. Rather, we are carried along, and the architecture of Poe's poem, so insistent in its textual form, is as it were submerged and swept away by the force of Hosokawa's music, with its "atmospheric and organic . . . colorings, pungently atonal harmonic writing, spectral textures and Asian-influenced melodic fragments."

In Noh drama, Hosokawa observes, "a ghost with deep sorrow and regret in its heart crosses the *hashigakari*, a bridge from the world of the dead to that of the living; this pitiable spirit then purifies its own grief through telling someone in this world its lamentable tale." The raven, according to this schema, would be the grieving soul, rather than a being delivering implacable news from beyond. But the raven and the man, as I suggested earlier, are at bottom one compound entity, a communicative circuit for the articulation of grief. One of the most extraordinary effects of Hosokawa's composition is the long and very quiet conclusion: the voice has been stilled, but grief itself "still is sitting, still is sitting" in what can only be called a sonic aftermath, the waters receded, winds whistling over the desolation.

Bridge and tunnel: Poe's poem addresses problems both ancient and contemporary for Hosokawa, Noh and Fukushima superimposed. He is thinking about incursion and grief, about cosmic forces and how to let them in. He builds a bridge and tunnel to give structure to the flow.

But Hosokawa's is hardly the only way to manage incursion. "I have to write a poem; I have no feeling, no sentiment, no inspiration." Tea was "served in the conservatory" and the poet remarked, "I so dislike the noise of bells to-night, I cannot write. I have no subject—I am exhausted." The poet is Poe, and the conservatory is that of his friend Mary Louise Shew

Houghton, who responds to Poe's complaints by writing the first lines of what will become a poem: "The bells, the little silver bells."

What prevents the poem becomes the poem: a sonic intrusion is contained and transformed in another ambiguous house, Poe's poem "The Bells."

But bells are not just any kind of sonic annoyance, not a squeaky floor or a neighbor's incessant cough. Bells are *designed* to be intrusive: for centuries they marked the rhythms and ceremonies of rural and civic life and, above all, the sacred calendar. Bells territorialize in a literal way: if you could hear them, you were part of that parish. To incorporate the sound of ringing bells in all their significance and variety—pleasure, alarm, celebration, mourning—into a single poem is to hijack their territorializing power for aesthetic purposes. The techniques need to be as direct and forceful as what they manage, and Poe's are: onomatopoeia and insistent repetition ("the bells, bells, bells, bells, bells, bells, bells").

In 1912, Sergei Rachmaninoff wrote *The Bells* (in Russian, *Kolakola*), a four-part choral symphony, the text of which was provided by Konstantin Balmont's translation of Poe's poem. Rachmaninoff describes it as an attempt to capture the sonic atmosphere of his life, and of his country: "The sound of church bells dominated all the cities of the Russia I used to know—Novgorod, Kiev, Moscow. . . . They accompanied every Russian from childhood to grave. . . . This love for bells is inherent in every Russian. . . . If I have been at all successful in making bells vibrate with human emotion in my works, it is largely due to the fact that most of my life was lived amid the vibrations of the bells of Moscow."

The comments sound nostalgic; Rachmaninoff speaks of the "love for bells . . . inherent in every Russian." But there is another note threading through it all: the bells "dominated" the cities, "accompanied" each Russian "from childhood to grave." And the piece itself could not possibly be described as reflective or "loving." It has been pointed out, for example, that Rachmaninoff insinuates the Dies Irae into each of the four movements, even the one celebrating marriage. The gargantuan energies stirred up in Rachmaninoff's composition are at times simply frightening, especially the third movement, dedicated to alarm bells, which has been accurately described as an "intense orchestral conflagration."

What does Poe's poem make available to Rachmaninoff? It offers the idea of channeling an entire sonic atmosphere, rehousing it in musical form.

Rachmaninoff borrows the four-part structure from Poe (and Balmont) as well, with the bells running the gamut of ideas of joy, marriage, crisis, and death, "childhood to grave," as it were. Hosokawa had channeled an incursion, and he devised a "house" to let the force pass through. Rachmaninoff's encounter with sonic atmosphere is less otherworldly, more a matter of territory and social power. It is his sense of *belonging* as a Russian that is at stake in this clanging atmosphere, a belonging that has a history and—possibly—a future. In Hosokawa we hear the sound of a desolate aftermath; in Rachmaninoff we cannot help wondering what the tolling bells portend.

As we have seen, many of Poe's tales and poems are dramas of sound, allegories of the effort to capture it—or they are allegories of the *failure* of that effort of containment, the cat's cry escaping from within the tomb. Either way, sound does not respect human thresholds: we are *in* it, whether we hear it or not. Poe's starkest image of such immersion is in "A Descent into the Maelstrom": "As far as the eye could fathom it, was a smooth, shining, and jet-black wall of water, inclined to the horizon at an angle of some forty-five degrees, speeding dizzily round and round with a swaying and sweltering motion, and sending forth to the winds an appalling voice, half shriek, half roar, such as not even the mighty cataract of Niagara ever lifts up in its agony to Heaven."

J. M. Turner's famous canvas *Snow-Storm: Steam-Boat off a Harbour's Mouth* (1842) "tries to show what it was like to be *in* the scene, enveloped by its energies, and not to be detached from that experience by the security of a cabin, a frame, or secure sense of perspective." For Turner or Poe, the vortex or maelstrom represents an experiential intensification of its cognate form, the spiral: "The change may be described most simply as the movement from the form as a spiral, arabesque, or serpentine line that cuts across our line of vision, to the image of a vortex or maelstrom that surrounds the line of vision and seems to suck us in with a force that may be simultaneously alluring and threatening." The spiral "arabesque" and the vortex are both metaphors of form, and Poe knew them both.

To be "enveloped by the energies" of the maelstrom, to be immersed in it, is more about noise and roar than about the "sense of perspective." In fact, the Norwegian sailor who narrates his "descent" has a keen eye and unobstructed view. Noticing that objects of different weight descend the walls of the maelstrom at different rates—the lighter the object, the slower the descent—the sailor lashes himself to a small barrel and jumps ship.

What looks like the most irrational act is in fact the most rational one: the only way to survive the maelstrom is by throwing oneself into its teeth, becoming one with the threat.

The image of the maelstrom, perhaps via Poe's story, became a touchstone for Theodor Adorno in his account of modernity. "In central passages of Poe and Baudelaire the concept of newness emerges," he writes in one of the final entries of *Minima Moralia*, seizing on the line in which Poe's narrator remarks on the "bewildering sense of the *novel* which confounds the beholder" of the maelstrom. The wild grasping after the new characteristic of capitalist modernity finds its natural emblem in the maelstrom: the "breathlessly spinning yet in a sense stationary movement" of the maelstrom describes a world in which everything gets caught up in violent motion, and yet nothing really changes. Thus Adorno. But as we just saw, things *do* change in the maelstrom, and the sailor's life is saved because he notices this fact.

Poe and Baudelaire are "heralds of modernity" for Adorno because they understand they are immersed in the forces that threaten them, and because, faced with that realization, they plunge "au fond du gouffre, Enfer ou Ciel, qu'importe?" One cannot escape the maelstrom of modernity, one can only throw oneself at it: "Modern works relinquish themselves mimetically to reification, their principle of death." In *Aesthetic Theory* (1970), the vortex or maelstrom describes modernity as a self-consuming force and temporal sinkhole. Perhaps the sailor's desperate leap into the maelstrom, lashed to a barrel, could be described as "relinquishing" himself "mimetically." We might call it going with the flow, in an extreme sense.

It may seem strange, given how closely Adorno seems to have read Poe's tale and given how central music was to his understanding of modernity, that he ignores the maelstrom as an image of an immersion in *sound*, odd that its "appalling voice, half roar, half shriek" draws no comment from him. Because modernity was, if nothing else, *noisy*. Urban and industrial cacophony and—especially starting in the 1920s—the mass-mediated sonic saturation brought about by radio, sound film, and phonography created new urgency to the questions of threshold and immersion. Art music made many efforts, from the Futurist Luigi Russolo's fabricated noise instruments—the *intonarumori*—to John Cage's 4′33″ to make music from "noise."

From the late nineteenth century, sound—in which I include noise (and silence), performance and recording, the status of sonic *imitation* (in program music, by instruments imitating worldly sounds such as bells, in the use of recorded sounds in live performance)—was a key battleground for the understanding of modern art and mass culture. Adorno's many writings on music, mass culture, and radio testify vividly to his deep understanding of this fact. And yet he did not invoke Poe's deafening maelstrom in this context.

Others did. In 1986, the Adelaide Festival of the Arts presented *A Descent into the Maelstrom*, an hour-long piece for chamber orchestra and dancers by Philip Glass, from whom the festival had commissioned it. It is very far from the sonic violence—"half shriek, half roar"—that Poe describes. Rather, we are given Glassian minimalism: shimmering arpeggiated gestures sliding one on top of another, in and out of phase, creating a range of tonal colors. The impression is one of constancy above all: the music is uninterrupted, morphing into distinct enough sections to allow for Poe's narrative to become vaguely articulated, but never developing into something wholly different. The music changes, we might say, but never alters. The structure of the piece is cyclical and fluid. In this sense, at least, it is like Poe's maelstrom.

There's a witty piece by music critic Tom Johnson called "What Is Minimalism Really About?" An earnest young man and a critic have just experienced a concert of minimalist music. The young man asks the critic what is supposed to be going on with the music. Johnson mimics the compositional devices of minimalism—overt and insistent repetition (the question is always the same; much of the language repeats itself verbatim throughout) punctuated by slight variations: "'What is it all about?' I thought for a moment about what I ought to say and settled for a brief generalization: 'It has a lot to do with repetition.'" The young man decides repetition is not very interesting and asks again: "What is it all about?" It's about "tiny variations," "it has something to do with hyper-clarity," "it has something to do with encouraging more subtle perceptions," "it has something to do with making music less dramatic," and so on. Johnson's piece manages to describe minimalism, express doubt about its musical interest, and be interesting in just the way minimalism is interesting—all at the same time.

Adorno might have seen Glass as throwing himself into the maelstrom, mimetically reproducing the death-dealing regime of remorseless repetition peppered with "tiny variations" that are interesting only because they *are* variations. Johnson's answers to the young man, suggesting that a listener to minimalist music is meant to develop "subtle perceptions," even a "hyper-clarity" about "tiny variations" within an endless whirl of repetition, recall what the Norwegian sailor had to manage on the fly, as it were: in the face of imminent destruction, he attains a "hyper-clarity" that notes the different speeds of descent of objects, and he jumps. What seems most dramatic actually "has something to do with making [things] less dramatic." Perhaps Glass's listener is meant to develop the sang-froid of Poe's sailor.

Glass seizes on Poe's "Descent" to explore sonic immersion. As I have suggested, Glass's *Descent* captures some of the "hyper-clarity" of Poe's story, but it misses the sheer terror. One never really feels disoriented within this sonic universe, even if one does not know exactly where one is going. What's missing in the Glass is what Poe's tale calls the "appalling voice." There can be a machinic quality to Glass's music. Like most composers of his generation, he readily embraces electric and synthesized sound (sometimes to slightly comic effect: an ironic comment online suggests that the synthesizer octaves with which *Descent* begins are reminiscent of "Funky Town"). But to my ear, Glass's musical idiom is almost always infused with an irrefutably human idiom of gesture and voice—*Descent* features an important part for solo soprano. What might seem likely to feel alienating—obsessive, machinic repetition—rarely does. Glass's maelstrom does not appall you the way Poe's maelstrom does.

In the early 1950s, the jazz pianist Lennie Tristano built a home recording studio and started to experiment with overdubbing, changing speeds in playback, and other possibilities presented by tape recording. There had been a lot of avant-garde experimentation in this area, as early as the 1920s, and Pierre Schaefer's epochal explorations in musique concrète date from 1948. In the realm of popular music, there was less activity along these lines, though Les Paul (always ahead of the curve) and, more surprisingly, Sidney Bechet, who released a performance of "The Sheik of Araby" in 1941 in which he played all the parts, are exceptions. Tristano's work is a bit different.

Some results of this period of experimentation can be found on the 1956 album titled, simply, *Tristano*. There are four compositions featuring Tristano overdubbing himself, the most striking of which is "Turkish Mambo," which layers motifs in four different time signatures on top of one another. *Tristano* caused something of a controversy, with fans and critics objecting to this frank embrace of technological solutions to musical problems, an embrace all the more incongruous in a music dedicated to improvisation. Perhaps anticipating this, *Tristano*'s second side featured a live performance.

One recording from this period in his home studio was "A Descent into the Maelstrom," which was only released in the 1970s. You do not so much listen to this three-and-a-half-minute free-form composition as you enter it. You feel as if you have been caught in a sudden squall. The rhythmic identity is pulsating rather than metric, but this more organic sense of measure oddly makes the whole thing feel less human rather than more. The pulsations are watery and tidal and atmospheric. Tinkling droplets hover over low brooding currents. We are constantly being swept away.

In a way that would become increasingly prevalent within the experi-mentations of free jazz, Tristano's "Descent" is not only an improvisa-tion: it is *about* improvisation. There is a good recent book about free improvisation—collectively produced music with no score, no given motifs, no leader, no set time limit—titled *Into the Maelstrom: Music, Improvisation, and the Dream of Freedom*. Its author, David Toop, is bor-rowing the figure from both Poe and Tristano (the book cover is Harry Clarke's illustration of Poe's tale), and it is meant to refer to the sense of immersion, risk, and disorientation that is so common when one par-ticipates in such events, the "static turbulence," the "radial wheeling," the "overwhelming sensation of unpredictable volition" (all descriptions of Tristano's performance).

Like Glass, Tristano finds in Poe's tale a provocation to sonic immersion. But Tristano's "Descent" brings out the risk and disorientation present in Poe's tale in a way Glass does not. Repetition is everywhere present in his Tristano's recording, repetition enabled by technological augmentation of human performance, but it does not feel machinic (as Glass sometimes does). It certainly does not behave like the engine of reification, as repeti-tion does in Adorno, though Adorno might have seen Tristano's solicita-tion of sonic chaos as anything but a "dream of freedom."

But this music is not antihuman. It is extra-human. You are in it; you are no less human, but you are much more than that as well. Tristano's ver-sion of "Maelstrom" produces an atmospheric aesthetics that does not fret about meaninglessness. Our role in the midst of this all-encompassing sonic squall is to keep our head, just as the Norwegian sailor does. Mean-ing is not something we build out from ourselves—we do not compose it. Meaning is a matter of selecting from a surfeit; it is seizing a detail to which we can lash ourselves as we go down.

We have looked at dramas of sonic incursion—otherworldly spirits, clanging bells. We have looked at experiences of sonic immersion. Poe's tales are probably best remembered, however, for how sound *explodes* the various structures the characters have built: the cat's cry, the beating heart, and—in "The Cask of Amontillado"—a tiny tinkling bell.

Recall Poe's tale: Montresor, the narrator, meets his rival Fortunato in the street—it's carnival, and Fortunato is in motley, a cap and bells on his head. Montresor lures Fortunato into the catacombs, where eventually he surprises his victim, chains him, and bricks him up behind a wall. It's one of Poe's most chilling tales—and one of his most sonically saturated. The pretense of polite banter at one point yields to pure sound: first a moan, then silence, a furious clanking of the chains, then bellowing. Montresor simply bellows back: "I re-echoed, I aided, I surpassed them in volume and in strength." Eventually, this: "I hearkened in vain for a reply. I grew impatient. I called aloud—'Fortunato!' No answer. I called again—'Fortunato!' No answer still. I thrust a torch through the remaining aperture and let it fall within. There came forth in reply only a jingling of the bells. My heart grew sick."

In narrative terms, the "jingling of the bells" works like the cat's cry from within the bricked-up niche, or like the beating of the heart: just when the task of enclosure and eclipse seems to have attained its aim, something escapes. In "The Black Cat" and "The Tell-Tale Heart," the sounds betray the murderer, but not here. We know about the jingling only because Montresor tells us about it, fifty years later. Perhaps because of the very delicacy of this sonic event, or because of its delayed action, the tiny jingling of the bells has always struck me as the most terrifying example of sonic explosion in all of Poe. There is something monstrous in it, something beyond explanation—What does it mean? *Does* it mean at all?—that makes it seem to come from a different dimension.

After his stage collaboration with Robert Wilson, Reed compiled an expanded homage to Poe titled simply *The Raven* (2003). It is not easy to characterize this body of work: the script and songs are Reed's, and he sings many of them, but the recording also features many other prominent actors and musicians—Ornette Coleman, David Bowie, Laurie Anderson,

Blind Boys of Alabama, Willem Dafoe, Steve Buscemi. These last two appear in "The Cask," Reed's take on Poe's tale.

Poe's power was frankly literary for Reed (an English major and former student of Delmore Schwartz): "The language is so beautiful. I spent so many hours with the dictionary, because some of these words were already arcane when he used them. He was a show-off in that way. My God, what a vocabulary." But "the physical push" of Poe's language speaks to Reed's idiom, and in fact provides him with "an idea of what rock could be."

In "The Cask," Reed cast Steve Buscemi as a loudmouth Fortunato—"You can kiss my ass!"—and Willem Dafoe as the murderous Montresor. A shambling rhythmic figure accompanies the two as they trade their jibes and make their way to the crypt. But, as in Poe's tale, in the closing section something monstrous shows itself. Having realized his fate, Buscemi cries, "For the love of God, Montresor!" and a background distorted rumble swells menacingly, eventually completely engulfing the sonic space. The story has gone black, as it were, behind a wall of noise, in place of Poe's brick and mortar.

Reed is interested in both the wall and what escapes it, just as Poe is. Out of the wall of noise there emerges a single, piercing note. It grows louder and louder and escapes, an assaultive interpretation of Fortunato's tiny jingling. Reed understands Poe's narrative, its flight to aggression and noise, and its focus on the escape of sound as a kind of emancipation that is also a kind of terror: all this *could* be rock. Reed fashions an ambiguous house in which literature feeds back.

Ambient Diptych

I want to close this chapter—and this book—with two starkly different treatments of sonic atmosphere, both from the 1990s. One of them—an episode of *SpongeBob SquarePants*—is heir to the decades-long exploration of sonic plenitude to be found in animated cartoons. The other half of my diptych is a more groping affair, literally: to play *The Dark Eye* (1995), you must move a disembodied hand around, grasping objects to discover which ones yield the possibility of action—standard for point-and-click games of the era. *The Dark Eye* is, in its way, as compelled by the idea of ambient sound as the episode from *SpongeBob*, but while the latter is about the saturation of sound, *The Dark Eye*, with its extraordinary voice-over by William S. Burroughs, is finally about gaps and fallout, seemingly revealing a species of mutism at the heart of the universe.

Found sound, recorded sound, live performance, fabricated instruments—anything was fair game as the period of sound cinema got off the ground in the late 1920s and 1930s. The early animated cartoons were industry leaders in the use of sound linked to moving image. A year after *The Jazz Singer* (1927) inaugurated the "talkies," Disney's *Steamboat Willie*, featuring Mickey Mouse banging out "Turkey in the Straw" on a variety of farm animals and kitchen implements, took sound in film to a new level. So precise was Disney's "sound synchronization" that this aspect of the art became known in the business as "mickey mousing."

Sound was not a layover or an additive in Disney cartoons—it was primary: "The nature of [Disney's] material forced upon him something like the right solution," namely, "making his sound strip first and working his animated figures in distortion and counterpoint to the beat of the sound." But even when the animations are assembled differently (as they are today), sound remains elemental to the form: "Voices, sounds, and music [are] spread out over the bodies of both characters and objects . . . whether a squeaking elbow joint, fly footsteps, [or] flesh ripped off to play a rib-cage xylophone." The result is that the "visual experience of animated cartoons [is] itself animated by sound." In the cartoon cosmos, sound comes first. To be alive—to be animated—is to be *in* sound. There is nothing in the world, no matter how insignificant or inanimate we normally take it to be, that does not have, in principle, its own unique and prior sound identity.

Cartoon sound is extreme, aggravated. In fact, it is aggravating—intentionally so. It is manic and crude, and often very funny. Which brings me to my first example: the episode titled "Squeaky Boots" from the first season of *SpongeBob SquarePants* first aired in September 1999. Mr. Krabs has disappointed his daughter, Pearl, by failing to get her the "flipper slippers" all the kids are wearing, offering instead a large pair of rubber fishing boots. Fobbing the rejected boots off on SpongeBob—who is of course delighted—Mr. Krabs sets himself up for auditive torture. The boots make a terrible squeaking, a wet, squishy sound with every movement. Like any self-respecting child with control over an annoying sound, SpongeBob sees the magic in these noisy boots, performing remarkable physical feats with their aid, and will not be parted from them.

But Mr. Krabs takes a page from Poe's playbook, steals the boots while SpongeBob is sleeping, and buries them underneath the floorboards of the Krusty Krab. The squeaking just spreads, however—now everyone is *speaking* in squeaks—and Mr. Krabs is driven insane, eventually confessing: "I did it! Make it stop! It's the squeaking of the hideous boots!" as he pulls up the floorboards (see plate 18).

The online Encyclopedia SpongeBobia informs us that this episode was one of the first to be produced for the series. In fact, creator Stephen Hillenburg had used the idea for this episode in his initial pitch for the series, which included a sketch of SpongeBoy (as he was initially called) striding around in his boots. Something basic about Hillenburg's very conception for the series is tied up with this idea of "Squeaky Boots," his remake of "The Tell-Tale Heart."

Poe's tale, as this book has amply demonstrated, is part of our stock of plots, and its narrative economy recommends itself to a form that demands extreme compression—these reasons alone might suggest why it makes good pitch material. The executives will recognize it, and they'll see that it's a good idea for a remake. Perhaps they imagine that some parents might recognize the subtext, thus securing approval from an essential audience. But most important is that "Squeaky Boots" delivers, in spades, what cartoons must have: agitated, amplified, annoying sound.

The episode tells the story of conflict between parents and children over aggravating ambient noise. SpongeBob is relentlessly inventive in finding ways to squeak his boots. It's a celebration of the power of noisemaking. To be in the world is to make noise. Note that the squeaking that drives Mr. Krabs crazy is also quite likely to drive real-world parents crazy, an annoying addition to the ambient noise in the house. "Squeaky Boots" uses the exorbitance of the faculty of hearing in Poe's tale to make a joke about a contemporary exorbitance of sonic atmosphere as mediated by children's TV. The episode allegorizes its own conditions of consumption—and the allegory is available to both parents and children, each in their own way. No wonder Hillenburg's pitch was successful.

The Dark Eye creates gameplay from three of Poe's tales: "Berenice," "The Cask of Amontillado," and "The Tell-Tale Heart." (There is also a frame narrative, as well as two slideshows with recitations by Burroughs—"Annabel Lee" and "The Masque of the Red Death," both quite compelling). Each of these three tales can be experienced from the point of view of both the victimizer and the victim. That you can play the victim, probably the most unusual feature of the game's design, makes sense in terms of Poe's tales, where the reader is forced to see the story through the eyes of the violent narrators but also where another terror comes from our imagining ourselves also into the positions of the victim—how it would feel to be walled up alive, to take the example of "The Cask of Amontillado." Insofar as *The Dark Eye* is a role-playing game, the medium here brings forward in a forthright way a narrative effect that remains tacit in literary form.

As the game's creator, Russell Lees, remarked in a recent podcast interview, *The Dark Eye*, like most games of its time, restricts play within defined narrative arcs. In *Grand Theft Auto*, by contrast, we remain ourselves, as it were, just a version of ourselves that likes to steal cars. You are free to walk away and fiddle around in the outskirts of the game's narrative core. But *The Dark Eye* doubles down on the narrative constriction common to games of its type and era: if we play from the point of view of the killer in "The Tell-Tale Heart," we are required to kill the old man; if we play from the victim, we must be killed.

We may construe these constraints on gameplay as powerful interpretations of Poe's tales (I think they are), but it affects the experience in significant ways. One contemporary commentator suggests that "You don't beat *The Dark Eye*, you explore it." Lees has described this exploration as providing the player with backstory for our character. What a live actor would have worked up in advance of performance, we must discover as we walk through the vaguely empty game-space. In a sense, we "play" to find out *who we are* and why we must perform or suffer the terrible events that are our destiny.

These features contribute to the oppressive atmosphere in this game: "Instead of puzzles, *The Dark Eye* gives you atmosphere—all the atmosphere you can inhale, enough atmosphere to send you running to a less pressurized room of your house after spending a while in its company." But the atmosphere in *The Dark Eye* is not a matter of air or claustrophobia. It is not even primarily a matter of visual design, though the hideous puppet figures and desolate visual backgrounds surely contribute, and the slide shows with the Burroughs recitations are disturbing in their way. I think, however, the source of atmosphere in this game is sound and voice.

"Interactivity" is an equivocal value in the world of video games. On the one hand, it seems a defining feature: "The activity of gaming . . . only ever comes into being when the game is actually played. [It] is an undivided act wherein meaning and doing transpire in the same gamic gesture." This requirement to act produces medium specificity: "If photographs are images, and films are moving images, then video games are actions." There are other opinions: "Interactivity is a debatable concept which has been so over-applied as to be rendered meaningless, and the sense of agency that videogame players experience is illusory."

The Dark Eye seems intent on exposing the equivocalness that resides at the heart of the idea of interactivity. On the one hand, nothing happens if we do not make it happen: this is in the nature of point-and-click games. Within this context, our agency is well-nigh Olympian. On the other hand, as the choice to confine us to killer or victim indicates, our godlike agency is on the order of Oedipus's: you can act, but it always leads to the same conclusion.

This alienation of agency is not just in the script—it is in the gameplay: as we wander around, finding our way to the story, everything and everybody waits on us. Of course, *The Dark Eye* is hardly unique in this regard. *Myst*, contemporary with *The Dark Eye*, is similar: but a lot of what waits for us in *Myst* are vaguely steampunk mechanisms, while in *The Dark Eye*, it's mostly people, so-called non-player characters (NPCs). We get so used to this aspect of gameplay—NPCs just idling while we decide if we want to them bring into action again—that it does not seem weird. But it can be recalled to its uncanniness. David Cronenberg's *eXistenZ* (1999) has scenes in which live actors revert to the inertness and lassitude of NPCs in games: the effect is both creepy and funny. In the case of *The Dark Eye*, the uncanniness emerges also as a function of sound. You are on a bridge in Venice, searching for Montresor or Fortunato (depending on who you are playing). It's carnival, so there are revelers. They call out drunkenly and so on. You turn away. Silence. You turn back: they call out, and with exactly the same words and incoherent cries.

Again, people got used to this kind of thing quickly, of course, just like they got used to the spookiness of radio. But it remains fundamentally alienating. In the real world, one is never without ambient noise (even in a sensory deprivation chamber, as Cage discovered). Games have soundtracks, it's true, increasingly elaborate ones, and they contribute atmosphere the way soundtracks do in film. But even here, the soundtracks are subordinate in basic ways to the player's decisions. In a video game like *The Dark Eye*, sonic ambience usually only appears when we make it appear.

In a way, this makes it the opposite of the cartoon world of *SpongeBob SquarePants*. The cosmos presented in children's cartoons is saturated in sound; noise is an index of plenitude, the emblem of animation itself. Although children, in the nature of things, have limited agency, the noise-making in cartoons provides a compensatory power: it testifies to real if relative freedom. In *The Dark Eye*, by contrast, our ability to activate the ambient noise combines unconstrained agency with unfreedom.

Which brings us, at long last, to William S. Burroughs. No artist of the past one hundred years has been more committed to exploring the estrangement of voice characteristic of the Pythian cosmos than Burroughs. From his early writings through his various experiments with "cut-up" techniques, Burroughs has been throwing his voice, as it were: as one contemporary critic puts it, "Voices in Burroughs' writing are rarely isolated to their supposed source . . . but often drift as forces and subjects all their own. The vocal utterances of Burroughs' characters vary between immediate, embodied voices and mediated, disembodied voices."

I am not aware of any accounts explaining Burroughs's decision to participate in *The Dark Eye*. Creator Russell Lees apparently did not sign Burroughs but was presented with his involvement as a fait accompli, and it was Lees who worked with Burroughs during the taping. Burroughs died in 1997, so this voice work was surely one of his last creative acts, recorded in his home studio in Lawrence, Kansas. Perhaps Burroughs saw this work—recording a couple of recitations and snippets of dialogue that would be repeated according to the demands of the gameplay—as a continuation of his lifelong interest in how voice is both intimate and estranging, natural and machinic, embodied and disembodied.

Of course, there is the unforgettable and unique timbre of Burroughs's voice, its "vocal fry." In *The Dark Eye*, he leans into that timbre mostly at the end of phrases, when he drops pitch suddenly. "We must take immediate actionnnnnn," Burroughs rasps, the last syllable dropping pitch as if retreating into a space of brooding reflection. "Immediate action!" he barks next, to make sure we note the different deliveries. This pitch-dropping is especially prominent, and oddly affecting, in his recitation of "Annabel Lee," "in a kingdom by the seeeeeaaaa."

Some of Burroughs's effect is a matter of simple vocal acting; for example, the weariness or resignation with which he enunciates a line like "scratched out his own eyes in a fit of frenzy." But other times, it seems almost as if Burroughs is performing a snippet, a cut-up, knowing it is a snippet and wanting us to know that he knows it. It is a shard of language that is not expressed so much as activated in an alien world. So strange is the performance that one finds oneself wondering, when Burroughs's speech is slurred, whether it's a choice or a condition. Probably the latter: Lees notes that they continued recording well past three o'clock in the afternoon, the hour at which Burroughs started in on his vodka and Sprite.

This concluding chapter has argued that sound in Poe's work—as theme, as narrative device, as treatment of voice—is cosmic, pervasive, and estranging. It is, in my characterization, Pythian not Pythagorean: that is, it is not a symbol of unchanging order but a point of access to a metamorphic continuum that extends from human voice to animal, natural, and machinic expression. Form and medium are always determining for the capture of such sonic forces. In our concluding ambient diptych, the medium of animated children's cartoons demands—almost as its metaphysics—a world of sonic saturation in which the individual affirms a place in an overmastering reality by making noise. But the medium of the point-and-click video game *The Dark Eye* produces a sonic experience of the world as riddled with silences, with the presence of absence, as if our attainment of agency came at the cost of our every phrase reverting to rasping sound in a dying fall and a return to silence.

Afterword

The task I set myself in this book was to explore the vastness and various-ness of the archive of works inspired by Poe without getting lost along the way or extending the exploration so far that my readers would get bored. This required me to be generous with the range of my examples, but also selective, and because these examples came from such different media and historical moments, I had to stick close to the objects themselves, rather than launch from them into more purely historical or theoretical excurses. Historical and theoretical issues are raised throughout but rarely engaged directly. I saw no way to avoid this if I wanted to produce an enjoyable and manageable text. If the title of this book implies a maritime setting for the "travels" undertaken, then my job was to plot an island-hopping itinerary of interest and variety, while making sure we never stayed in port too long.

I had started, as I explained in the introduction, with a sense that the vernacular aesthetic descriptors of "graphic" and "atmospheric" aligned with very basic perceptions of Poe's work—namely, that he wrote highly memorable scenes of graphic violence and that his works were often menacing, vague, and otherworldly in a way that could be described as atmospheric. This commitment to the vernacular made me want to build out from my examples rather than land on them from above, armed with established or developing bodies of theory. That said, in this afterword I will try to gather up some threads with an eye to some general conclusions about what the uptake of Poe, across so many different media, tells us about modern aesthetics.

Tragic, comic, mythic—these ancient terms name very basic ways in which we give narrative shape to facets of the human condition: plots that end with death or marriage, or the often-surreal mythic narratives meant to explain how our very real world came to be. Despite their shared *-ic* endings, *graphic* and *atmospheric* are different. Northrop Frye, who thought a lot about the narrative typologies of the tragic, mythic, and comic, was also a great admirer of Poe who appreciated what was essentially modern in his achievement. Poe was a "radical abstractionist" and "anti-realist," according to Frye, someone who "specializes in setting down the traditional formulas of storytelling without bothering with much narrative logic." All of this was in the service, thought Frye, of the goal of producing "fragmentary intensity"—what Poe called "unity of effect." Frye captures the formal abstractness of Poe, the "pattern-making" that animates his fictions—and that proves so alluring to creators in other media. These traits taken together, suggests Frye, explain why Poe has had such an outsize "influence on our [twentieth] century."

In his short time at West Point, Poe was trained as an "artificer"—that is, someone who manages and engineers explosive devices. This biographical fact is suggestive not just in the case of Poe, whose carefully wrought narrative constructions so often blow up in some way, but also for all those making use of Poe for their own purposes, who follow his aesthetic program of combining powerful effects with the foregrounded exhibition of the technical mastery necessary to produce such effects.

In his field-defining book, *The American Renaissance* (1941), F. O. Matthiessen relegated Poe to a footnote on the ground of his "factitiousness." The *Oxford English Dictionary* offers as its third definition of "factitious" the following: "Got up; made up for a particular occasion or purpose; arising from custom, habit, or design; not natural or spontaneous; artificial, conventional." Most of this definition seems applicable to any sort of art-making: surely, all art is "made up for a particular occasion or purpose," even if only the artist's desire to fabricate something, and surely it makes sense that art arises always out of some mixture of "custom, habit, or design." By process of elimination, we must conclude that when Matthiessen criticizes Poe's work as "factitious," he means "not natural or spontaneous."

Matthiessen subscribes to an essentially Romantic idea of the artwork as "natural or spontaneous" rather than "got up," a plant and not a gizmo. Poe set his face against this aesthetic philosophy: "It is to be hoped that common sense, in the time to come, will prefer deciding upon a work of art . . . by the impression it makes" rather than inappropriate ideas of originality or "naturalness" (recall Poe's sarcasm, in his discussion of Wordsworth: "I love a sheep from the bottom of my heart"). The artwork's "effect" is all that matters, the "impression it makes," and if it works, that's because the artist structured it so as to have that effect.

What Matthiessen disliked about Poe, however, is just what so many others, in so many nonliterary media, liked about him. It was the whole "factitious" enterprise of Poe's work—its experimental method, its embrace of short forms, its frank desire to produce an "effect," its understanding that art is "got up" for a particular purpose—that served as an example and an inspiration for the hundreds of short-form specialists that come after him—the filmmakers, illustrators, animators, comics artists, game designers, and so on. The factitiousness that sidelined Poe in Matthiessen's eyes made him central in the eyes of the artists that followed in his wake—the fabricators, the artificers.

The "graphic" and the "atmospheric," as aesthetic categories, belong to this world of the "artificer." I have remarked several times how openly and often those remediating Poe foreground not simply the effects they produce but the means to such effects—how often medium becomes a theme, in other words. Jean Epstein's *La chute de la maison Usher* is a film about filmmaking, about the possibilities of film as a medium, as much as it is about a house, or the return of the dead. Lennie Tristano's "Descent into the Maelstrom" is more than simply a tone poem; it is an experiment in combining improvisation and overdubbing, and an argument against jazz traditionalists that understood the two as necessarily antithetical. Pierre Huyghe's art installation that borrows from *Pym* is ultimately about art (and the impossibility of cordoning it off from the "real").

Even when medium is less ostentatiously foregrounded, a little interpretive pressure reveals how these artists explore the limits and conditions of their medium. Odilon Redon hangs eyeballs in black space in part because he wants to destabilize the relation between seer and seen and thus make the visual medium part of his story. Edgar G. Ulmer was given a story ("The Black Cat") about subterranean spaces and walled-up corpses, but he worked in a medium based on light: when he transforms the coffins into well-lighted vitrines, we can almost hear him exulting: "See how cleverly I have solved this problem!" Manet's images for *Le corbeau* constitute a powerful interpretation of the poem's story, but they are also a celebration of pure markmaking transcending the demands of figuration. Clarke wants us to see how he uses his frames, Breccia how he uses his panels and gutters. Toshio Hosokawa, addressing Poe and Noh drama alike, devises a compositional form adequate to the hosting of cosmic forces: his monodrama on "The Raven" is as much about music's capacities in the face of unleashed energies as it is about Poe.

All this points to the fact that the "graphic" and the "atmospheric" are terms appropriate to a world of artifice and of self-consciousness about media. I observed that Poe himself, with his coining of the term "graphicality" and his comments about photography, glimpsed aspects of the image-saturated mediatized world that would adapt him so often and so variously. Likewise, what was "atmospheric" was understood already in Poe's day to point to a condition of being environed by interrelated forces beyond human control, whether those were frankly supernatural, climatic, or semiotic. To talk about atmosphere was to talk about media. "Atmosphere" and an array of related terms—"pneumatics, air, spirit, *Stimmung*, field, gloom . . . haze, vagueness, cloud, . . . smoke, gas chamber, breath, and mist"—"provided an indispensable lexicon for theorising an array of processes, practices and instruments that are now typically discussed under the rubrics of 'mediation' and the 'medium.'" We might say that that the atmospheric became abstracted as figure for mediatedness tout court, for the fact that neither subject nor object determines the commerce between them, but that something always is left over, remains obscure, flows away.

But the story that emerges from the interpretations offered here is not just about a focus on media and technique, from Poe to the present, or merely a celebration of it. There is a darker note as well. I suggested that in both traditional graphic arts and in photographic/cinematic production, something like a self-destructive drive is at work. Poe's harassment of human vision, at its limit rendered useless in a black box, is peculiarly provocative for many artists, as though what they wanted to do was not merely celebrate the regnant visual media but rather to touch their limits—illegibility or unwatchability.

Something similar is at work with explorations of the "atmospheric." But here the limit is not a sense modality; it is the art object itself, as that implodes, gives way, or disappears, in the face of atmosphere. In its foregrounding of mediatedness (insofar as one can foreground a background condition), the atmospheric indexes a situation in which form and medium feed back into each other. In the hands of a filmmaker such as Jean Epstein, atmosphere is a motif—rustling curtains, for example—but also a mood enclosing and exceeding the diegetic action: these two dimensions then feed back into the medium itself, exemplifying what for Epstein is film's unique power of presenting continuity where all we normally see is discontinuity. We see a distinct human being, but film can see behind or beneath that human being to another reality in which a human being is really only a "gaseous cloud."

For philosopher Yves Michaud, art itself has become "gaseous." We are suffering from a "hyper-aestheticization of reality" itself, a condition "in which things means less than processes, objects less than ambiance, qualities less than shades of quality, facts less than their effects and the echoes they create, substances less than flux, entities less than relations." One expression of this development Michaud describes is frankly commercial: "Back in the early 1970s, the marketing professor Philip Kotler coined the term 'atmospherics' to designate a new field of research and practical intervention which revolved around the idea that '[i]n some cases, the place, more specifically the *atmosphere* of the place, is more influential than the product itself in the purchase decision.'"

But as we have seen over the course of this book, commercial or mass-cultural expressions often find an echo in avant-garde practices. Consider the famous debate instigated by Michael Fried's essay "Art and Object-hood," from 1967. Fried criticized minimalist artists—or "literalists" as he called them—such as Donald Judd and Robert Morris. Fried quotes Morris: "[The] object is but one of the terms in the newer aesthetic. It is in some way more self-reflective because one's awareness of oneself existing in the same space as the work is stronger than in previous work, with its many internal relationships." Fried draws the conclusion: "The experience of literalist art is of an object in a *situation*—one that, virtually by definition, *includes the beholder*." Fried, it seems fair to say, feels bullied by his unilateral inclusion as beholder. He might as well be in the theater: "The literalist espousal of objecthood amounts to nothing more than a plea for a new genre of theater, and theater is now the negation of art."

Whatever we think about Fried's most prescriptive comments, he was right to identify the acceleration of an approach to art that is finally more interested in the situation than the object per se. This kind of minimalism might emphasize the singular (no internal relations to speak of) and simple thereness of the art object—this was the approach of Judd and Morris and others like them. Or it might, at a limit, emphasize the evanescence of the art object itself. In Pierre Huyghe's conceptual art installation, the disappearance of the artwork into its environment is indexed several ways, but nowhere more forthrightly than in the boat fabricated out of ice, slowly melting as the exhibition goes forward.

In this book, we have seen visual artists who celebrate their medium's powers but feel driven to expose its limits, and artists of "atmosphere" who pursue an environmental vision to the point of exposing the artwork's ephemerality, even its dispensability. Why? What provokes this limit-chasing? The history of photographic and cinematic media I touched on briefly in chapter 2 may help us toward a hypothesis. As Comolli observed, the "frenzy of the visible" is coincident with the "grave of the eye." The medium giveth, and the medium taketh away. The idea that "*nothing must be left unseen*" can lead to an alarmed or despairing view that a "sex-and-violence spiral is a logical and even inevitable tendency in the development of the cinematic and televisual media." With whatever justification, people often think of media as autonomous, beyond human control—not a tool but a condition.

This may be even more obviously the case with "atmosphere," which at its broadest names an environment conditioning human activity. This can be comforting, as Spitzer's account of ancient notion of atmosphere suggests. But for us moderns, it names an existential powerlessness in the face of environment. Part of the current increase of interest in the "atmospheric" as a term of aesthetic analysis is surely due to terror brought on by the slow-motion catastrophe of climate change.

"Graphic" and "atmospheric," then, are terms appropriate to an age in which mediatedness is experienced as a pressing fundamental condition, and in which human beings oscillate between the self-aggrandizement enabled by the powers of their technical media and the helplessness that so often shadows it or becomes its consequence. If nothing else, this book has shown that Poe has proved an essential resource to artists for the past 170 years. This is because Poe provided those in his wake with a method and a vision appropriate for an era of saturated media: an experimental method emphasizing the fabrication of complex and flexible artifices, and a vision in which the power of human reason is everywhere limited by its exposure to sensory extremes and incomprehensible violence.

Acknowledgments

The seeds of this book lie in a lecture I gave, and subsequently published, in South Africa in 1996. What I thought of as a coda to my then-recently published book on Poe turned out to be the beginning of this book. So much thinking gets worked out in public exchanges that I want to begin my thanks with the many places in which I have been fortunate enough to share my thoughts, starting with that 1996 lecture at the Association of University English Teachers of Southern Africa (AUETSA), in Bellville, South Africa. Lloyd Pratt invited me to Oxford University; Stephen Dougherty to Agder i Universiteit, in Kristiansand, Norway; Adam Frank to the University of British Columbia; Jarkko Toikkanen to Tampere University, in Finland; Meredith McGill and Brad Evans to Rutgers University; and Thomas Ford to the University of Melbourne.

I have also shared parts of this book at conferences—in Kyoto, Japan; Boston, MA; Brighton, United Kingdom; Baltimore, MD; New York, NY; Chicago, IL. My thanks to organizers, fellow panelists, and all the conferees.

Along the way, many people encouraged me in this project, sending me to texts or sources that I did not know. Jerome McGann first told me about the Peirce transcriptions at Harvard; Megan Hines generously shared her knowledge of the artist Pierre Huyghe; Garrett Stewart alerted me to the new translation of Jean Epstein's *The Intelligence of a Machine*; Greg Waller forwarded a tidbit on Alice Guy-Blaché's *Pit and the Pendulum*; Ian Balfour informed me about Northrop Frye's appreciation of Poe; Terry Borton very generously shared the magic-lantern slide included here—more than once!; Suzanne Ebraheem first made the music video by Anthony Roth Costanzo known to me, and her interpretation of it has influenced me; Dan Bashara generously shared a document at MOMA he had dug up for his own research on UPA Studios; Joan Hawkins gave me innumerable suggestions, including directing me to the wonderful article on William S. Burroughs's "vocal fry." With all these material accomplices, I discussed the book, always to my benefit. I have bent the ear of others too: Ed Dallis-Comentale, Jim Naremore, Darlene Sadleier, John Tresch, Emily Ogden, Maurice Lee, Scott Peeples, Meredith McGill, Brad Evans, Emron Esplin, J. Gerald Kennedy, Jana L. Argesinger. None of what I say in this book would have been possible if I had not spent thirty years learning from colleagues working on Poe's strange work and outsize influence.

I have also learned from many of my students over a number of years. Two classes in particular proved transformative to me: a graduate seminar in fall 2017 at Indiana University and an undergraduate seminar at Hebrew University in 2019. Thanks to all students in these two classes, who opened my eyes to so much.

Two of my published essays contain material that reappears in altered form in this book: "Poe and the Avant-Garde" in *The Oxford Handbook of Edgar Allan Poe*, edited by J. Gerald Kennedy and Scott Peeples (Oxford: Oxford University Press, 2019), 700–717; and "Peirce, Poe, and Proto-plasm," *Poe Studies* 52 (2019): 29–49. I thank the editors of these texts for permission to reprint parts of these essays in this book.

Concerted writing on this book began in the bizarre year of 2020, when I was extremely fortunate to have a year's fellowship as the Carl and Betty Pforzheimer Research Fellow in American Culture, from the America Council of Learned Societies. Such a gift of time is invaluable, and I am very grateful for it.

Indiana University has been supportive of my research in every way a scholar could wish. It has been a great place to spend a career. I was especially lucky to have concrete advice and support from Rebecca Bauman, Rachel Stoeltje, Naz Pantaloni, Alexander Teschmacher, and Carmel Curtis. I thank Tony Brewer for advice on images.

Over the years, I have had several research assistants who helped me get a handle on this vast archive and helped me finalize the product: thanks to Sam Tett, Maddie Parker, and, for final image-wrangling, Evan Leake.

Two discerning and detailed reader's reports gave me both the endorsement I needed and specific passages to rethink and rewrite. I am very grateful to Alan Thomas at the University of Chicago Press, who waited patiently for delivery of the text, and who made it better.

Once writing was well and truly underway, I had the benefit of readers for different chapters and parts of chapters: Mitch Breitwieser, Adam Bresnick, Jen Fleissner, Donald Gray, Susan Gubar, Paul Gutjahr, Chad Luck, Hirsch Perlman, and Bret Rothstein. Alexandra Morphet is in a class by herself, and I thank her for everything.

And all the way to the bitter end, I had two remarkably generous interlocutors and editors: Andrew Miller and Michel Chaouli. I thank all my readers very much, but with these last two my thanks go *up to eleven.*

Notes

Introduction

1   "SEEN THEM KICKING EDGAR ALLAN POE": "I Am the Walrus," track 6 on the Beatles, *Magical Mystery Tour*, Apple Records, 1967, vinyl LP album.

1   "WITH EYES UPTURNED IN PASSIONATE PRAYER": Griswold, ed., "Memoir of the Author," in *The Works of the Late Edgar Allan Poe*, 3:xxxviii.

2   THE "ULTIMA THULE" DAGUERREOTYPE: The title is derived from Poe's poem "Dream-Land": "I have reached these lands but newly / From a ultimate dim Thule" (Poe, *Poetry and Tales*, 79). A good reproduction of the daguerreotype's, with notes about its history and naming, is in Deas, *The Portraits and Daguerreotypes of Edgar Allan Poe*, 36–41.

3   LIES COILED IN POE'S DARK EYES: Howell, "Facts in the Case of Edgar Allan Poe."

3   CONFLATED WITH THE SPEAKER IN "THE RAVEN": Peeples, "'That Name'll Never Be Worth Anything!': Poe's Image on Film."

3   SOLVE A GRISLY SERIES OF MURDERS: Cooper, *The Pale Blue Eye*.

5   THE ENTRANCE TO "NEVERMORE: THE MADNESS OF EDGAR ALLAN POE": Halloween Horror Nights Wiki, "Nevermore: The Madness of Poe."

5   "TAKES YOU CLOSER TO THE BRINK OF INSANITY": Halloween Horror Nights Wiki, "Nevermore: The Madness of Poe."

5   EFFECTIVELY INAUGURATING THE "HAUNTED ATTRACTION INDUSTRY": Heller, "A Brief History of the Haunted House."

5   "VACANT EYE-LIKE WINDOWS": Poe, *Poetry and Tales*, 318.

6   "ACT OF SHOWING AND EXHIBITION": Gunning, "The Cinema of Attraction[s]," 381.

6   "FRENZY OF THE VISIBLE": Comolli, "Machines of the Visible," 122.

6   "THE ULTIMATE IDEOLOGICAL *CONCLUSION*": Eisenstein, "Montage of Attractions," 78.

6   A FELT SENSE OF THE "UNITY" OF THE EFFECT: Poe, *Essays and Reviews*, 572.

6   "THE PRECISION AND RIGID CONSEQUENCE OF A MATHEMATICAL PROBLEM": Poe, "The Philosophy of Composition" in *Essays and Reviews*, 15.

7   "RAREFYING THEM INTO MORE CONCENTRATED FORMS": Tresch, *The Reason for the Darkness of the Night*, 68.

8   "HIDEOUS VELOCITY": Poe, *Poetry and Tales*, 1179.

9   HE WAS LOW ENOUGH ON THE PUBLISHING PECKING ORDER: See Cantalupo, *Poe and the Visual Arts*, for a full account of Poe's relation to illustrations and the visual arts.

9   "GRAPHICALITY": Poe, *Essays and Reviews*, 1173.

9   "INFINITELY": Poe, "The Daguerreotype."

9   A FUNDAMENTAL HOMELESSNESS, DISORIENTATION, OR DETERMINISM: Spitzer, "Milieu and Ambiance."

9   ILLUSTRATION OF THIS DISORIENTATION AND DETERMINISM: Spitzer, "A Reinterpretation of 'The Fall of the House of Usher.'"

10   "CLASSICAL AND CHRISTIAN IDEAS OF WORLD HARMONY": Spitzer, "Classical and Christian Ideas of World Harmony."

Chapter One

17   "MAY LEAD A FILM TO RECEIVE AN R OR NC-17 RATING": Motion Picture Association of America, *G Is for Golden: The MPAA Ratings at 50.*

19   "AND THUS RID MYSELF OF THE EYE FOREVER": Poe, *Poetry and Tales*, 555.

20   "HIGHLY GRAPHIC IN ITS STYLE OF COMPOSITION": Poe, *The Collected Works of Edgar Allan Poe*, 2:130.

20   "LESS BY ITS FEATURES THAN BY ITS EFFECTS": Poe, *Essays and Reviews*, 1173.

21   "STUPENDOUS PLASTICITY": Dostoevsky, "Edgar Allan Poe."

21   "THE MYSTERY WHICH DEFIES FURTHER SCRUTINY": Nathaniel Beverly Tucker, quoted in González-Moreno and Rigal-Aragón, *The Portrayal of the Grotesque*, 50.

22   "DOES NOT LEAVE A PIN OR BUTTON UNNOTICED": James Russell Lowell, quoted in González-Moreno and Rigal-Aragón, *The Portrayal of the Grotesque*, 50.

22   "THE RELATION OF WARP AND WOOF": Mitchell, *Iconology: Image, Text, Ideology*, 43.

23   "VICTORIAN ODDITY": Pollin, *Images of Poe's Works*, 7.

23   COMMISSIONED BY HARPER & BROTHERS IN THE UNITED STATES: Pollin, *Images of Poe's Works*, 243; Doré, "Gustave Doré's 'Raven.'"

24   "HUMAN THIRST FOR SELF-TORTURE": Poe, *Essays and Reviews*, 24.

24   "SHALL BE LIFTED—NEVERMORE!": Poe, *Poetry and Tales*, 86.

24   "SHADOW THAT LIES FLOATING ON THE FLOOR": Poe, *Poetry and Tales*, 81, 83, 86.

25   COMPARED TO THE PROTO-CINEMATIC MEDIUM: Le Men, "Manet et Doré: L'illustration du *Corbeau* de Poe," 13.

25   "PRESENTATIONAL APPROACH": Musser, *The Emergence of Cinema*, 36.

25   PAINTED BY JOSEPH BOGGS BEALE AND DATED BY EXPERTS TO 1894: Borton and Borton, *Before the Movies*, 104.

25   "RARE AND RADIANT MAIDEN WHOM THE ANGELS NAME LENORE": Poe, *Poetry and Tales*, 85.

25   IT MAKES SENSE TO DEPICT A SCENE WITH THE WORD "RADIANT" IN IT: For a more complete treatment of Beale's "Raven," see Borton, "Magic Lantern Art."

26   "'TALKED INCESSANTLY' OF POE AND BAUDELAIRE": Gamboni, *The Brush and the Pen*, 108.

26   "DECLARING THE AUTONOMY OF THE SERIES OF PLATES": Le Men, "Manet et Doré," 5 (my translation).

26   WIDELY VIEWED AS THE FIRST "ARTIST'S BOOK": Le Men, "Manet et Doré," 4; Hannoosh, "From *Nevermore* to Eternity," 37.

26   "SOME OTHER UNKNOWN THING BY POE TO DO": Arnar, *The Book as Instrument,* 126

26   TO MAKE THE PAINTER, IN FACT, A KIND OF AUTHOR: Le Men, "Manet et Doré," 6.

26   "SHARING THE BASIC TOOLS OF THE TRADE: PAPER AND INK": Arnar, *The Book as Instrument,* 75.

27   "QUALITIES CENTRAL TO THE CONSTRUCTION OF MODERNITY": Arnar, *The Book as Instrument,* 77.

27   "INTENSE AND IDIOSYNCRATIC MARKMAKING": Arnar, *The Book as Instrument,* 108.

27   THEY ARE IN FACT TRANSFER LITHOGRAPHS: Pop, *A Forest of Symbols,* 61. See also Wilson-Bareau and Mitchell, "Tales of a Raven."

27   "NOT POSSIBLE FOR A SERIOUS PUBLISHING HOUSE TO PUBLISH IT": Arnar, *The Book as Instrument,* 118.

27   "PRESSED INTO THE CHAIR, ALMOST EROTICALLY": Rubin, *Manet's Silence and the Poetics of Bouquets,* 145.

27   "HAS ARGUABLY NO EQUIVALENT IN THE HISTORY OF ILLUSTRATION": Hannoosh, "From *Nevermore* to Eternity," 53.

27   "STRUCK BY THE STARK AND 'BRUTAL' SIMPLICITY OF MANET'S BROAD UNMODULATED STROKES": Arnar, *The Book as Instrument,* 106.

29   "IT IS NEITHER FIGURATIVE, NOR ABSTRACT, NOR EXPRESSIVE": Florence, *Mallarmé, Manet, and Redon,* 36.

29   "BLANK DARKNESS OF WHICH THEY ARE SIMULTANEOUSLY PART": Hannoosh, "From *Nevermore* to Eternity,"53.

30   "SHADOW AND SIGNATURE REPRESENT NOTHING OTHER THAN A GRAPHISME": Le Men, "Manet et Doré," 8–9 (my translation).

30   "GRANDLY GRIM AND SELF-CONTAINED": Arnar, *The Book as Instrument,* 125. Hannoosh, "From *Nevermore* to Eternity," 46, notes the "claustral setting" of Manet's images.

30   THE "INDECIPHERABLE" AND "ILLEGIBILITY": Rubin, *Manet's Silence,* 148 ("indecipherable"); Len Men, "Manet et Doré," 9 ("illegibility").

31   "LEST THERE SHOULD BE NOTHING TO SEE": Poe, *Poetry and Tales,* 493.

33   "REACH THE UNKNOWN THROUGH THE UNSETTLING OF *ALL THE SENSES*": Rimbaud, "Unsettling of All the Senses," 138.

33   HISTORIANS OF SCIENCE, OF ART, AND OF MEDIA HAVE SHOWN: See, among others, Brain, *The Pulse of Modernism;* Crary, *Techniques of the Observer;* Crary, *Suspensions of Perception;* Fretwell, *Sensory Experiments;* Sterne, *The Audible Past;* Kittler, *Gramophone, Film, Typewriter;* Kittler, *Optical Media;* Tresch, "Estrangement of Vision"; Tresch, "The Prophet and the Pendulum"; Tresch, *The Reason for the Darkness of the Night.*

33   ASKING QUESTIONS ABOUT VISION AND SIGHT: On the camera obscura, see Kittler, *Optical Media,* 69; Crary, *Techniques of the Observer,* 39; Sweeney, "The Horror of Taking a Picture in Poe's 'The Tell-Tale Heart.'"

34   "ALL OBJECTS OF SIGHT, AND THE IDEAS OF THEM": John Locke, quoted in Crary, *Techniques of the Observer*, 41–42.

34   "CUT OFF FROM A PUBLIC EXTERIOR WORLD": Crary, *Techniques of the Observer*, 39.

34   ONLY TO PROVIDE A DARK PARODY OF IT: Tresch, "Estrangement of Vision."

34   "OR CONCEAL THE ILLUMINATION ALTOGETHER": Sweeney, "The Horror of Taking a Picture," 148.

34   "AND FELL UPON THE VULTURE EYE": Poe, *Poetry and Tales*, 555.

34   FIVE YEARS BEFORE THE STORY'S PUBLICATION: See Sweeney, "The Horror of Taking a Picture."

35   "ALL TO OBTAIN AN IMAGE OF SOMEONE ELSE": Sweeney, "The Horror of Taking a Picture," 143.

36   "THE *LITTÉRATEURS* WHO MADE UP HIS FIRST ADMIRERS": Gamboni, *The Brush and the Pen*, 124.

36   "WITH A MAXIMUM OF FREEDOM AND AUTONOMY": Gamboni, *The Brush and the Pen*, 106.

36   "I CAN ONLY THINK OF TRANSMISSION, OF INTERPRETATION": Odilon Redon, quoted in Figura "Redon and the Lithographed Portfolio," 83.

38   "A KIND OF EDGAR POE OF THE GRAPHIC ARTS": Alfred Paulet, quoted in Gamboni, *The Brush and the Pen*, 128.

39   "FALLS UPON THE EYE OF AN OLD MAN": Gamboni, *The Brush and the Pen*, 111.

40   "THE SOUL OF THE READER IS AT THE WRITER'S CONTROL": Poe, *Essays and Reviews*, 572.

42   "MR. CLARKE CAN MAKE A DAISY LOOK CORRUPT": Sullivan, "Harry Clarke's Natural World," 101.

42   "EVINCES A *HORROR VACUI*": Bowe, *The Life and Work of Harry Clarke*, 120.

49   "AND BATHED THE WHOLE IN A GHASTLY AND INAPPROPRIATE SPLENDOR": Poe, *Poetry and Tales*, 325.

53   "CLOSURE": McCloud, *Understanding Comics*, chap. 3.

55   "FAIR AND STATELY PALACE": Poe, *Poetry and Tales*, 76.

56   "FRONTISPICIUM, FROM FONS (FOREHEAD) AND SPECIO (LOOK)": Piper, *Book Was There*, 28–29.

57   "LINEWORK WOVEN INTO THEM": Poe, *The Haunted Palace*, front flap.

57   "HE WANTED IN COMBINATION OF TEXT AND DRAWING": Poe, *The Haunted Palace*, front flap.

57   "AND CONTINUOUS FLOW OF THE BOOK AS A WHOLE": Poe, *The Haunted Palace*, back flap.

57   "ELECTRIC INFORMATION AGE BOOK": Schnapp and Michaels, *The Electronic Information Age Book*.

59   "THE SCHISM UNDERLYING THE EMERGENCE OF KITSCH": Tiffany, *My Silver Planet*, 42.

59   "I LOVE A SHEEP FROM THE BOTTOM OF MY HEART": Poe, *Essays and Reviews*, 10.

59   "REFRACTORY AND MILITANT FORM OF POETICISM": Tiffany, *My Silver Planet*, 42.

62   "TO IMITATE AND TO SIGNIFY; TO LOOK AND TO READ": Foucault, *This Is Not a Pipe*, 21.

62   "AND LINGUISTIC REFERENCE (WHICH EXCLUDES IT)": Foucault, *This Is Not a Pipe*, 32.

62   "AN INDEFINITE AND REVERSIBLE RELATION OF THE SIMILAR TO THE SIMI-
LAR": Foucault, *This Is Not a Pipe*, 44.

62   "WE SEE LETTERS AND WE READ FACES": Piper, *Book Was There*, 31.

63   "ONE OF THE GREAT MERCIES OF GOD THAT 'ER LASST SICH NICHT LESEN.'":
Poe, *Poetry and Tales*, 396.

63   THEMATIZATIONS OF THE PROBLEMS OF READING/SEEING: See Irwin, *American Hieroglyphics*.

64   POE SCHOLARS HAVE ALSO DEMONSTRATED: For title page, see Tresch, "The
Compositor's Reversal"; for symmetry more generally in *Pym*, see Kopley,
"The Hidden Journey of 'Arthur Gordon Pym,'" and Kopley, "The Secret of
Arthur Gordon Pym: The Text and the Source."

64   PERHAPS MAGRITTE, EVER A FAN OF PLAY WITH FRAMES, IS THINKING OF
THAT: See Allmer, *René Magritte: Beyond Painting*, 164.

64   PLAYS GAMES WITH FACIAL (UN)RECOGNIZABILITY: Weinstein, "*La reproduction interdite*: Magritte's Reproduction of *Pym*."

64   ECHOED POWERFULLY THEIR OWN EXPERIENCES OF VISION: Allmer, *René
Magritte: Beyond Painting*, 112–16; Umland, *Magritte: The Mystery of the Ordinary*,
18–19.

64   "OR IN THE TYPOGRAPHY OF A BOOK": Poe, *Poetry and Tales*, 227.

64   THE "MYSTERIOUS QUALITY" OF THE "MOLDINGS ON A DOOR": Magritte,
quoted in Umland, *Magritte: The Mystery of the Ordinary*, 19.

64   ANY AESTHETIC IDEOLOGY OF GROWTH OR MATURITY: Poe's *Eureka* demonstrates an aesthetic vision of growth, but vision of cyclical repetition, as universes explode and implode one after another, is not best described as being
about development.

Chapter Two

67   "A FRENZY OF THE VISIBLE": Comolli, "Machines of the Visible," 122.

67   "'GET CLOSER' TO THINGS": Benjamin, "The Work of Art in the Age of Its Mechanical Reproducibility," 255 (italics in original).

67   "THAN ANY PAINTING BY HUMAN HANDS": Poe, "The Daguerreotype."

67   "A MORE PERFECT IDENTITY OF ASPECT WITH THE THING REPRESENTED":
Poe, "The Daguerreotype."

68   "SUPREMENESS OF ITS PERFECTION": Poe, "The Daguerreotype."

69   "NOT VIEWING AND WANTING TO WATCH": Geimer, "The Incommensurable,"
82 (italics in original).

69   "THE TRIUMPH AND THE GRAVE OF THE EYE": Comolli, "Machines of the Visible," 122.

69   "DENIGRATION OF VISION": Jay, *Downcast Eyes*.

70   "AT THE EXPENSE OF NARRATIVE COHERENCE AND CONVENTION": Schaefer,
"Bold! Daring! Shocking! True!": A History of Exploitation Films, 90–93.

70   "THESE THINGS ARE INVARIABLY SOUGHT AFTER WITH AVIDITY": Poe to
Thomas W. White, April 30, 1835, in Poe, *The Collected Letters of Edgar Allan Poe*.

70   "THE SINGULAR WROUGHT OUT INTO THE STRANGE AND MYSTICAL": Poe to
Thomas W. White, April 30, 1835, in Poe, *The Collected Letters of Edgar Allan Poe*.

71   THE DURABLE TRADITION OF MERGING POE'S LIFE AND HIS WORKS: Peeples,
"'That Name'll Never Be Worth Anything!': Poe's Image on Film."

71   "THE MOST ORIGINAL POETIC GENIUS EVER PRODUCED BY AMERICA": Smith, *The Poe Cinema*, 8.

71   AND PERHAPS THAT IS TRUE: See Leitch, *Adaptation and Its Discontents*, 308n38: "The point of the film's ambiguous historical setting, as in its allusion to two quite different literary sources, is that consistency and fidelity are less important values than the impressiveness the institutions of literature and history can lend his project."

71   EARLY INSTANCES OF CROSSCUTTING: Jurgess, "Continuity, the Weight of the Suture."

72   "HAVE BEEN ILLUSTRATED BY THE SOLAX PRODUCER": Smith, *The Poe Cinema*, 10. For more on the film, see Hayes, "Alice Guy's *The Pit and the Pendulum* (1913)."

72   "WE SEE SKULLS AND CRAWLING SERPENTS": Smith, *The Poe Cinema*, 10.

72   "A MORE POWERFUL EFFECT MAY BE GAINED BY SUGGESTION": R. R., "The Pit and the Pendulum," 7. My thanks to Greg Waller for sharing this text with me.

72   AND JOSEPH BREEN, PUBLICIST AND PROMINENT CATHOLIC LAYMAN, WAS PUT IN CHARGE: See Leff and Simmons, *The Dame in the Kimono*.

73   "CONTAINS LITTLE, IF ANYTHING, THAT IS REASONABLY CENSORABLE": Mank, *Bela Lugosi and Boris Karloff*, 193.

73   "HOW DID ULMER GET THIS FAR WITH SO PERVERSE A SCRIPT?": Mank, *Bela Lugosi and Boris Karloff*, 163.

73   BY DEVISING A FORMULA AND ITERATING A SERIES: Edwards, "House of Horrors."

73   HIS FILM HAS "NOTHING" TO DO WITH POE'S STORY: Bogdanovich, "Interview with Edgar G. Ulmer," 388.

73   "DEPRAVITY, MELANCHOLY, PSYCHOLOGICAL TRAUMA, AND SADISM": Edwards, "House of Horrors," 20.

75   DEDICATED ABOVE ALL TO THE PRESENTATION OF WHITENESS: Dyer, *Whiteness*.

76   IN THE WORDS OF ONE HISTORIAN OF HORROR CINEMA: Everson, *Classics of the Horror Film*, 122.

76   "THE FEARFUL COLOURED INTO THE HORRIBLE": Poe to Thomas W. White, April 30, 1835, in Poe, *Collected Letters*.

76   "LIGHTHEARTED, EVEN CORNY, MOMENTS": Friedrich, *City of Nets*, 198.

76   BANNED OR CUT IN ALL THOSE PLACES: Mank, *Bela Lugosi and Boris Karloff*, 193.

77   "TO BE A RESPECTABLE RIVAL TO THE PULPS": Auden, preface to *Edgar Allan Poe: Selected Prose and Poetry*, xvi.

77   "AND I READ ALL OF POE'S STORIES": Roger Corman, quoted in Nashawaty, *Crab Monsters, Teenage Cavemen, and Candy Stripe Nurses*, 29.

77   "DARK TALE OF NECROPHILIA, SADISM, AND TORTURE": Smith, *The Poe Cinema*, 45.

77   "THE INTELLECT OF A HIGHLY-GIFTED PERSON BEFORE PUBERTY": Eliot, "From Poe to Valéry," 330, 331, 335.

77   CITING THE BLOOD-SMEARED RAZOR IN "THE MURDERS IN THE RUE MORGUE": Legman, *Love & Death*.

78   "GRAPHIC INSANITY": Sterling North, quoted in Hajdu, *The Ten-Cent Plague*, 40.

78   "UR-MODERNISTIC CRIME WRITERS LIKE EDGAR ALLAN POE": Naremore, *More Than Night: Film Noir in Its Contexts*, 255.

78   "FOR THE COVER OF A HORROR COMIC": Gaines, "Testimony of William Gaines."

78   "DID TERRIBLE THINGS TO THEIR HORRIBLE LOVED ONES AND FRIENDS": Chabon, *The Amazing Adventures of Kavalier and Clay*, 601, 566.

79   "BUT I DON'T THINK IT DOES THEM A BIT OF HARM, EITHER": Gaines, "Testimony of William Gaines."

80   "IDEAS SEEM TO BE *ENTERTAINED* RATHER THAN BELIEVED": Eliot, "From Poe to Valéry," 335.

80   "THE HERESY OF *THE DIDACTIC*": Poe, *Essays and Reviews*, 75.

81   BUT NOT THE STORY WITH THE CAT: See, for example, Hajdu, *The Ten-Cent Plague*, 179.

81   "SERIES OF MERE HOUSEHOLD EVENTS": Poe, *Poetry and Tales*, 597.

82   "WHICH IS ONE REASON HIS INFLUENCE ON OUR CENTURY" IS SO DIRECT: Frye, *Anatomy of Criticism: Four Essays*, 139.

82   "HIS EVENTUAL ACCEPTANCE OF THE COMPLEXITY OF LIFE": Warshow, "Paul, the Horror Comics, and Dr. Wertham," 77.

83   "WHICH, TO BE SURE, WOULD BE BETTER": Warshow, "Paul, the Horror Comics, and Dr. Wertham," 73.

83   MAD'S REDUCTION OF "ALL CULTURE TO INDISCRIMINATE ANARCHY": Warshow, "Paul, the Horror Comics, and Dr. Wertham," 80.

83   "THAT I HAD ANYTHING TO DO WITH IT": Warshow, "Paul, the Horror Comics, and Dr. Wertham," 80.

84   WHAT WE HAVE COME TO CALL *MIDCENTURY MODERNISM*: for one recent compelling treatment, see Nieland, *Happiness by Design*.

84   "CAN BE USED FOR ANY KIND OF STORY": United Productions of America, Production Notes, 1. My thanks to Dan Bashara for sharing his copies of this file from the archive.

84   "EVER PRODUCED IN THE MEDIUM OF ANIMATED FILM": United Productions of America, Production Notes, 1.

85   *LANGUAGE OF VISION* TO ALL NEW EMPLOYEES: Bashara, *Cartoon Vision*, 102.

85   "AND THE EXTENSION OF VISION INTO INFINITY": Bashara, *Cartoon Vision*, 149–50.

86   ITS FIRST-EVER X RATING FOR AN ANIMATED WORK: Robertson, *The British Board of Censors*. My thanks to the British Board of Film Classification feedback team for sharing the notes on the animation that exist in their archives.

86   "WE COULD SEE THAT HE WAS GOING FOR SOMETHING NEW": Martin Scorsese, quoted in Nashawaty, *Crab Monsters*, 21.

87   HAVE VIOLENT HORROR AND EXPLOITATION FILMS AS A CORE: For one argument along these lines, see Sconce, "'Trashing' the Academy."

89   "MEN, WOMEN, AND CHAINSAWS": Clover, *Men, Women, and Chainsaws*.

89   "DENIGRATION OF VISION": Jay, *Downcast Eyes*.

89   "MORE THAT I AM POWERLESS NOT TO SEE": Shaviro, *The Cinematic Body*, 47.

89   "AN EXTREME POINT OF IMPLOSION AND SELF-ANNIHILATION": Shaviro, *The Cinematic Body*, 53–54.

90   WAS A LIFELONG READER OF POE: McDonagh, *Broken Mirrors / Broken Minds*, 210.

91   "RELENTLESS SEARCH FOR THE OUTER LIMITS OF STYLE": McDonagh, *Broken Mirrors / Broken Minds*, 204.

91   ARE NOT ABOUT REALISM: Shaviro, *The Cinematic Body*, 100. Shaviro puts it this way: "Romero's trilogy, and the many horror films produced in its wake, do not try to suture the spectator into a seamless world of false plenitude and ideological mystification. Rather, they blithely dispense with the canons of realistic conviction. They indulge themselves in the production of 'special effects,' in the double sense of grotesque visual effects and of affective and physiological effects."

91   "SHOCK AS A CONSUMER COMMODITY": Adorno, *Minima Moralia*, 236.

91   "SEEN BY A CLOSED EYE THAT HAS RECEIVED A BLOW": Adorno, *Minima Moralia*, 236.

92   "COMET-LIKE, REMOTE, ULTIMATE NEWNESS": Adorno, *Minima Moralia*, 237.

92   "EXTREME CINEMA": Frey, *Extreme Cinema*.

92   "NOT VIEWING AND WANTING TO WATCH": Geimer, "The Incommensurable," 82 (italics in original).

93   "BASE ITSELF ON POE'S TALE OF TORTURE": Hughes, "Evolutions in Torture."

93   "IMPLOSION AND SELF-ANNIHILATION": Shaviro, *The Cinematic Body*, 53–54.

Chapter Three

97   A PRIMITIVE IMAGE OF "PROTECTED INTIMACY": Bachelard, *The Poetics of Space*, 4, 3.

97   "VAULTED AND FRETTED CEILING": Poe, *Poetry and Tales*, 320.

97   "A GREAT DREAMER OF CURTAINS": Bachelard, *Poetics of Space*, 39.

98   "WHICH DID NOT INSPIRE HIM WITH HORROR": Poe, *Poetry and Tales*, 322.

98   "WITHOUT PASSING AWAY INTO THE DISTANCE": Poe, *Poetry and Tales*, 331 (italics mine).

98   "THE DECAYED TREES WHICH STOOD AROUND": Poe, *Poetry and Tales*, 327.

98   "DULL, SLUGGISH, FAINTLY DISCERNIBLE, AND LEADEN-HUED": Poe, *Poetry and Tales*, 329.

99   ATTUNED TO NATURE, GOD, AND THE UNIVERSE: Spitzer, "Milieu and Ambiance"; Spitzer, "Classical and Christian Ideas of World Harmony"; Heidegger, "Building Dwelling Thinking."

99   "IS DETERMINISM MADE POETIC, 'ATMOSPHERIC'": Spitzer, "A Reinterpretation of 'The Fall of the House of Usher,'" 356.

99   POINTS TO OUR CURRENT CRISIS OF GLOBAL WARMING: Two especially astute essays in what is a large and fast-growing literature are Menely, "Anthropocene Air," and Ford, "Aura in the Anthropocene."

100   "WHAT THE AMERICAN ROMANCER NEEDS": Hawthorne, *The Blithedale Romance*, 2.

100   "YET OF MIGHTY INFLUENCE": Durand, "On Landscape Painting," *The Crayon*, 146.

100   "AND PALPABLE IN THE DISTANCE": Durand, "On Landscape Painting," 146.

100   "IN CONSTANT VIGOROUS ACTION AND RE-ACTION": Horace Bushnell, quoted in Modern, *Secularism in Antebellum America*, 30.

101   "THAT ALL IS IN ITS PROPER PLACE": Durand, "On Landscape Painting," 146.

101   "RATHER THAN WHAT THEY ARE": Griffero, *Atmospheres*, 83.

102   "ART IN A GASEOUS STATE": Michaud, *L'art à l'état gazeux*.

102   "PRODUCES INFORMATION ABOUT ART EVENTS": Groys, *In the Flow*, 4.

102   "A NATURAL, EVEN OBLIGATORY, PHENOMENON": Claude Debussy, quoted in Walsh, *Debussy: A Painter in Sound*, 195.

103   "NOT DROWNED BUT STRANGLED AT BIRTH": Walsh, *Debussy: A Painter in Sound*, 102.

103   "AND THE NEED TO UNDERLINE EVERYTHING": Debussy, quoted in Walsh, *Debussy: A Painter in Sound*, 5.

103   "THAT ONE MUST SUBMERGE TONALITY": Debussy, quoted in Walsh, *Debussy: A Painter in Sound*, 102.

104   "PRACTICALITIES OF THE OPERATIC STAGE": Walsh, *Debussy: A Painter in Sound*, 195.

104   "THAN A PRACTICAL CREATIVE PROJECT": Walsh, *Debussy: A Painter in Sound*, 196.

104   "IN SPITE OF ALL MY EFFORTS": Debussy, quoted in Walsh, *Debussy: A Painter in Sound*, 195–96.

105   "ONLY MOVEMENTS AND DEEDS OF PEOPLE, BUT NOT PEOPLE": Lukács, "Thoughts on an Aesthetics of Cinema," 12.

105   "THE NEVER-RESTING CHANGE OF THINGS": Lukács, "Thoughts on an Aesthetics of Cinema," 13.

105   "UNLIKE DRAMA'S TRAGIC FOCUS ON FINITUDE AND FATE": Lukács, "Thoughts on an Aesthetics of Cinema," 13.

105   "YET GAINS HIS BODY IN RETURN": Lukács, "Thoughts on an Aesthetics of Cinema," 14.

105   "AN INSTRUMENT READY FOR HIS SCENIC YEARNING": Lukács, "Thoughts on an Aesthetics of Cinema," 15.

105   DURING THE FILMING OF LA CHUTE: Cortade, "The 'Microscope of Time,'" 168.

106   "SHOULD NOT TELL STORIES": Bordwell, *French Impressionist Cinema: Film Culture, Film Theory, and Film Style*, 245.

106   "THE FILM IS BAD": Epstein, "For a New Avant-Garde," 350.

106   MERGED IN THE DEPTHS OF THE BODY: On Epstein's ideas about "coenesthesis," see Wall-Romana, *Jean Epstein: Corporeal Cinema and Film Philosophy*, 74–76.

106   "FOLLOWS A STRICT TEMPO": Bordwell, *French Impressionist Cinema*, 205.

107   "CHEEKS OF HER WHO SATE BESIDE HIM": Poe, *Poetry and Tales*, 483 (italics in original).

109   "LA LUMIÈRE CENDRÉE": Epstein, *Écrits sur le cinema*, 188 (my translation).

109   WRITES ONE CONTEMPORARY CRITIC: Wall-Romana, *Jean Epstein: Corporeal Cinema and Film Philosophy*, 39–40.

109   "ONLY ONE REALM REMAINS: LIFE": Epstein, *The Intelligence of a Machine*, 3.

109   "ALIENATING QUALITY OF CINEMA'S RELATION TO REALITY": Bordwell, *French Impressionist Cinema*, 106.

110   "YOU WILL BELIEVE IN A BETRAYAL": Epstein, "La lyrosophie," 283.

110   NOT TO MAKE ANY MORE MOVIES: Hames, "Jan Švankmajer, Interview with Peter Hames," 100.

111   "DRAG ABOUT FOR THE REST OF OUR LIFE": Johnson, *Jan Švankmajer*, 160.

111   "CRAMMED WITH DESCRIPTIONS OF THE TACTILE": Hames, "Jan Švankmajer, Interview with Peter Hames," *Dark Alchemy*, 109.

111   "AND MAKING THEM CONSIDERABLY INTENSIVE": Hames, "Jan Švankmajer, Interview with Peter Hames," *Dark Alchemy*, 109.

111   "TRANSFERRING TACTILE SENSATIONS TO THE VIEWER": Jan Švankmajer, quoted in Johnson, *Jan Švankmajer*, 156.

113   "AND EVEN OF MAKING THEM VISIBLE": Švankmajer, *Touching and Imagining*, 149.

113   BROUGHT HIS INSTALLATION *L'EXPÉDITION SCINTILLANTE*: For a description of *L'expédition scintillante*, I have relied on Barikin, *Parallel Presents: The Art of Pierre Huyghe*; Morton, "Bon Voyage: Pierre Huyghe"; and Lally, "Overlooked the Day Before: The Work of Pierre Huyghe." See also Hines, "A Journey That Wasn't." My thanks to Megan Hines from whose presentation I first heard of Huyghe's installation.

114   "REFERRED TO AS THE 'SUNRISE/SUNSET CEILING'": Barikin, *Parallel Presents*, 193.

115   "IT IS A DEFORMATION OF THE SAME": Huyghe, quoted in Barikin, *Parallel Presents*, 183.

115   A FEW YEARS LATER AS *A JOURNEY THAT WASN'T*: See Barikin, *Parallel Presents*, 200, and Hines, "A Journey That Wasn't."

116   "PRODUCES INFORMATION ABOUT ART EVENTS": Groys, *In the Flow*, 4.

117   MIGHT BE CALLED A DISASSEMBLED *GESAMTKUNSTWERK*: On this performance, see Box Burners, "Countertenor Anthony Roth Costanzo Pushes Opera-Goers."

118   "AND ENTERING ANOTHER HUMAN BODY": Costanzo, quoted in Box Burners, "Countertenor Anthony Roth Costanzo Pushes Opera-Goers."

119   "NO MATTER HOW CLOSE IT MAY BE": Benjamin, "The Work of Art in the Age of Its Mechanical Reproducibility," 255.

119   "ESSENTIALLY UNAFFECTED BY THE ROLE": Cavell, *A Pitch of Philosophy*, 137.

120   "IS NOT HE, BUT SHE": Hélène Cixous, quoted in Cavarero, *For More Than One Voice*, 122.

120   "A BOY WHO SINGS LIKE A GIRL": Costanzo, quoted in Box Burners, "Countertenor Anthony Roth Costanzo Pushes Opera-Goers."

120   LOOKS TO POE'S TALE AS MUCH AS GLASS'S OPERA: Sanders, "How All Living Things Breathe."

121   "VACANT EYE-LIKE": Poe, *Poetry and Tales*, 317.

Chapter Four

123   "SOME DEEP CAVERN WITHIN THE EARTH": Poe, *Poetry and Tales*, 839.

123   "AND NOT FROM THE LIPS OF THE SUFFERER": Poe, *Poetry and Tales*, 839. Adam Frank has suggested that this bizarre scene of communication is Poe's allegorization of telegraphy. See Frank, "Valdemar's Tongue, Poe's Telegraphy."

123   "GELATINOUS": Poe, *Poetry and Tales*, 839.

123   THE IDEA OF A "MUSIC OF THE SPHERES": For the idea of "music of the spheres" see Spitzer, "Classical and Christian Ideas of World Harmony," and Heller-Roazen, *The Fifth Hammer*.

123   INTO HUMAN, IF OBSCURE, SPEECH: On the Pythia and voice, see Cavarero, *For More Than One Voice*, 19.

124   A COSMIC HOLDING ENVIRONMENT: Spitzer, "Classical and Christian Ideas of World Harmony."

124   "ATTUNEMENT TO THE *NOTHING*": Brenkman, *Mood and Trope*, 53 (italics in original).

124   "SECOND-ORDER EXCEPTION TO A SPECTRUM OF NOISE": Kittler, *Gramophone, Film, Typewriter*, 23. See also Kahn, *Noise Water Meat*, 9, 16, and Sterne, *The Audible Past*, 23.

125   "THAT MAN HAS EVER SAID OR WOMAN WHISPERED": Babbage, "The Ninth Bridgewater Treatise."

125   "THE AGE OF THE COSMIC": Deleuze and Guattari, *A Thousand Plateaus*, 342.

125   "BUT THE COSMIC ARTISAN": Deleuze and Guattari, *A Thousand Plateaus*, 345.

125   "IT MAKES US WANT TO DIE": Deleuze and Guattari, *A Thousand Plateaus*, 348. For a skeptical view concerning this idea of sound "invading" us, see Sterne, *The Audible Past*, 15.

126   "VOICES ABSENT TO THEMSELVES": Sterne, *The Audible Past*, 290.

126   "CARVES OUT A TERRITORY AND CONSTRUCTS A HOUSE": Deleuze and Guattari, *What Is Philosophy?*, 183.

126   "LIKE SOUND WALLS AROUND EVERY HOUSEHOLD AND MARK TERRITORIES": Deleuze and Guattari, *A Thousand Plateaus*, 311.

126   "MAKES THEM WHIRL AROUND LIKE WINDS": Deleuze and Guattari, *What Is Philosophy?*, 183.

127   "AND HAVE HEARD IT": Poe, *Poetry and Tales*, 334.

127   "I HEARD MANY THINGS IN HELL": Poe, *Poetry and Tales*, 555.

127   "NOT ATTACHED TO ANY OF THE SENSES": Empson, *Seven Types of Ambiguity*, 16.

127   "A 'MOOD,' AN 'ATMOSPHERE'": Empson, *Seven Types of Ambiguity*, 17.

128   "THE EXPERIENCE OF READING A PARTICULAR POET": Empson, *Seven Types of Ambiguity*, 17.

128   "WRITTEN BY CRITICALLY SENSITIVE PEOPLE": Empson, *Seven Types of Ambiguity*, 17.

128   "THE JINGLE MAN": Howells, *Literary Friends and Acquaintance*, 58.

128   "DO SOMEHOW STICK IN THE MEMORY": Eliot, "From Poe to Valéry," 330.

129   "OR MOTION OF THE MOTOR": Francis M. Criswell and James A. E. Criswell, Phonograph. For more on the Criswells' patent, see Gitelman, *Scripts, Grooves, and Writing Machines*.

129   "HAVE COMBINED THEREWITH A PHONOGRAPH": Criswell and Criswell, "Phonograph," 1.

130   "AS FAR AS HUMAN RECOGNITION IS CONCERNED, CAN END HERE": Doten, *Poems from the Inner Life*, 157.

130   "MADE A LIVING AS A TRANCE SPEAKER": Braude, "Trance Lecturers in Antebellum America," 488.

130   "MOST POPULAR SPIRIT VISITORS TO MEDIUMS": Richards, "'Lyric Telegraphy': Women Poets, Spiritualist Poetics, and the Phantom Voice of Poe," 270. Richards refers to Poe's poetic "brand" in "Poe's Lyric Media," 203.

130   "ELATE WITH HOPE AWAY": Doten, *Poems from the Inner Life*, 162.

131   "SHALL BE LIFTED EVERMORE": Doten, *Poems from the Inner Life*, ii.

131   "IMPOSSIBLE TO OVERLOOK": Poe, *Essays and Reviews*, 18.

133   "HUMAN THIRST FOR SELF-TORTURE": Poe, *Essays and Reviews*, 24.

133   "BY HIM [POE] IN THE EARTH-LIFE": Wallace, *Edgar Allan Poe*, 6.

133   "TO GAIN A REPUTATION": Wallace, *Edgar Allan Poe*, 13–14.

134   "A LIAR ANY WAY YOU PUT IT": Riley, "Mr. Riley Wrote Poem Leonaine [*sic*]."

134   THAT HE EXTENDED OVER FIVE SEPARATE TRIALS: For more on these transcriptions, see Elmer, "Peirce, Poe, and Protoplasm."

134   "AT THE HEAD OF THE SCHOOL": Ketner, *His Glassy Essence*, 135.

135   "AND OTHER BLOOD-CURDLING POEMS": Ketner, *His Glassy Essence*, 134.

136   "PHONIC-SEMANTIC KNOT": Winner, "Peirce and Literary Studies," 282.

136   "HAUNTED": On "haunted" media, see Sconce, *Haunted Media*; a range of perspectives on this idea can be sampled from Mowitt, *Radio*; Warner, *Phantasmagoria*; Babich, "Radio Ghosts"; Sterne, *The Audible Past*; Kahn, *Noise Water Meat*.

136   "IT SUGGESTS SOMETHING 'BEHIND' IT": Adorno, *Current of Music*, 373.

137   "AND YET QUITE FAR AWAY": Adorno, *Current of Music*, 349.

137   "LISTENER GETS ACCUSTOMED TO THE TOOL": Adorno, *Current of Music*, 381.

137   "WARM ATMOSPHERE CREATED BY CENTRAL HEATING": Bazin, "Adaptation."

137   "SPUN IN HIS GRAVE HAD HE HEARD IT": Dunning, "Poe on the Radio," 5.

138   "MANY THINGS IN HELL": Poe, *Poetry and Tales*, 555.

138   "THINGS THAT DON'T EVEN EXIST": Karloff, "The Tell-Tale Heart."

138   "THE *GLORIOUS* FEELING THAT GOES WITH REGULARITY": Karloff, "The Tell-Tale Heart."

139   "IMAGINARY SPACE": Brenkman, "On Voice."

139   WHAT SUCH REPRODUCED VOICES SOUNDED LIKE: For accounts of early recording, I have relied on Sterne, *The Audible Past*; Kittler, *Gramophone, Film, Typewriter*; Gitelman, *Always Already New*; Smith, *Vocal Tracks*; Rubery, "Thomas Edison's Poetry Machine."

139   "STRUGGLING UP FROM THE UNDERWORLD": Rubery, "Thomas Edison's Poetry Machine," 3–4.

139   "THE UNCANNY ASSOCIATED WITH POE'S WRITING": Rubery, "Thomas Edison's Poetry Machine," 20.

139   "EVERY UTTERANCE OF WHICH THE HUMAN VOICE IS CAPABLE": Smith, *Vocal Tracks*, 18.

139   "DEMONSTRATIONS FLAUNTED IT": Rubery, "Thomas Edison's Poetry Machine," 7.

139   THE ELEVEN MINUTES PER SIDE OF A 78 RPM RECORD: American Foundation for the Blind, "The Making of a Talking Book."

139   UNDER THE DIRECTION OF LEOPOLD STOKOWSKI: Stokowski, "1932 Recordings."

139   ADDED NOISE IN THE PLAYBACK: Stokowski, "1932 Recordings."

140   THE PREFERENCE WAS FOR MINIMAL THEATRICALITY: Rubery, *The Untold Story of the Talking Book*.

140   BETWEEN TENTATIVE TINKLING AND MUSIC HALL BOUNCINESS: Hemus and Heinrich, "The Raven."

140   TO PRODUCE HIS OWN RECORDING, *THE RAVEN*: Willner, *Closed on Account of Rabies*; Reed, *The Raven*.

141   "ENVELOPED EVERY READER": Willner, *Closed on Account of Rabies*, liner notes.

141   "SPRAYED WITH LURID FEEDBACK": Willner, *Closed on Account of Rabies*, liner notes.

141   "INTENSIFIED BY ELECTRONIC DYNAMICS": Gehr, "Mourning in America," 117.

142   "OR THE BOUNDLESS ENVELOPMENT OF OCEANIC SPACE": Toop, *Oceans of Sound*, 85.

142 "TO FIND A SMALL LIGHT IN THE DARKNESS": Toshio Hosokawa, quoted in Morioka, "Report on 'The Vibrating Path toward a Musical Dream.'"

142 "MONODRAMA WITH MEZZO-SOPRANO AND ENSEMBLE": Hosokawa, *The Raven*.

143 "LYRICALLY ALLURING FLIGHTS TO BURSTS OF SOARING INTENSITY": Tommasini, "Poe's Lost Lenore Lives in Song and Dance," 1.

143 "SPECTRAL TEXTURES AND ASIAN-INFLUENCED MELODIC FRAGMENTS": Tommasini, "Poe's Lost Lenore Lives in Song and Dance," 1.

143 "THROUGH TELLING SOMEONE IN THIS WORLD ITS LAMENTABLE TALE": Hosokawa, quoted in Morioka, "Report on 'The Vibrating Path toward a Musical Dream.'"

143 "I HAVE NO SUBJECT—I AM EXHAUSTED": Poe, "The Bells," *The Collected Works of Edgar Allan Poe*, 1:429 (editorial notes).

144 OF RURAL AND CIVIC LIFE AND, ABOVE ALL, THE SACRED CALENDAR: See Corbin, *Village Bells*.

144 "LIVED AMID THE VIBRATIONS OF THE BELLS OF MOSCOW": Rachmaninoff quoted in Houston Symphony, "Apocalyptic Prophecy."

144 INTO EACH OF THE FOUR MOVEMENTS, EVEN THE ONE CELEBRATING MARRIAGE: Houston Symphony, "Apocalyptic Prophecy"; see also Lowery, "Bells of Death."

144 "INTENSE ORCHESTRAL CONFLAGRATION": Houston Symphony, "Apocalyptic Prophecy."

145 "NIAGARA EVER LIFTS UP IN ITS AGONY TO HEAVEN": Poe, *Poetry and Tales*, 434–35.

145 "OR SECURE SENSE OF PERSPECTIVE": Mitchell, "Metamorphoses of the Vortex," 140.

145 "SIMULTANEOUSLY ALLURING AND THREATENING": Mitchell, "Metamorphoses of the Vortex," 133.

146 "THE CONCEPT OF NEWNESS EMERGES": Adorno, *Minima Moralia*, 235.

146 "WHICH CONFOUNDS THE BEHOLDER": Poe, *Poetry and Tales*, 435.

146 "YET IN A SENSE STATIONARY MOVEMENT": Adorno, *Minima Moralia*, 236.

146 "ENFER OU CIEL, QU'IMPORTE?": Baudelaire, "The Voyage," 400.

146 "TO REIFICATION, THEIR PRINCIPLE OF DEATH": Adorno, *Aesthetic Theory*, 182.

146 AS A SELF-CONSUMING FORCE AND TEMPORAL SINKHOLE: For representative passages, see Adorno, *Aesthetic Theory*, 32, 38, 98.

146 TO MAKE MUSIC FROM "NOISE": Kahn, *Noise Water Meat*.

147 ALL AT THE SAME TIME: Johnson, "What Is Minimalism Really About?"

148 EXPLORATIONS IN MUSIQUE CONCRÈTE DATE FROM 1948: Kahn, *Noise Water Meat*, 100.

149 WAS ONLY RELEASED IN THE 1970S: Tristano, "Descent into the Maelstrom."

149 "OVERWHELMING SENSATION OF UNPREDICTABLE VOLITION": Toop, *Into the Maelstrom*, 104–5.

150 "MY HEART GREW SICK": Poe, *Poetry and Tales*, 854.

151 "AN IDEA OF WHAT ROCK COULD BE": Lou Reed, quoted in Pareles, "MUSIC; Lou Reed, The Tell-Tale Rocker," 1.

152 A SPECIES OF MUTISM AT THE HEART OF THE UNIVERSE: See NintendoComplete, "The Dark Eye (PC) Playthrough."

152 "USE OF SOUND LINKED TO MOVING IMAGE": Kahn, *Noise Water Meat*, 148.

152   "MICKEY MOUSING": Kahn, *Noise Water Meat*, 148.

152   "ANIMATED BY SOUND": Kahn, *Noise Water Meat*, 149.

153   ONE OF THE FIRST TO BE PRODUCED FOR THE SERIES: Encyclopedia Sponge-Bobia, "Squeaky Boots."

154   "YOU DON'T BEAT *THE DARK EYE*, YOU EXPLORE IT": Maher, "The Dark Eye."

154   "AFTER SPENDING A WHILE IN ITS COMPANY": Maher, "The Dark Eye."

155   "TRANSPIRE IN THE SAME GAMIC GESTURE": Galloway, *Gaming*, 104.

155   "THEN VIDEO GAMES ARE ACTIONS": Galloway, *Gaming*, 2.

155   "SENSE OF AGENCY THAT VIDEOGAME PLAYERS EXPERIENCE IS ILLUSORY": Stang, "This Action Will Have Consequences."

155   EVEN IN A SENSORY DEPRIVATION CHAMBER, AS CAGE DISCOVERED: On Cage's experience in an anechoic chamber, see Kahn, *Noise Water Meat*, 179–81.

156   "AND MEDIATED, DISEMBODIED VOICES": Palmer, "The Disembodied Fry," 101–02. Thanks to Joan Hawkins for pointing me to Palmer's essay.

157   STARTED IN ON HIS VODKA AND SPRITE: Rose, "Russell Lees & Inscape's The Dark Eye Retrospective."

Afterword

160   EXPLAIN WHY POE HAS HAD SUCH AN OUTSIZE "INFLUENCE": Frye, *Anatomy of Criticism*, 139.

160   MANAGES AND ENGINEERS EXPLOSIVE DEVICES: Peeples, *The Man of the Crowd*, 42.

160   "FACTITIOUSNESS": F. O. Matthiessen, *The American Renaissance*, xii.

160   "ARTIFICIAL, CONVENTIONAL": *Oxford English Dictionary*, compact edition (1971), s.v. "factitious."

160   "BY THE IMPRESSION IT MAKES": Poe, *Essays and Reviews*, 72.

160   "I LOVE A SHEEP FROM THE BOTTOM OF MY HEART": Poe, *Essays and Reviews*, 10.

162   "THE RUBRICS OF 'MEDIATION' AND THE 'MEDIUM'": Ford, *Wordsworth and the Poetics of Air*, 13, 2. A very rich archaeology of atmosphere and media from an art-historical perspective can be found in Bruno, *Atmospheres of Projection*.

163   "ENTITIES LESS THAN RELATIONS": Michaud, *L'art, c'est bien fini* (my translation).

163   "THE MARKETING PROFESSOR PHILIP KOTLER COINED THE TERM 'ATMO-SPHERICS'": Borch, *Architectural Atmospheres*, 82.

163   "WITH ITS MANY INTERNAL RELATIONSHIPS": Fried, "Art and Objecthood," 153.

163   "ONE THAT, VIRTUALLY BY DEFINITION, *INCLUDES THE BEHOLDER*": Fried, "Art and Objecthood," 153.

163   "AND THEATER IS NOW THE NEGATION OF ART": Fried, "Art and Objecthood," 153.

164   "IN THE DEVELOPMENT OF THE CINEMATIC AND TELEVISUAL MEDIA": Black, *The Reality Effect*, 25, 10.

Bibliography

Adamson, Joseph. "Frye and Poe." *The Educated Imagination: A Website Dedicated to Northrop Frye* (blog), December 16, 2012. https://macblog.mcmaster.ca/fryeblog/2012/12/16/frye-and-poe-2/.

Adorno, Theodor W., *Aesthetic Theory*. Translated and edited by Robert Hullot-Kentor, London: Bloomsbury, 1997.

———. *Current of Music: Elements of a Radio Theory*. Translated and edited by Robert Hullot-Kentor. Cambridge: Polity Press, 2009.

———. *Minima Moralia: Reflections from Damaged Life*. Translated by E. F. N. Jephcott. London: Verso Books, 2010.

Allmer, Patricia. *René Magritte: Beyond Painting*. Manchester: Manchester University Press, 2009.

American Foundation for the Blind. "The Making of a Talking Book." AFB Talking Book Exhibit: Early History. https://www.afb.org/about-afb/history/online-museums/afb-talking-book-exhibit/early-history-why/making-talking-book.

Anderson, Paul Allen. "Neo-Muzak and the Business of Mood." *Critical Inquiry* 41, no. 4 (Summer 2015): 811–40.

Andriopoulos, Stefan. *Ghostly Apparitions: German Idealism, the Gothic Novel, and Optical Media*. New York: Zone Books, 2013.

Arnar, Anna Sigríður. *The Book as Instrument: Stéphane Mallarmé, the Artist's Book, and the Transformation of Print Culture*. Chicago: University of Chicago Press, 2011.

Auden, W. H., ed. Preface to *Edgar Allan Poe: Selected Prose and Poetry*. By Edgar Allan Poe. New York: Holt, Rinehart, and Winston, 1955.

Babbage, Charles. "The Ninth Bridgewater Treatise: A Fragment." 2nd ed. London: John Murray, 1838. https://victorianweb.org/science/science_texts/bridgewater/intro.htm.

Babich, Babette. "Radio Ghosts: Phenomenology's Phantoms and Digital Autism." *Thesis Eleven* 153, no. 1 (2019): 57–74.

Bachelard, Gaston. *The Poetics of Space*. Translated by Maria Jolas. Boston: Beacon Press, 1964.

Baker, George. "An Interview with Pierre Huyghe." *October*, no. 110 (2004): 80–106.

Barikin, Amelia. *Parallel Presents: The Art of Pierre Huyghe*. Cambridge, MA: MIT Press, 2012.

Barker, Martin. *A Haunt of Fears: The Strange History of the British Horror Comics Campaign.* Jackson: University Press of Mississippi, 1992.

Bashara, Dan. *Cartoon Vision: UPA Animation and Postwar Aesthetics.* Berkeley: University of California Press, 2019.

Baudelaire, Charles. "The Voyage." In *The Flowers of Evil: A Selection,* edited by Marthiel Mathews and Jackson Mathews, 133–46. New York: New Directions, 1955.

———. *Selected Writings on Art and Artists.* Translated by P. E. Charvet. New York: Penguin Books, 1993.

Bazin, André. "Adaptation; or, Cinema as Digest." *Esprit,* July 1948.

Benjamin, Walter. "The Work of Art in the Age of Its Mechanical Reproducibility: Third Version." In *Walter Benjamin: Selected Writings.* Vol. 4, *1938–1940,* edited by Howard Eiland and Michael W. Jennings, 251–83. Cambridge, MA: Harvard University Press, 2003.

Bennett, Jane. *Vibrant Matter: A Political Ecology of Things.* Durham, NC: Duke University Press, 2010.

Black, Joel. *The Reality Effect: Film Culture and the Graphic Imperative.* New York: Routledge, 2001.

Bogdanovich, Peter. "Interview with Edgar G. Ulmer." In *Kings of the Bs: Working Within the Hollywood System: An Anthology of Film History and Criticism,* edited by Todd McCarthy and Charles Flynn, 377–410. New York: E. P. Dutton, 1975.

Böhme, Gernot. "Atmosphere as the Fundamental Concept of a New Aesthetics." *Thesis Eleven* 36 (1993): 113–26.

———. *Atmospheric Architectures: The Aesthetics of Felt Spaces.* Translated and edited by Tina Engels-Schwarzpaul. London: Bloomsbury, 2017.

Borch, Christian, ed. *Architectural Atmospheres: On the Experience and Politics of Architecture.* Basel, Switzerland: Birkhaüser, 2014.

Bordwell, David. *French Impressionist Cinema: Film Culture, Film Theory, and Film Style.* PhD thesis, University of Iowa, 1974. Ann Arbor: Xerox University Microfilms.

Borton, Terry. "Magic Lantern Art: Joseph Boggs Beale, First Great Screen Artist of the American Screen." Unpublished manuscript, last modified April 12, 2023.

Borton, Terry, and Deborah Borton. *Before the Movies: American Magic-Lantern Entertainment and the Nation's First Great Screen Artist, Joseph Boggs Beale.* New Barnet, UK: John Libbey Publishing, 2014.

Bowe, Nicola Gordon. *The Life and Work of Harry Clarke.* Dublin: Irish Academic Press, 1989.

Box Burners. "Countertenor Anthony Roth Costanzo Pushes Opera-Goers— Literally—with Glass Handel." All Arts TV. February 22, 2020. YouTube video, 10:53. https://www.youtube.com/watch?v=5HRREezzzdc.

Brain, Robert. *The Pulse of Modernism: Physiological Aesthetics in Fin-de-Siècle Europe.* Seattle: University of Washington Press, 2015.

Braude, Ann. "Trance Lecturers in Antebellum America." In *Religions of the United States in Practice, Volume 1,* edited by Colleen McDannell, 483–91. Princeton, NJ: Princeton University Press, 2001.

Breccia, Alberto. *Le coeur révélateur et autres histoires extraordinaires d'Edgar Allan Poe.* Translated by Sylvestre Zas. Paris: Rackham, 2018.

Brenkman, John. *Mood and Trope: The Rhetoric and Poetics of Affect.* Chicago: University of Chicago Press, 2020.

———. "On Voice." *NOVEL: A Forum on Fiction* 33, no. 3 (Summer 2000): 281–306.

Brinkema, Eugenie. *The Forms of the Affects*. Durham, NC: Duke University Press, 2014.

———. *Life-Destroying Diagrams*. Durham, NC: Duke University Press, 2014.

Bruhn, Jørgen, Anne Gjelsvik, and Eirik Frisvold Hanssen, eds. *Adaptation Studies: New Challenges, New Directions*. London: Bloomsbury, 2013.

Bruno, Giuliana. *Atmospheres of Projection: Environmentality in Art and Screen Media*. Chicago: University of Chicago Press, 2022.

Calinescu, Matei. *Five Faces of Modernity: Modernism Avant-Garde Decadence Kitsch Postmodernism*. Durham, NC: Duke University Press, 1987.

Cantalupo, Barbara. *Poe and the Visual Arts*. University Park, PA: Penn State University Press, 2014.

———. "Poe's Visual Legacy." In *The Oxford Handbook of Edgar Allan Poe*, edited by J. Gerald Kennedy and Scott Peeples, 676–700. Oxford: Oxford University Press, 2019.

Cantril, Hadley, and Gordon W. Allport. *The Psychology of Radio*. New York: Arno Press, 1971.

Carlson, Eric. *Critical Essays on Edgar Allan Poe*. Boston: G. K. Hall & Co., 1987.

Cavarero, Adriana. *For More than One Voice: Toward a Philosophy of Vocal Expression*. Stanford, CA: Stanford University Press, 2005.

Cavell, Stanley. *A Pitch of Philosophy: Autobiographical Exercises*. Cambridge, MA: Harvard University Press, 1994.

Chabon, Michael. *The Amazing Adventures of Kavalier and Clay*. New York: Random House, 2000.

Clover, Carol. *Men, Women, and Chainsaws: Gender in the Modern Horror Film*. Princeton, NJ: Princeton University Press, 1993.

Comolli, Jean-Louis, "Machines of the Visible." In *The Cinematic Apparatus*, edited by Teresa de Lauretis and Stephen Heath, 121–42. New York: St. Martin's Press, 1980.

Coombs, Neil. *Studying Surrealist and Fantasy Cinema*. London: Auteur, 2008.

Cooper, Scott, dir. *The Pale Blue Eye*. Netflix, 2023.

Corbin, Alain. *Village Bells: Sound and Meaning in the Nineteenth-Century French Countryside*. Translated by Martin Thom. New York: Columbia University Press, 1998.

Cortade, Ludovic. "The 'Microscope of Time': Slow Motion in Jean Epstein's Writings." In *Jean Epstein: Critical Essays and New Translations*, edited by Sarah Keller and Jason N. Paul, 161–76. Amsterdam: Amsterdam University Press, 2012.

Costanzo, Anthony Roth, Les Violons du Roy, and Jonathan Cohen, conductor. *ARC: Glass/Handel*. Decca Gold B0028648-02, 2018, compact disc.

Crary, Jonathan. *24/7: Late Capitalism and the Ends of Sleep*. London: Verso, 2013.

———. *Suspensions of Perception: Attention, Spectacle, and Modern Culture*. Cambridge, MA: MIT Press, 2001.

———. *Techniques of the Observer: On Vision and Modernity in the Nineteenth Century*. Cambridge, MA: MIT Press, 1990.

Criswell, Francis M., and James A. E. Criswell. Phonograph. US Patent 470,477, filed June 16, 1891, and issued March 8, 1892.

Deas, Michael J. "The 'Ultima Thule' Daguerreotype." In *The Portraits and Daguerreotypes of Edgar Allan Poe*. Charlottesville: University of Virginia Press, 1989. https://www.eapoe.org/papers/misc1921/deas107a.htm.

Deleuze, Gilles, and Félix Guattari, *A Thousand Plateaus: Capitalism and Schizophrenia*. Translated by Brian Massumi. Minneapolis: University of Minnesota Press, 1987.

———. *What Is Philosophy?* Translated by Hugh Tomlinson and Graham Burchell. New York: Columbia University Press, 1994.

Dennett, Daniel. *Darwin's Dangerous Idea: Evolution and the Meanings of Life.* New York: Simon & Schuster, 1995.

Dolar, Mladen. *A Voice and Nothing More.* Cambridge, MA: MIT, 2006.

Donald, James, ed. *Fantasy and the Cinema.* London: British Film Institute, 1989.

Doré, Gustave. "Gustave Doré's 'Raven.'" Illustrated Books, Graphic Arts Collection, Special Collections, Firestone Library, Princeton University, March 2018. https://graphicarts.princeton.edu/2018/03/29/gustave-dores-raven/.

Dostoevsky, Fyodor. "Edgar Allan Poe." In *Critical Essays on Edgar Allan Poe,* edited by Eric Carlson, 78–79. Boston: G. K. Hall & Co., 1987.

Doten, Lizzie. *Poems From the Inner Life.* Boston: William White and Company, 1864.

Draper, Jason. "Who's Who on the Beatles' 'Sgt. Pepper's Lonely Hearts Club Band' Album Cover." Udiscovermusic, May 26, 2023. https://www.udiscovermusic.com/stories/whos-who-on-the-beatles-sgt-peppers-lonely-hearts-club-band-album-cover/.

Drost, Christian. "Illuminating Poe: The Reflection of Edgar Allan Poe's Pictorialism in the Illustrations for Tales of the Grotesque and Arabesque." PhD diss., Universität Hamburg, 2006.

Drucker, Johanna. *Graphesis: Visual Forms of Knowledge Production.* Cambridge, MA: Harvard University Press, 2014.

Dubensky, Arcady. "The Raven." Performed by Benjamin DeLoache. Victor Program Transcription. Victor, 1932. Audio recording. https://www.stokowski.org/sitebuilderfiles/321209_Dubensky_Raven_H.mp3.

Dunning, John. "Poe on the Radio." *The Edgar Allan Poe Review* 1, no. 2 (2000): 3–9.

Durand, Asher B. "On Landscape Painting." *The Crayon* 1, no. 10 (March 7, 1855): 145–46.

Dyer, Richard, *Whiteness: Essays on Race and Culture.* London: Routledge, 1997.

Edwards, Kyle. "'House of Horrors': Corporate Strategy at Universal Studios in the 1930s." In *Merchants of Menace: The Business of Horror Cinema,* edited by Richard Nowell, 13–30. New York: Bloomsbury, 2014.

Eisenstein, Sergei. "Montage of Attractions: For 'Enough Stupidity for Every Wiseman.'" Translated by Daniel Gerould. *The Drama Review: TDR* 18, no. 1 (March 1974): 77–85.

Eliot, T. S. "From Poe to Valéry." *The Hudson Review* 2, no. 3 (Autumn 1949): 327–42.

Elkins, James. *The Object Stares Back: On the Nature of Seeing.* New York: Harcourt, 1996.

Elliott, Kamilla. *Theorizing Adaptation.* Oxford: Oxford University Press, 2020.

Elmer, Jonathan. "Peirce, Poe, and Protoplasm." *Poe Studies: Dark Romanticism* 52 (2019): 29–49.

———. "Poe and the Avant-Garde." In *The Oxford Handbook of Edgar Allan Poe,* edited by J. Gerald Kennedy and Scott Peeples, 700–717. Oxford: Oxford University Press, 2019.

Empson, William. *Seven Types of Ambiguity.* New York: New Directions, 1947.

Encyclopedia SpongeBobia. "Squeaky Boots." Fandom. Accessed March 12, 2022. https://spongebob.fandom.com/wiki/Squeaky_Boots.

Epstein, Jean. *Écrits sur le cinéma, 1921–1953.* Vol. 1, *1921–1947.* Paris: Seghers / Cinéma Club, 1974.

———. "For a New Avant-Garde." In *French Film Theory and Criticism*, edited by Richard Abel, 349–52. Vol. 1, *1907–1939*. Princeton, NJ: Princeton UP, 1988.

———. *The Intelligence of a Machine*. Translated by Christophe Wall-Romana. Minneapolis, MN: Univocal Press, 2014.

———, dir. *La chute de la maison Usher*. 1928. Blanche. Posted September 29, 2017. YouTube video, 1:02:58. https://www.youtube.com/watch?v=Tf8Kv4YSBq4.

———. "La lyrosophie." In *Jean Epstein: Critical Essays and New Translations*, edited by Sarah Keller and Jason N. Paul, 281–86. Amsterdam: Amsterdam University Press, 2012.

Esper, Dwayne, dir. *Maniac*. 1934. Timeless Classic Movies. Posted April 24, 2017. YouTube video, 50:56. https://www.youtube.com/watch?v=yfDZH0Vr5p8.

Everson, William. *Classics of the Horror Film*. Secaucus, NJ: Citadel Press, 1974.

Favret, Mary A. *War at a Distance: Romanticism and the Making of Modern Wartime*. Princeton, NJ: Princeton University Press, 2010.

Figura, Star. "Redon and the Lithographed Portfolio." In *Beyond the Visible: The Art of Odilon Redon*, edited by Jodi Hauptman, 76–98. New York: Museum of Modern Art, 2005.

Florence, Penny. *Mallarmé, Manet, and Redon: Visual and Aural Sign and the Generation of Meaning*. Cambridge: Cambridge University Press, 1986.

Ford, Thomas H. "Aura in the Anthropocene." *Symploke* 21, no. 1–2 (2013): 65–82.

———. *Wordsworth and the Poetics of Air: Atmospheric Romanticism in a Time of Climate Change*. Cambridge: Cambridge University Press, 2018.

Foseca-Wollheim, Corinna da. "Handel and Philip Glass, but Make It Fashion." *New York Times*, September 21, 2018. https://www.nytimes.com/2018/09/21/arts/music/anthony-roth-costanzo-philip-glass-handel.html.

Foucault, Michel. *This Is Not a Pipe*. Illustrated by René Magritte. Translated by James Harkness. Berkeley: University of California Press, 1983.

Frank, Adam. *Transferential Poetics, from Poe to Warhol*. New York: Fordham University Press, 2015.

———. "Valdemar's Tongue, Poe's Telegraphy." *ELH* 73, no. 2 (2005): 635–62.

Fretwell, Erica. *Sensory Experiments: Psychophysics, Race, and the Aesthetics of Feeling*. Durham, NC: Duke University Press, 2020.

Frey, Mattias. *Extreme Cinema: The Transgressive Rhetoric of Today's Art Film Culture*. New Brunswick: Rutgers University Press, 2016.

Fried, Michael. "Art and Objecthood." In *Art and Objecthood: Essays and Reviews*. Chicago: University of Chicago Press, 1998.

Friedrich, Otto. *City of Nets: A Portrait Hollywood in the 1940's*. Berkeley: University of California Press, 1997.

Frye, Northrop. *Anatomy of Criticism: Four Essays*. Princeton, NJ: Princeton University Press, 1957.

Gaines, William. "Testimony of William Gaines." *Juvenile Delinquency (Comic Books): Hearings before the Subcommittee to Investigate Juvenile Delinquency*. Committee on the Judiciary, United States Senate, 83rd Congress (1954). http://www.thecomicbooks.com/gaines.html.

Galloway, Alexander. *Gaming: Essays on Algorithmic Culture*. Minneapolis: University of Minnesota Press, 2006.

Gamboni, Dario. *The Brush and the Pen: Odilon Redon and Literature*. Translated by Mary Whittal. Chicago: University of Chicago Press, 2011.

Gehr, Richard. "Mourning in America: Diamanda Galás." *Artforum*, May 1989.

Geimer, Peter. "The Incommensurable." In *Unwatchable*, edited by Nicholas Baer, Maggie Hennefeld, Laura Horak, and Gunnar Iverson, 82–85. New Brunswick: Rutgers University Press, 2019.

Gitelman, Lisa. *Always Already New: Media, History, and the Data of Culture.* Cambridge, MA: MIT, 2008.

———. *Scripts, Grooves, and Writing Machines: Representing Technology in the Edison Era.* Stanford, CA: Stanford University Press, 2000.

Gitelman, Lisa, and Geoffrey B. Pingree, eds. *New Media, 1740–1915.* Cambridge, MA: MIT Press, 2003.

Glass, Philip. *Descent into the Maelström.* Orange Mountain Music OMM0140, 2019, compact disc.

Golden, Catherine. *Serials to Graphic Novels: The Evolution of the Victorian Illustrated Book.* Gainesville, FL: University of Florida Press, 2017.

González-Moreno, Fernando, and Margarita Rigal-Aragón. *The Portrayal of the Grotesque in Stoddard's and Quantin's Illustrated Editions of Edgar Allan Poe (1884): An Interdisciplinary Analysis of the Relations Between the Visual and the Verbal.* Lewiston, NY: Edwin Mellen Press, 2017.

Goodman, Steve. *Sonic Warfare: Sound, Affect, and the Ecology of Fear.* Cambridge, MA: MIT Press, 2012.

Gregg, Melissa, and Gregory J. Siegworth, eds. *The Affect Theory Reader.* Durham, NC: Duke University Press, 2010.

Griffero, Tonino. *Atmospheres: Aesthetics of Emotional Spaces.* Translated by Sarah de Sanctis. London: Routledge, 2014.

———. *Quasi-Things: The Paradigm of Atmospheres.* Translated by Sarah de Sanctis. Albany, NY: SUNY Press, 2017.

Groys, Boris. *In the Flow.* London: Verso, 2016.

Gumbrecht, Hans Ulrich. *Atmosphere, Mood, Stimmung: On a Hidden Potential of Literature.* Translated by Erik Butler. Stanford, CA: Stanford University Press, 2012.

Gunning, Tom. "The Cinema of Attraction[s]: Early Film, Its Spectator and the Avant-Garde." In *The Cinema of Attractions Reloaded*, edited by Wanda Strauven, 381–88. Amsterdam: Amsterdam University Press, 2006. https://www.jstor.org/stable/j.ctt46n09s.27.

Hajdu, David. *The Ten-Cent Plague: The Great Comic-Book Scare and How It Changed America.* New York: FSG, 2008.

Halloween Horror Nights Wiki. "Nevermore: The Madness of Poe." Fandom. Accessed January 18, 2020. https://halloweenhorrornights.fandom.com/wiki/Nevermore:_The_Madness_of_Poe.

Hames, Peter. "Jan Švankmajer, Interview with Peter Hames." In *Dark Alchemy: The Films of Jan Švankmajer*, edited by Peter Hames. Westport, CT: Greenwood Press, 1995.

Hannoosh, Michèle. "From *Nevermore* to Eternity: Mallarmé, Manet and 'The Raven.'" In *The Dialogue Between Painting and Poetry: Livres d'artistes, 1874–1999*, edited by Jean Khalfa, 37–57. Cambridge: Black Apollo Press, 2001.

Hansen, Miriam. *Babel & Babylon: Spectatorship in American Silent Film.* Cambridge, MA: Harvard University Press, 1991.

Hawkins, Joan. "Culture Wars: Some New Trends in Art Horror." *Jump Cut*, no. 51 (2009).

———. *Cutting Edge: Art-Horror and the Horrific Avant-Garde*. Minneapolis: University of Minnesota Press, 2000.

Hawkins, Joan, and Alex Wermer-Colan, eds. *William S. Burroughs: Cutting Up the Century*. Bloomington: Indiana University Press, 2019.

Hawthorne, Nathaniel. *The Blithedale Romance*. New York: Penguin Books, 1986.

Hayes, Kevin. "Alice Guy's *The Pit and the Pendulum* (1913)." *The Edgar Allan Poe Review* 2, no. 1 (Spring 2001): 37–42.

Heidegger, Martin. "Building Dwelling Thinking." In *Poetry, Language, Thought*. Translated by Albert Hofstadter. New York: Harper & Row, 1971.

Heller, Chris. "A Brief History of the Haunted House." *Smithsonian Magazine*, October 31, 2017. https://www.smithsonianmag.com/history/history -haunted-house-180957008/.

Heller-Roazen, Daniel. *The Fifth Hammer: Pythagoras and the Disharmony of the World*. New York: Zone Books, 2011.

Hemus, Percy, vocalist, and Max Heinrich, composer. "The Raven." By Edgar Allan Poe. Library of Congress. Victor, 1913. Audio recording. https://www.loc.gov/ item/jukebox-133400/.

Herzfeld, Gregor. *Poe in der Musik: Eine versatile Allianz*. Münster, Germany: Waxmann, 2013.

Hess, Brian Allan. "A Rhetorical Analysis of the Entertaining Comics Group's 'New Trend' Series, 1950–56." Regent University, 2003.

Heyer, Paul. *The Medium and the Magician: Orson Welles, the Radio Years, 1934–52*. Lanham, MD: Rowman and Littlefield, 2005.

Hines, Megan. "A Journey That Wasn't: Huyghes' Graphic Film." *Edgar Allan Poe Review* 22, no. 1 (Spring 2021): 167–83.

Hosokawa, Toshio, composer. *The Raven: Monodrama for Mezzo-Soprano and 12 Players Based on 'The Raven' by Edgar Allan Poe*. Tokyo: Schott Music Co. Ltd., 2012. https://en.schott-music.com/shop/the-raven-no305256.html.

Houston Symphony. "Apocalyptic Prophecy: Rachmaninoff's *The Bells*." *Houston Symphony* (blog), April 19, 2019. https://houstonsymphony.org/rachmaninoff -bells/.

Howell, Laura. "Facts in the Case of Edgar Allan Poe." In *Nevermore: A Graphic Adaptation of Edgar Allan Poe's Short Stories*, edited by Dan Whitehead, 127–28. London: SelfMadeHero, 2007.

Howells, W. D. *Literary Friends and Acquaintance*. Vol. 32 of *A Selected Edition of W. D. Howells*, edited by David F. Hiatt and Edwin H. Cady. Bloomington: Indiana University Press, 1968.

Huckvale, David. *Poe Evermore: The Legacy in Film, Music, and Television*. Jefferson, NC: McFarland and Co., 2014.

Hughes, Sandra. "Evolutions in Torture: James Wan's *Saw* as Poe for the Twenty-First Century." In *Adapting Poe: Re-Imaginings in Popular Culture*, edited by Dennis R. Perry and Carl H. Sederholm, 71–80. New York: Palgrave Macmillan, 2012.

Hutcheon, Linda. *A Theory of Adaptation*. 2nd ed. New York: Routledge, 2012.

Inge, M. Thomas. *The Incredible Mr. Poe: Comic Book Adaptations of the Works of Edgar Allan Poe, 1943–2007*. Richmond: Poe Museum, 2008.

———. "Poe and the Comics Connection." *Edgar Allan Poe Review* 2, no. 1 (Spring 2001): 2–29.

Irwin, John. *American Hieroglyphics: The Symbol of the Egyptian Hieroglyphics in the American Renaissance*. Baltimore: Johns Hopkins University Press, 1980.

Isenberg, Noah. *Edgar G. Ulmer: A Filmmaker at the Margins*. Berkeley: University of California Press, 2014.

Jackson, Christine A. *The Tell-Tale Art: Poe in Modern Culture*. Jefferson, NC: McFarland and Co., 2012.

Jackson, Wendy. "The Surrealist Conspirator: An Interview with Jan Švankmajer." *Animation World Magazine*, 3.2, (June 1997). https://www.awn.com/mag/issue2 .3/issue2.3pages/2.3jacksonsvankmajer.html.

Jankélevitch, Vladimir. *Music and the Ineffable*. Translated by Carolyn Abbate. Princeton, NJ: Princeton University Press, 2003.

Jay, Martin. *Downcast Eyes: The Denigration of Vision in Twentieth-Century French Thought*. Berkeley: University of California Press, 1993.

Johnson, Keith Leslie. *Jan Švankmajer*. Contemporary Film Directors. Champaign: University of Illinois Press, 2017.

Johnson, Tom. "What Is Minimalism Really About?" Editions75: Works by Tom Johnson, June 13, 1977. https://editions75.com/tvonm/articles/1977/ what-is-minimalism-really-about.html.

Jones, Steve. *Torture Porn: Popular Horror After "Saw."* Basingstoke, UK: Palgrave Macmillan, 2012.

Jurgess, Todd. "Continuity, the Weight of the Suture (*The Sealed Room*, 1909)." *D. W. Griffith, Some Readings* (blog), August 4, 2014. https://griffithreadings .wordpress.com/2014/08/04/continuity-the-weight-of-the-suture-editing-3/. Site discontinued.

Kahn, Douglas. *Noise Water Meat: A History of Sound in the Arts*. Cambridge, MA: MIT Press, 1999.

Kahn, Douglas, and Gregory Whitehead, eds. *Wireless Imagination: Sound, Radio, and the Avant-Garde*. Cambridge, MA: MIT Press, 1992.

Karloff, Boris, performer. "The Tell-Tale Heart." By Edgar Allan Poe. *Inner Sanctum*, August 3, 1941. Heirloom Radio. Soundcloud sound recording, 26:42. https:// soundcloud.com/user-693593010/inner-sanctum-the-tell-tale-heart-starring -boris-karloff-8-3-41.

Keller, Sarah, and Jason N. Paul, eds. *Jean Epstein: Critical Essays and New Translations*. Amsterdam: Amsterdam University Press, 2012.

Kermode, Mark. "The British Censors and Horror Cinema." In *British Horror Cinema*, edited by Julian Petley and Steve Chibnall, 10–22. London: Routledge, 2001.

Kerner, Aaron Michael. *Torture Porn in the Wake on 9/11: Horror, Exploitation, and the Cinema of Sensation*. New Brunswick, NJ: Rutgers University Press, 2015.

Ketner, Kenneth Laine. *His Glassy Essence: An Autobiography of Charles Sanders Peirce*. Nashville: Vanderbilt University Press, 1998.

Kittler, Friedrich. *Gramophone, Film, Typewriter*. Translated by Geoffrey Winthrop-Young and Michael Wutz. Stanford, CA: Stanford University Press, 1999.

———. *Optical Media: Berlin Lectures 1999*. Translated by Anthony Enns. Cambridge: Polity Press, 2009.

Kopley, Richard. "The Hidden Journey of 'Arthur Gordon Pym.'" *Studies in the American Renaissance*, 1982, 29–51.

———. "The Secret of Arthur Gordon Pym: The Text and the Source." *Studies in American Fiction* 8, no. 2 (Autumn 1980): 203–18.

Krauss, Rosalind. *"A Voyage on the North Sea": Art in the Age of the Post-Medium Condition.* London: Thames & Hudson, 2000.

Lally, Sean. "Overlooked the Day Before: The Work of Pierre Huyghe." *Architectural Design* 79, no. 3 (2009): 64–69.

Lamberti, Edward, ed. *Behind the Scenes at the BBFC: Film Classification from the Silver Screen to the Digital Age.* British Film Institute, 2012.

Larson, Barbara. *The Dark Side of Nature: Science, Society, and the Fantastic in the Work of Odilon Redon.* University Park: Penn State University Press, 2005.

———. "Evolution and Degeneration in the Early Work of Odilon Redon." *Nineteenth-Century Art Worldwide* 2, no. 2 (Spring 2003). https://www.19thc-artworldwide .org/spring03/220-evolution-and-degeneration-in-the-early-work-of-odilon-redon.

Leff, Leonard J., and Jerrold L. Simmons. *The Dame in the Kimono: Hollywood, Censorship, and the Production Code.* Lexington: University of Kentucky Press, 2013.

Legman, Gershon. *Love & Death: A Study in Censorship.* New York: Breaking Point, 1949.

Leitch, Thomas. *Adaptation and Its Discontents: From "Gone with the Wind" to "The Passion of the Christ."* Baltimore: Johns Hopkins University Press, 2007.

Le Men, Ségolène. "Manet et Doré: L'illustration du corbeau de Poe." *Nouvelles de l'estampes,* no. 78 (1984): 4–21.

Lewis, Jayne Elizabeth. *Air's Appearance: Literary Atmosphere in British Fiction, 1660–1794.* Chicago: University of Chicago Press, 2012.

Lewis, Jon. *Hollywood v. Hard Core: How the Struggle over Censorship Saved the Modern Film Industry.* New York: NYU Press, 2000.

Lowery, Madeleine. "Bells of Death: Rachmaninoff's Use of the Dies Irae in His Choral Symphony, Kolakola." Honors Thesis, University of Southern Mississippi, 2016. https://core.ac.uk/download/pdf/301297245.pdf.

Lukács, Georg. "Thoughts on an Aesthetics of Cinema" (1913). In *German Essays on Film,* edited by Richard W. McCormick and Alison Guenther-Pal, 11–16. New York: Continuum Books, 2004.

Macdonald, Dwight. *Masscult and Midcult: Essays Against the American Grain.* Edited by John Summers. New York: New York Review of Books, 2011.

Maher, Jimmy. "The Dark Eye." *The Digital Antiquarian* (blog), November 5, 2021. https://www.filfre.net/2021/11/the-dark-eye/.

Mandell, Paul. "Edgar Ulmer and The Black Cat." *American Cinematographer* 65, no. 9 (October 1984): 34–47.

Mank, Gregory William. *Bela Lugosi and Boris Karloff: The Expanded Story of a Haunting Collaboration.* Jefferson, NC: McFarland and Company, 2009.

Mattey, Gareth. "Opera Meets Film: A Deep Dive into Anthony Roth Costanzo's 'Glass Handel' (Part One)." *Operawire* (blog), December 17, 2020. https:// operawire.com/opera-meets-film-a-deep-dive-into-anthony-roth-costanzos -glass-handel-part-one/.

Matthiessen, F. O. *The American Renaissance: Art and Expression in the Age of Emerson and Whitman.* Oxford: Oxford University Press, 1941.

McCarthy, Todd, and Charles Flynn, eds. *Kings of the Bs: Working within the Hollywood System: An Anthology of Film History and Criticism.* New York: E. P. Dutton, 1975.

McCloud, Scott. *Understanding Comics: The Invisible Art*. New York: William Morrow, 1994.

McDonagh, Maitland. *Broken Mirrors / Broken Minds: The Dark Dreams of Dario Argento*. Minneapolis: University of Minnesota Press, 2010. Project MUSE https://muse.jhu.edu/book/24467.

McGill, Meredith L. *American Literature and the Culture of Reprinting, 1834–1853*. Philadelphia: University of Pennsylvania Press, 2007.

Menely, Tobias. "Anthropocene Air." *Minnesota Review* 83 (2014): 93–101.

Menely, Tobias, and Jesse Oak Taylor, eds. *Anthropocene Reading: Literary History in Geologic Times*. University Park: The Pennsylvania State University Press, 2017.

Michaud, Yves. *L'art à l'état gazeux: Essai sur le triomphe de l'esthétique*. Paris: Stock, 2003.

———. *L'art, c'est bien fini: Essai sur l'hyper-esthétique et les atmosphères*. Paris: Gallimard, 2021.

Mitchell, W. J. T. *Iconology: Image, Text, Ideology*. Chicago: University of Chicago Press, 1986.

———. "Metamorphoses of the Vortex: Hogarth, Turner, Blake." In *Articulate Images: The Sister Arts from Hogarth to Tennyson*, edited by Richard Wendorf, 125–68. Minneapolis: University of Minnesota Press, 1983.

Modern, John Lardas. *Secularism in Antebellum America*. Chicago: University of Chicago Press, 2011.

Morioka, Miho. "Report on 'The Vibrating Path toward a Musical Dream: From Noh-Theater to a New Operatic Form—Opera *Erdbeben. Traüme* and Other Works': The Japan Foundation Award 2018 Commemorative Lecture by Toshio Hosokawa." *Web Magazine Wochi Kochi*, June 28, 2019. https://www.wochikochi.jp/english/foreign/2019/06/award2018-hosokawa-repo-en.php.

Morton, Timothy. *Ecology without Nature: Rethinking Environmental Aesthetics*. Cambridge, MA: Harvard University Press, 2007.

Morton, Tom. "Bon Voyage: Pierre Huyghe," *Frieze*, no. 74 (April 2003). https://www.frieze.com/article/bon-voyage.

Motion Picture Association of America. *G Is for Golden: The MPAA Film Ratings at 50*. Research Report. October 29, 2018. https://www.motionpictures.org/wp-content/uploads/2018/11/G-is-for-Golden.pdf.

Mowitt, John. *Radio: Essays in Bad Reception*. Berkeley: University of California Press, 2011.

———. *Sounds: The Ambient Humanities*. Berkeley: University of California Press, 2015.

Musser, Charles. *The Emergence of Cinema: The American Screen to 1907*. New York: Charles Scribner's Sons, 1990.

Naremore, James. *More than Night: Film Noir in Its Contexts*. Berkeley: University of California Press, 1998.

Nashawaty, Chris. *Crab Monsters, Teenage Cavemen, and Candy Stripe Nurses: Roger Corman, King of the B Movie*. New York: Abrams Books, 2013.

Neale, Steve. "Art Cinema as Institution." *Screen* 22, no.1 (1981): 11–40.

Nelson, Maggie. *The Art of Cruelty: A Reckoning*. New York: W. W. Norton and Co., 2011.

Ngai, Sianne. *Our Aesthetic Categories: Zany, Cute, Interesting*. Cambridge, MA: Harvard University Press, 2012.

Nieland, Justus. *Happiness by Design: Modernism and Media in the Eames Era*. Minneapolis: University of Minnesota Press, 2019.

NintendoComplete. "The Dark Eye (PC) Playthrough." October 20, 2016. YouTube video, 2:14:49. https://www.youtube.com/watch?v=eX7r7QVJDEM.

Olalquiaga, Celeste. *The Artificial Kingdom: On the Kitsch Experience*. Minneapolis: University of Minnesota Press, 1998.

O'Pray, Michael. "Jan Švankmajer: A Mannerist Surrealist." In *Fantasy and the Cinema*, edited by Donald James, 254–68. Westport, CT: Greenwood Press, 1989.

Oshima, Nagisa. *Nagisa Oshima, Cinema, Censorship, and the State: The Writings of Nagisa Oshima, 1956–1978*. Edited by Annette Michaelson. Translated by Dawn Lawson. Cambridge, MA: MIT Press, 1992.

Palmer, Landon. "The Disembodied Fry: William S. Burroughs and Vocal Performance." In *William S. Burroughs: Cutting Up the Century*, edited by Joan Hawkins and Alex Wermer-Colan, 97–111. Bloomington: Indiana University Press, 2019.

Pareles, Jon. "MUSIC; Lou Reed, The Tell-Tale Rocker." *New York Times*, November 25, 2001, sec. 2.

Peeples, Scott. *The Man of the Crowd: Edgar Allan Poe and the City*. Photographs by Michelle Van Parys. Princeton, NJ: Princeton University Press, 2020.

———. "'That Name'll Never Be Worth Anything!': Poe's Image on Film." *The Edgar Allan Poe Review* 16, no. 2 (Autumn 2015): 169–83.

Perry, Dennis R., and Carl H. Sederholm, eds. *Adapting Poe: Re-imaginings in Popular Culture*. New York: Palgrave Macmillan, 2012.

Peters, John Durham. *The Marvelous Clouds: Toward a Philosophy of Elemental Media*. Chicago: University of Chicago Press, 2015.

Piper, Andrew. *Book Was There: Reading in Electronic Times*. Chicago: University of Chicago Press, 2013.

Poe, Edgar Allan. *The Bells and Other Poems*. Illustrated by Edmund Dulac. London: Hodder and Stoughton, 1912.

———. *The Collected Letters of Edgar Allan Poe*. Vol. 1. 3rd ed. Edited by John Ward Ostrom, Burton R. Pollin, and Jeffrey A. Savoye. New York: Gordian Press, 2008. https://www.eapoe.org/works/ostlttrs/pl081000.htm.

———. *The Collected Works of Edgar Allan Poe*. Edited by T. O. Mabbott. 3 vols. Cambridge, MA: Belknap Press, 1978.

———. "The Daguerreotype." *Alexander's Weekly Messenger*, January 15, 1840, 2. http://www.daguerreotypearchive.org/texts/P8400008_POE_ALEX -WEEKLY_1840-01-15.pdf.

———. *Essays and Reviews*. Edited by G. R. Thompson. New York: Library of America, 1984.

———. *The Fall of the House of Usher*. Illustrated by Abner Epstein. New York: Cheshire House, 1931.

———. *The Haunted Palace*. Illustrated by Heinz Veuhoff. New York: H. Schiskowsky, 1963.

———. *Histoires extraordinaires et Nouvelles histoires extraordinaires*. Translated by Charles Baudelaire. Illustrated by Carlo Farneti. 2 vols. Paris: KRA, 1927–28.

———. *Le corbeau*. Translated by Stéphane Mallarmé. Paris: Richard Lesclide, 1875.

———. *Poetry and Tales*. Edited by Patrick Quinn. New York: Library of America, 1984.

———. *Quattro racconti di Edgardo Allan Poë*. Illustrated by Pietrino Vicenzi. Urbino: R. Istituto d'arte di Urbino, 1940.

———. *The Raven*. Illustrated by Gustave Doré. New York: Harper & Brothers, 1884.

———. *Selected Prose and Poetry*. Edited by W. H. Auden. Revised edition. New York: Rinehart and Co., 1955.

———. *Tales of Mystery and Imagination*. Illustrated by Harry Clarke. New York: George Harrap & Co., 1919.

———. *The Works of Edgar Allan Poe*. Edited by Richard Henry Stoddard. 6 vols. London: Kegan Paul, Trench & Co., 1884.

———. *The Works of the Late Edgar Allan Poe*. Edited by Rufus Wilmot Griswold. 4 vols. New York: J. S. Redfield, 1850–1856. https://www.eapoe.org/works/editions/griswold.htm.

Pollin, Burton, comp. *Images of Poe's Works: A Comprehensive Descriptive Catalogue of Illustrations*. Westport, CT: Greenwood Press, 1989.

Pop, Andrei. *A Forest of Symbols: Art, Science, and Truth in the Long Nineteenth Century*. New York: Zone Books, 2019.

Powell, Anna. "The Feel of the House of Usher." *The Cine-Files*, no. 10 (Spring 2016): 1–7.

Reed, Lou. *The Raven*. Sire, 2003, compact disc.

Richards, Eliza. "'Lyric Telegraphy': Women Poets, Spiritualist Poetics, and the Phantom Voice of Poe." *Yale Journal of Criticism* 12, no. 2 (Fall 1999): 270–91.

———. "Poe's Lyric Media: The Raven's Returns." In *Poe and the Remapping of Antebellum Print Culture*, edited by J. Gerald Kennedy and Jerome McGann, 200–224. Baton Rouge: Louisiana State University Press, 2012.

Riedel, Friedland, and Juha Torvinen, eds. *Music as Atmosphere: Collective Feelings and Affective Sounds*. London: Routledge, 2020.

Riley, James Whitcomb. "Mr. Riley Wrote Poem Leonaine [*sic*]: Hoosier Poet Replies to Attack of Alfred Russell [*sic*] Wallace in *Fortnightly Review*." *Indianapolis Sentinel*, n.d. Riley MSS. Bloomington: Lilly Library, Indiana University.

Rimbaud, Arthur. "The Unsettling of All the Senses." In *Symbolist Art Theories: A Critical Anthology*, edited by Henri Dorra, 136–38. Berkeley: University of California Press, 1994.

Robertson, James C. *The British Board of Censors: Film Censorship in Britain, 1896–1950*. London: Croom Helm, 1985.

Rose, Emily. "Russell Lees & Inscape's The Dark Eye Retrospective," *The RE:BIND.io Podcast*, episode 15, May 4, 2020. Audio recording, 1:20:41. https://podtail.com/en/podcast/the-re-bind-io-podcast/the-re-bind-podcast-episode-15-russell-lees-inscap/.

R. R. "The Pit and the Pendulum. A Study in Suspense." *The Exhibitors' Times*, 1913, 6–7.

Rubery, Matthew. *Audiobooks, Literature, and Sound Studies*. New York: Routledge, 2011.

———. "Thomas Edison's Poetry Machine." *19: Interdisciplinary Studies in the Long Nineteenth Century*, no. 18 (2014). https://doi.org/10.16995/ntn.678.

———. *The Untold Story of the Talking Book*. Cambridge, MA: Harvard University Press, 2016.

Rubin, James H. *Manet's Silence and the Poetics of Bouquets*. Cambridge, MA: Harvard University Press, 1994.

Sanders, Rupert, dir. "How All Living Things Breathe." From *The Fall of the House of Usher*, composed by Philip Glass. Anthony Roth Costanzo. November 16, 2018. YouTube video, 4:21. https://www.youtube.com/watch?v=oJC_gDoZcbk.

Schaefer, Eric. *"Bold! Daring! Shocking! True!": A History of Exploitation Films, 1919–1959*. Durham: Duke University Press, 1999.

Schjeldahl, Peter. *Let's See: Writings about Art from "The New Yorker"*. New York: Thames & Hudson, 2008.

Schnapp, Jeffrey T., and Adam Michaels. *The Electronic Information Age Book: McLuhan/Agel/Fiore and the Experimental Paperback*. Princeton, NJ: Princeton Architectural Press, 2012.

Sconce, Jeffrey. *Haunted Media: Electronic Presence from Telegraphy to Television*. Durham, NC: Duke University Press, 2000.

———. "Spectacles of Death: Identification, Reflexivity, and Contemporary Horror." In *Film Theory Goes to the Movies*, edited by Jim Collins, Hilary Radner, and Ava Preacher Collins, 103–19. New York: Routledge, 1994.

———. "'Trashing' the Academy: Taste, Excess, and an Emerging Politics of Cinematic Style." *Screen* 36, no. 4 (1995): 372–93.

Shaviro, Steven. *The Cinematic Body*. Minneapolis: University of Minnesota Press, 1989.

Sloterdijk, Peter. *Bubbles: Spheres Volume 1: Microspherology*. Translated by Wieland Hoban. Cambridge, MA: Semiotext(e), 2011.

———. *Globes: Spheres Volume 2: Macrospherology*. Translated by Wieland Hoban. Cambridge, MA: Semiotext(e), 2014.

———. *Foams: Spheres Volume 3: Plural Spherology*. Translated by Wieland Hoban. Cambridge, MA: Semiotext(e), 2016.

Smith, Don G. *The Poe Cinema: A Critical Filmography of Theatrical Releases Based on the Works of Edgar Allan Poe*. Jefferson, NC: McFarland & Company, 1999.

Smith, Jacob. *Spoken Word: Postwar American Phonograph Cultures*. Berkeley: University of California Press, 2011.

———. *Vocal Tracks: Performance and Recorded Sound*. Berkeley: University of California Press, 2008.

Smith, Ronald L. *Poe in the Media: Screen, Songs, and Spoken Word Recordings*. New York: Garland Publishing, 1990.

Sorenson, Thomas. "Reading for Atmosphere: A Pedagogical Approach." *PMLA* 138.1 (2023): 188–93.

Spadoni, Robert. "Horror-Film Atmosphere as Anti-narrative (and Vice Versa)." In *Merchants of Menace: The Business of Horror Cinema*, edited by Richard Howell, 109–28. London: Bloomsbury, 2014.

Spitzer, Leo. "Classical and Christian Ideas of World Harmony: Prolegomena to an Interpretation of the Word 'Stimmung' (Part 2)." *Tradition* 3 (1945): 307–64.

———. "Milieu and Ambiance: An Essay in Historical Semantics." *Philosophy and Phenomenological Research* 3, no. 2 (1942): 169–218.

———. "A Reinterpretation of 'The Fall of the House of Usher.'" *Comparative Literature* 4, no. 4 (1952): 351–63.

Stang, Sarah. "'This Action Will Have Consequences': Interactivity and Player Agency." *Game Studies* 19, no. 1 (2019). https://gamestudies.org/1901/articles/stang.

Sterne, Jonathan. *The Audible Past: Cultural Origins of Sound Reproduction*. Durham, NC: Duke University Press, 2003.

Stokowski, Leopold. "1932 Recordings of Leopold Stokowski and the Philadelphia Orchestra." *The Stokowski Legacy* (blog), https://www.stokowski.org/1932_Electrical_Recordings_Stokowski.htm.

Sullivan, Kelly. "Harry Clarke's Natural World." In *Harry Clarke and Artistic Visions of the New Irish State*, edited by Angela Griffith, Marguerite Helmers, and Róisín Kennedy, 101–30. Newbridge: Irish Academic Press, 2019.

Švankmajer, Jan. *Touching and Imagining: An Introduction to Tactile Art*. Edited by Cathryn Vasseleu. Translated by Stanley Dalby. London: I. B. Tauris & Co., 2014.

Sweeney, Susan Elizabeth. "The Horror of Taking a Picture in Poe's 'The Tell-Tale Heart.'" *The Edgar Allan Poe Review* 18, no. 2 (Autumn 2017).

Tannenbaum, Libby. "The Raven Abroad." *Magazine of Art*, April 1944.

Taylor, Timothy D., Mark Katz, and Tony Grajeda, eds. *Music, Sound, and Technology in America: A Documentary History of Early Phonograph, Cinema, and Radio*. Durham, NC: Duke University Press, 2012.

Thomas, Dwight R., and David K. Jackson. Chapter 3 of *The Poe Log: A Documentary Life of Edgar Allan Poe, 1809–1849*, 111–43. Boston: G. K. Hall & Co., 1987.

Thrift, Nigel. *Non-representational Theory: Space, Politics, Affect*. London: Routledge, 2008.

Tiffany, Daniel. *My Silver Planet: A Secret History of Poetry and Kitsch*. Hopkins Studies in Modernism. Baltimore: Johns Hopkins University Press, 2013.

Tommasini, Anthony. "Poe's Lost Lenore Lives in Song and Dance." *New York Times*, May 30, 2014, sec. C.

Toop, David. *Into the Maelstrom: Music, Improvisation and the Dream of Freedom: Before 1970*. London: Bloomsbury, 2016.

———. *Oceans of Sound: Ambient Sound and Radical Listening in the Age of Communication*. London: Serpent's Tail, 1995.

Tresch, John. "The Compositor's Reversal: Typography, Science, and Creation in Poe's *Narrative of Arthur Gordon Pym*." *History and Theory* 56 (December 2018): 8–31.

———. "Estrangement of Vision: Edgar Allan Poe's Optics." In *Observing Nature-Representing Experience: The Osmotic Dynamics of Romanticism, 1800–1850*, edited by Erna Fiorenti, 155–86. Berlin: Reimer Verlag, 2007.

———. "Extra! Extra! Poe Invents Science Fiction." In *The Cambridge Companion to Poe*, edited by Kevin J. Hayes, 113–32. Cambridge: Cambridge University Press, 2001.

———. "The Potent Magic of Verisimilitude: Edgar Allan Poe within the Mechanical Age." *British Journal for the History of Science* 30, no. 3 (September 1997): 275–90.

———. "The Prophet and the Pendulum: Sensational Science and Audiovisual Phantasmagoria around 1848." *Grey Room*, no. 43 (Spring 2011): 16–41.

———. *The Reason for the Darkness of the Night: Edgar Allan Poe and the Forging of American Science*. New York: FSG, 2021.

———. *The Romantic Machine: Utopian Science and Technology after Napoleon*. Chicago: University of Chicago Press, 2014.

———. "Technology." In *Edgar Allan Poe in Context*, edited by Kevin J. Hayes, 372–82. Oxford: Oxford University Press, 2012.

———. "The Uses of a Mistranslated Manifesto: Baudelaire's 'La genèse d'un poème.'" *L'esprit créateur* 43, no. 2 (Summer 2003): 23–35.

Tristano, Lennie. "Descent into the Maelstrom." 1953. Nekotaro Netakiri. Posted November 30, 2015. YouTube video, 3:30. https://www.youtube.com/watch?v=99UTNVHLgEk.

———. *Lennie Tristano*. Jazz Series 3. London Records LTZ-K15033, 1956, vinyl LP album.

Umland, Anne. *Magritte: The Mystery of the Ordinary, 1926–1938*. New York: Museum of Modern Art, 2013.

United Productions of America. Production Notes. *The Tell-Tale Heart*, directed by Ted Parmelee. Museum of Modern Art Archives, EMH III.26.a.

United States Senate. *Juvenile Delinquency (Comic Books): Hearings before the Subcommittee to Investigate Juvenile Delinquency*. Committee on the Judiciary, United States Senate, 83rd Congress (1954). April 21, 1954. https://www.thecomicbooks .com/clendenen.html.

Vallas, Léon. *Claude Debussy: His Life and Works*. Translated by Maire and Grace O'Brien. London: Oxford University Press, 1933.

Vasseleu, Cathryn. "The Švankmajer Touch." *Animation Studies—Animated Dialogues*, 2007:91–101. https://journal.animationstudies.org/wp-content/uploads/2009/ 07/ASADArt12CVasseleu.pdf.

Vines, Lois Davis, ed. *Poe Abroad: Influence, Reputation, Affinities*. Iowa City: University of Iowa Press, 1999.

Wallace, Alfred Russell [*sic*]. *Edgar Allan Poe: A Series of Seventeen Letters Concerning Poe's Scientific Erudition in Eureka and His Authorship of Leonainie*. New York: Privately Printed, n.d.

Wall-Romana, Christophe. *Jean Epstein: Corporeal Cinema and Film Philosophy*. Manchester, UK: Manchester University Press, 2013.

Walsh, Stephen. *Debussy: A Painter in Sound*. New York: Vintage, 2018.

Warner, Marina. *Phantasmagoria: Spirit Visions, Metaphors, and Media into the Twenty-First Century*. Oxford: Oxford University Press, 2006.

Warshow, Robert. "Paul, the Horror Comics, and Dr. Wertham." In *Arguing Comics: Literary Masters on a Popular Medium*, edited by Heet Jeer and Kent Worcester, 63–80. Jackson: University of Mississippi Press, 2004.

Webber, Melville, and James Sibley Watson Jr., dirs. *The Fall of the House of Usher*. 1928. Ryan Douglas Morgan. Posted December 14, 2016. YouTube video, 13:50. https://www.youtube.com/watch?v=D0oCj8uTsh0.

Weinstein, Cindy. "*La reproduction interdite*: Magritte's Reproduction of Pym." *Poe Studies* 55 (2022): 32–58.

White, Tim, and J. Emmett Winn. "Jan Švankmajer's Adaptations of Edgar Allan Poe." *Kinema*, Fall (2006). https://openjournals.uwaterloo.ca/index.php/ kinema/article/view/1124/1338.

Whitehead, Dan, ed. *Nevermore: A Graphic Adaptation of Edgar Allan Poe's Short Stories*. London: SelfMadeHero, 2007.

Willner, Hal, producer. *Closed on Account of Rabies: Poems and Tales of Edgar Allan Poe*. Mercury Records, 1997, compact disc.

Wilson-Bareau, Juliet, and Breon Mitchell. "Tales of a Raven: The Origins and Fate of *Le Corbeau* by Mallarmé and Manet." *Print Quarterly* 6, no. 3 (September 1989): 258–307.

Winner, Thomas G. "Peirce and Literary Studies." In *Peirce and Value Theory: On Peircean Ethics and Aesthetics*, edited by Herman Parret, 277–300. Amsterdam: John Benjamins Publishing, 1994.

Yousif, Keri. *Balzac, Grandville, and the Rise of Book Illustration*. London: Ashgate, 2012.

Zhang, Dora. "Notes on Atmosphere." *Qui Parle* 27, no. 1 (June 2018): 123–55.

Zwarg, Christina. "Temporal Effects: Trauma, Margaret Fuller, and 'Graphicality' in Poe." In *The Oxford Handbook of Edgar Allan Poe*, edited by J. Gerald Kennedy and Scott Peeples, 773–91. Oxford: Oxford University Press, 2019.

Index

Page numbers in italics refer to figures.